The Cheap Bastard's Guide® to
NEW YORK CITY

"A penny-pincher's nirvana—it's as if we wrote it!"
—*Arthur Frommer's Budget Travel Magazine*

"A book that reinforces one of the classic family values
that New Yorkers hold dear—never pay retail."
—Brian Lehrer, *WNYC New York Public Radio*

"But does it work? You bet. . . . Grader hilariously dissects
the city to come up with his innovative money savers."
—John Deiner, *The Washington Post*

"There are a lot of ideas worth considering. . . .
Plenty of attractions for the casual visitor."
—Richard P. Carpenter, *Boston Globe*

"The [money] you spend on this book
will be recouped in no time."
—*Brooklyn Parent Magazine*

"Brings on attitude and humor in its revelations
of how to obtain assorted freebies."
—*Publishers Weekly*

"The last word on living well and cheaply
in the Big Apple—and, no, it is not an oxymoron."
—June Sawyers, *Chicago Tribune*

"If you are planning a trip to the Big Apple, this book is a
must. . . . You will enjoy the wit and humor Grader has
inserted into this delightful guide."
—*Gillette News–Record* (Gillette, Wyo.)

Help Us Keep This Guide Up to Date

Every effort has been made by the author and editors to make this guide as accurate and useful as possible. However, many things can change after a guide is published—establishments close, phone numbers change, facilities come under new management, and so on.

We would love to hear from you concerning your experiences with this guide and how you feel it could be improved and kept up to date. While we may not be able to respond to all comments and suggestions, we'll take them to heart, and we'll also make certain to share them with the author. Please send your comments and suggestions to the following address:

The Globe Pequot Press
Reader Response/Editorial Department
P.O. Box 480
Guilford, CT 06437

Or you may e-mail us at:

editorial@GlobePequot.com

Thanks for your input, and happy travels!

The Cheap Bastard's Guide® to
NEW YORK CITY

A NATIVE NEW YORKER'S SECRETS OF LIVING THE GOOD LIFE—FOR FREE!

FOURTH EDITION

Rob Grader

travel

Guilford, Connecticut

The prices and rates listed in this guidebook were confirmed at press time. We recommend, however, that you call establishments to obtain current information before traveling.

Text and map design: M. A. Dubé © Morris Book Publishing, LLC
Spot art: Image Club
Lyrics on page 25 from "Grand Central Station, March 18, 1977" by Steve Forbert, reprinted by kind permission of Welk Music (ASCAP, adm. Lichelle Music Co.).

ISSN 1549-5116
ISBN 978-0-7627-4770-2

Printed in the United States of America
10 9 8 7 6 5 4 3 2 1

For Dad, the one, the true, the Original Cheap Bastard,
and for Mom, though not always cheap,
one true original in her own right.

Contents

"Misers aren't fun to to live with, but they make wonderful ancestors."

— David Brenner

ACKNOWLEDGMENTS

NO **ONE BECOMES** a Cheap Bastard on his own, and here are the names to prove it. There are many people I need to acknowledge who've helped me along the way. From the very beginning, I had training from the best, the ultimate Cheap Bastard himself, my dad, Jack Grader. Thanks also to Mom, Bernice Grader, and everyone in my family for their support, encouragement, and suggestions while I was putting this opus together. In particular, thanks to Scott Grader (with two *t*'s, right?) for all the free legal counseling, to Trish Lande Grader for all the free publishing know-how, and to all the rest of the Graders: Jessica, Michelle, Emily, Sally, Jonas, Jeff, Lisa, Stu, and Ellen. Special thanks to Shari Springer Berman and Bob Pulcini for all the free writing advice and consultations. I am also indebted to Steve Harper for the free proofreading services (and the constantly free ear!), to Harry Mizrahi of American Spectrum Realty for the free use of the office equipment and for giving me plenty of free time while I was working for him, to Hans Kriefall and his mom for the free Latin lesson, and to Chiori Miagowa, Suzi Takahashi, Nilaja Sun, Ignacio Lopez, Ken Bolden, Danny Weiss, Patricia Kelley, Bill Quigley, Bill Driscoll, Mark Farnan, Sue Barret, Helen Mandlin, and Karen Raksis (the best things in life are free!) for all giving so freely of their spirits. My gratitude also goes out to Mark S. Roy and Brian DeFiore of DeFiore and Company, and to Laura Strom, Shelley Wolf, Maureen Graney, Jennifer Quint, Mike Urban, and everyone at The Globe Pequot Press for their invaluable assistance. There is also a nasty little secret about New Yorkers I must expose: Contrary to popular belief, they truly are the friendliest, smartest, most generous, and helpful people in the world. Innumerable friends, acquaintances, associates, and strangers helped me out in countless ways throughout the development of this book. I'm sorry I cannot name you all, but please know you are appreciated. Thanks to all—you're a wonderful bunch of Bastards!

> "Truly, our greatest
> blessings are very
> cheap."
>
> —Henry David Thoreau

A FEW YEARS BACK WHILE I was visiting England, I found myself low on cash—but still wanting to see the sights. Not to be deterred by this minor detail, I proceeded to figure out ways to sneak into some of the Brits' most expensive and heavily guarded tourist attractions. My proudest feat was making my way into the impenetrable Tower of London. Take that, William the Conqueror! I was having such a good time getting around the system that I thought this would make a great first in a series of books—*Getting Around London: How to Sneak into Anywhere.* Upon further consideration (and after speaking with my brother the lawyer), it seemed there might be an array of legal problems with this kind of book. But somehow the idea wouldn't go away.

Then back home in New York, I watched the Pulitzer Prize–winning play *Wit* one evening for free (and legally!). After the show, I stopped by a favorite haunt of mine to get a little snack (free, thank you) and made it home to my spacious Upper West Side apartment (for which I pay $560 a month in rent and found without paying any broker's fee). As I sat relaxing in my leather easy chair (free, too!) and thinking about my yoga class the next morning (you guessed it, free), it dawned on me—I am one cheap bastard. I also understood that I have a mission in life to figure out how I can get or do practically anything I want without paying one red cent, and usually on the up and up. And I felt compelled to share this—my life's work—with the world. So I humbly offer to you *The Cheap Bastard's Guide to New York City*.

The *CB Guide* is not only a collection of specific destinations, listings, and tips on how to get almost anything imaginable for free or ridiculously cheap (more on my definition of these later), it's also a celebration of life on the cheap. The myth is that New York is a great place to live or visit if you have the money to enjoy it. The truth is, no place offers more for free than New York, but only if you know how to find it. And once you find it, oh the joy! Anyone can pay their way into a Broadway show, but when you get in for free, somehow the lights are brighter, the songs are sweeter, the drama so much more heartbreaking. There is no thrill in buying a dinner, but the taste of a free Buffalo wing is spiced with adventure, the crunch of a crisp free Granny Smith apple is the sound of triumph, and the kick of getting a free cup of coffee puts just that extra spring in your step.

A big part of the value of getting something for nothing is the story that goes with it—the history, the event. What can you tell me about any piece of furniture in your house that you bought? *I went to the store. I liked it. I bought it.* But everything in my house comes with a heritage. Every time I sit in my leather easy chair, I'm reminded of how I came to own this piece of furniture that by all rights I could never afford to buy. I was walking along a few blocks away from my apartment, my arms loaded down with books I was donating to my local library, when I saw a chair sitting on the curb waiting to be picked up by the next sanitation truck. While at first glance it looked like it might truly be ready for the trash heap, with its torn-up seat cushion, I knew right away I wanted it. Still, I couldn't stop to grab it then. I hurried to the library, dropped off my books, and rushed back to the chair. Of course, someone else was checking out the merchandise by the time I got back. I thought I had lost it. Who would pass up such a great find? I waited on the corner sending evil thoughts his way . . . and miraculously, he walked away. *Great, it's mine!* When I was in the middle of inspecting my chair, seeing if the cushion really was beyond repair, another guy walked up to offer his advice. "Eh, you don't want that, it's falling apart," he said. I thanked him for his words of wisdom and continued to poke and prod at the chair. He then walked away, and I noticed him heading back to his double-parked van just down the block. *Nice try, buddy,* I thought. I knew I had to grab it now or kiss it good-bye. I heaved it over my head, managed to lug it the few blocks home—and the rest is history. All I had to do was fashion a new cover for the cushion, which cost me no more than $30. The chair has now served me well for many years.

Each and every listing in this book offers you an opportunity for something more valuable than money: a memory, an experience, a story (and of course, the chance to save a boatload of cash ain't such a bad thing, either).

The listings in this book can be split into two categories: "Free" and "Ridiculously Cheap," with the vast majority of the listings being free. So let's define what I mean by these terms.

Simply stated, *free* is getting something without having to pay any money for it. So, here are some of the things you will *not* find in this book: "Buy One, Get One Free"; "First Month Free"; "Mention the Cheap Bastard and get in for half price"; or any other scheme that is ultimately about getting cash out of your wallet. What kind of free listings *will* you find in this book? Two basic kinds: free-free and free-with-a-catch. *Free-free* is just that: no-strings-attached, give-it-to-me-but-I'm-not-giving-you-anything free. For example, you can get a free personalized guided tour of any neighborhood in the five boroughs from Big Apple Greeters, plus they will even give you a free one-day unlimited metro card, no strings attached. *Free-with-a-catch* generally means you'll need to exchange some time or effort to get that something for free. For example, you can see almost any Off Broadway and some Broadway shows for free by being a volunteer usher. Show up an hour early, help seat the paying folks, and watch the show for nothing. I have tried to clearly lay out any catch you may need to know about by including the category "The Catch" (ingenious, eh?) wherever necessary.

"Ridiculously cheap" listings are those things that, yes, you will have to lay out some money to get. Still, the cost is so minimal that when you're asked to pay, you do it quickly for fear they'll realize their mistake. For example, does $75 a year for a gym membership sound pretty ridiculous to you?

Let me also mention what makes someone a Cheap Bastard. I see *Cheap Bastard* as a proud term referring to someone who enjoys the thrill of the hunt, not someone whose end-all and be-all is not spending money. This isn't someone who will deny himself or anyone else anything simply because it will cost some money. Most importantly, this isn't someone who is looking to cheat another person; nor is it to be confused with *stingy*. A Cheap Bastard is not out to beat another person out of a few cents; he is out to beat the system.

This book is intended for visitors and natives alike. Whether you're a backpacker from Australia who has just shown up in the city at the end of your round-the-world jaunt with less cash than you planned; a born-and-bred New Yorker who needs to stretch that paycheck a little farther; someone who's just moved to the city and working his first (low-paying) job out of college; a college student who needs to figure out how to make that student loan last all year; or even one of those folks for whom money is no worry, but, hey, you just like getting something for nothing (and who doesn't?)— this book is for you.

Finally, all the information in this guide is accurate as of press time, but things change quickly in New York, so I have included as much contact information as possible for each listing. Always call, check the Web site, or stop by to make sure all the information in this book is still accurate. If you have any thoughts, comments, corrections, or suggestions for future volumes, I would love to hear from you. Please send all correspondence to jivner@yahoo.com (you guessed it, that's a free e-mail address).

I've had a ball putting this book together, and I hope it helps you get the most out of the greatest city in the world.

Live well, live free,

Rob Grader
The Cheap Bastard
New York City
www.thecheapbastard.com

ENTERTAINMENT IN NEW YORK

"Of all men, physicians and playwrights alone possess the rare privilege of charging money for the pain they inflict on us."

—Santiago Ramón y Cajal

FROM THE BRIGHT LIGHTS of Broadway to the cutting-edge antics of the downtown performance world, New York is the undisputed capital of the theater world. Any day of the week, there are literally hundreds of performances going on in every corner of the city. And while the top ticket prices for a Broadway show have surpassed $400, you can spend endless evenings in the theaters of New York without spending a cent. By taking on the role of a volunteer usher, you can make your way into some Broadway shows and almost any Off Broadway show absolutely free. You can also keep yourself very busy attending any of the many just-plain-free performances at theaters throughout the city. These run the gamut from full productions to staged readings of new plays and musicals.

3

VOLUNTEER USHERING

Every time you walk into a theater to see a show, some kind person takes your ticket and shows you to your seat. Often you find that these folks are just thrilled to be doing this job. Ever wonder why? Well, this isn't their regular job; they're just there to see the show, like you. The only difference is, they haven't paid a cent to get in. Yes, they're volunteer ushers, and you'll find them at almost all Off Broadway and some Broadway theaters. Considering the ticket prices of these shows (from $25 to more than $400), volunteer ushers get "paid" very well for basically one hour's work, so why wouldn't they be pretty darn happy? And it's easy to join their ranks.

Each theater has its own protocol, but essentially all that's involved is making a reservation a week or two in advance, then showing up an hour before the curtain rises. The house manager will give you a quick rundown on the seating plan (warning: you do need to be able to count to twelve to understand this; sometimes you even need to count backward), then you help seat the paying folks. During the performance, enjoy the show. Ushers get to watch from seats that remain empty as the show is about to start. There are almost always good seats—many times the best seats in the house—for you to fill, even if the show is officially sold out. On the very rare occasion that there are absolutely no seats available, they will set up chairs for you, or in extremely rare cases, ask you to sit in the aisles. Occasionally you need to stay a couple of minutes after the show to help pick up stray playbills. It's as simple as that.

Dress the Part

While no special skills or training are needed to be a volunteer usher, a nice pair of black pants and a crisp white shirt are often required. Many theaters do ask you to look the role, even though you're only playing the part for one evening. The dress codes vary from black and white (black pants and a white shirt) to all black; some just ask you to look respectable (don't worry, no ties required). Be sure to ask what to wear when making reservations. Most theaters are flexible in these requirements, but some do take them very seriously and will not let you usher if you aren't dressed properly.

Why do theaters do this? Economics. It's cheaper to let you in for nothing than it is to hire a full-time ushering staff. You can even bring a friend. Most theaters need at least two ushers per show (some as many as ten) and are happy to let you reserve more than one slot. Some theaters that officially only use one usher per show will even let you bring a companion to usher with you if you ask nicely. Talk about your cheap dates!

BROADWAY

MANHATTAN THEATRE CLUB AT THE BILTMORE THEATRE

261 West 47th Street (between Broadway and Eighth Avenue)
(212) 394–3000, ext. 5463 (usher hotline)
volunteer@mtc-nyc.org
www.manhattantheatreclub.com
Ushers per performance: 5

Dedicated to producing and developing new plays and musicals, Manhattan Theatre Club has built a sterling reputation that began as a small Off-Off Broadway showcase thirty years ago and has now claimed some prime Broadway real estate for itself. Over the years they have presented new works by such acclaimed playwrights as Sam Shepard, Terrance McNally, A. R. Gurney, Harold Pinter, John Patrick Shanley, and countless others. The production often attracts big-name Hollywood and Broadway talent. Each year they present a full season of new plays. They usually begin taking phone or e-mail reservations two weeks before performances begin, but call their hotline earlier to find out the specific day they will start accepting reservations. The slots for the entire run usually fill up that day.

THE ROUNDABOUT THEATRE COMPANY

The American Airlines Theater
227 West 42nd Street (between Eighth Avenue and Broadway)
(212) 719–9393, ext. 523 (usher hotline)
www.roundabouttheatre.org
Ushers per performance: 6

After years of hopping from theater to theater, one of New York's most renowned theater companies has found a permanent home on Broadway. And since they remain a not-for-profit theater, this is one of the few opportunities to volunteer-usher on Broadway. They also maintain productions at Studio 54 and the Off Broadway performances at the Laura Pells Theatre (see below for information on these theaters). Their productions often attract star performers and are almost always of a high caliber (particularly the musicals). To book a slot at the American Airlines Theater, sign up with the security guard in the lobby of the theater Monday through Friday between 10:00 A.M. and 5:00 P.M. (but just from 10:00 A.M. to noon on Wednesday). They generally make dates available about two weeks before previews begin and fill the dates for the entire run on a first-come, first-served basis. These slots go fast, so sign up early. Call their hotline (listed above) to find out when they are accepting ushers. They are very serious about the black-and-white dress code for ushers.

STUDIO 54
254 West 54th Street (between Broadway and Eighth Avenue)
(212) 719–9393, ext. 523 (usher hotline)
www.roundabouttheatre.org
Ushers per performance: 10
The Roundabout Theatre Company has taken ownership of the legendary disco and turned it into its own permanent home for musicals and high-profile plays. After playing host to the longtime Broadway hit *Cabaret,* the Roundabout will now continue to fill this theater with its own brand of high-quality, often star-studded revivals and original musicals for both limited and extended runs. To nab yourself an ushering slot, stop by the theater Monday through Friday from 10:00 A.M. to 5:00 P.M. (but just 10:00 A.M. to noon on Wednesday.) Be sure to call the usher hotline before you head down there to find out when they accepting ushers.

OFF BROADWAY

ATLANTIC THEATER COMPANY
336 West 20th Street (between Eighth and Ninth Avenues)
(212) 645–8015 or (646) 216-1191 (usher hotline)
www.atlantictheater.org
Ushers per performance: 2
Founded by followers of the David Mamet school of acting and known for producing his works and others of the same ilk. Productions all have limited runs, and ushering slots fill quickly. They start taking ushering reservations three weeks prior to the start of performances and are usually "sold out" by the time the reviews come out.

BLUE MAN GROUP
Astor Place Theatre
434 Lafayette Street (between East 4th and 8th Streets)
(212) 254–4370, ext. 220
www.blueman.com
Ushers per night: 4
You've seen the long-running Off Broadway Blue Man Group on the Intel commercials, Jay Leno, David Letterman, and every other talk show imaginable, and if you still haven't seen enough of them, come on down to the theater where the whole thing started and see them for free (they don't need any more money). They will also ask you to stay about fifteen minutes after the show is over to clean up. Warning: It's a messy show. To make an ushering reservation, call about a week in advance, Monday through Friday from 9:00 A.M. to 9:00 P.M.

THE CHERRY LANE THEATRE
38 Commerce Street (between Bedford and Hudson Streets)
(212) 989–2020, ext. 23
www.cherrylanetheatre.com
Ushers per performance: 3
Since 1924 this theater has been home to many of the early works of such playwrights as Edward Albee, Beckett, Ionesco, Mamet, Pinter, Lanford Wilson, and Sam Shepard. In recent years it has played host to such successful Off Broadway shows as *Fully Committed, Nunsense, True West, Blown Sideways through Life,* and many others. Call a week to a month in advance. Very casual and easygoing atmosphere for ushers.

CLASSIC STAGE COMPANY (CSC)
136 East 13th Street (between Third and Fourth Avenues)
(212) 677–4210, ext. 56
cschousemanager@gmail.com
www.classicstage.org
Ushers per performance: 3
For more than thirty years, CSC has built a reputation for reinventing classic works of the theater—some well known, others less so. They have attracted a loyal following by working with some of the best-known actors, directors, and writers from New York, Hollywood, and around the country. E-mail for ushering reservations a week to a month in advance of the performance.

THE CULTURE PROJECT

55 Mercer Street (Between Broome and Grand Streets)
(212) 925–1806
www.cultureproject.org

Ushers per performance: 1

Since its inception in 1996, this theater company has been presenting award-winning and often star-studded productions that bring the national political conversation to the New York stage. Some of its most noteworthy productions include *The Exonerated, Bridge and Tunnel, My Trip to Al-Qaeda,* and many others. Call anytime from a few days to a few weeks in advance to make a reservation, depending on the popularity of the show.

DRAMA DEPARTMENT

9 Desbrosses Street (between Hudson and Greenwich Streets)
(212) 633–9108
www.dramadept.org

This high-profile theater collective is the love child of actress Cynthia Nixon (*Sex and the City*) and playwright Douglas Carter Beane (*As Bees in Honey Drown*). The members of this company are many of the most sought-after artists in film, TV, and the theater, and in turn tickets for their productions can be hard to come by (even if you are willing to pay for them). Fret not, if you are willing to donate an hour or two helping out around their offices, they will happily pay you with free tickets to their shows.

ENCORES

City Center
West 55th Street (between Sixth and Seventh Avenues)
(212) 763–1204
www.citycenter.org

Ushers per performance: 6–9

Presenting series of highly produced staged readings of musicals with star performers, Encores is considered one of the hottest tickets in town. Call far in advance to put your name on a list of volunteers to hawk CDs and other paraphernalia in the lobby to get into the shows. Warning: There is a waiting list about 12 miles long to get on the list, so be patient.

HERE PERFORMANCE ART CAFE

145 Sixth Avenue (between Spring and Domnich Streets)
(212) 647–0202
www.here.org

Ushers per performance: 1–2

Here is a downtown art center bringing together theater, performance art, music, dance, and visual art into one complex. With an ever-changing rotation of productions of all sorts in their three theaters and intriguing work on the walls and floors of their gallery, there is always something worthwhile to see here. Call the box office manager a couple of days to a week in advance to reserve an ushering slot.

IRISH ARTS CENTER
553 West 51st Street (between Tenth and Eleventh Avenues)
(212) 757–3318, ext. 203
info@irishartscenter.org
www.irishartscenter.org
Ushers per performance: 1–2

Presents a full season of productions by and about the Irish experience, as well as playing host to many imports from Ireland. Call to add your name to the list of volunteer ushers, and they will call when they need you.

IRISH REPERTORY THEATRE
132 West 22nd Street (between Sixth and Seventh Avenues)
(212) 255–0270
www.irishrepertorytheatre.com
Ushers per performance: 2

Call 10:00 A.M. to 6:00 P.M. Monday through Friday to schedule a date. This company has built a strong reputation for presenting the works of (believe it or not) Irish and Irish-American writers, both classical and contemporary. They have two theaters, and you may usher in either of them. Call at least two weeks in advance for an ushering reservation, more if you need a specific date.

THE JOYCE THEATER
175 Eighth Avenue (at 19th Street)
(646) 792–8355
www.joyce.org
Ushers per performance: 8

The leading theater for dance companies, the Joyce plays host to practically every major company from around the country and around the world. They begin taking ushering reservations two weeks before each performance.

THE LAMB'S THEATRE
130 West 44th Street (between Sixth Avenue and Broadway)
(212) 575–0300, ext. 28
www.lambstheatre.org
Ushers per performance: 3

Designed by noted architect Sanford White in 1904 and as the original home to the Lambs, America's oldest theatrical club, this building has played a leading role in the development of the American theater. It was here that Lerner met Lowe (*My Fair Lady, Camelot*), that Mark Twain wrote his first play, and here that Richard Rodgers set to work on a new musical called *Away We Go* (later renamed *Oklahoma!*). The upstairs residences were once home to the likes of John Wayne, Fred Astaire, and John Philip Sousa. These days, their two Off Broadway theaters have been hosts to such shows as *Smoke on the Mountain, Dames at Sea, Beau Jest,* and *The Countess.* Call for ushering reservations.

THE LAURA PELLS THEATRE
The Roundabout Theatre Company
111 West 46th Street (between Sixth and Seventh Avenues)
(212) 719–9393, ext. 523 (usher hotline)
www.roundabouttheatre.org
Ushers per performance: 6

The Roundabout Theatre Company has closed down shop at the Gramercy Theater and moved its Off Broadway productions into the old American Place Theater. Expect a season chock-full of classics, small-scale musicals, and new plays with cast lists punctuated with star names. Sign up for an ushering slot at the theater on Monday, Tuesday, Thursday, or Friday from 10:00 A.M. to 5:00 P.M.

LUCILLE LORTEL THEATER
121 Christopher Street (between Hudson and Bleecker Streets)
(212) 924–2817, ext. 207
www.lortel.org
Ushers per performance: 3

This venerable Off Broadway theater has been the home of many major productions over its fifty-plus-year history, such as *Cloud 9, Steel Magnolias, Three Penny Opera, As Bees in Honey Drown,* and many others. Call anywhere from a few days to a few weeks in advance to make an ushering reservation, depending on the popularity of the show.

MANHATTAN THEATRE CLUB (MTC)
City Center (theater and box office)
West 55th Street (between Sixth and Seventh Avenues)
311 West 43rd Street, eighth floor (administrative offices)
(212) 247–0430, ext. 240
mtchousemanager@nycitycenter.org
www.manhattantheatreclub.com
Ushers per performance: 4 on Stage 1, 1 on Stage 2

MTC is a major producer of new plays, many of which end up transferring to larger commercial Broadway theaters, including *Proof, The Tale of the Allergist's Wife, Ain't Misbehavin',* and many others over the years. See them before they move, because you can't usher for them once they hit the Great White Way. To get an ushering reservation, e-mail them at least a few weeks in advance with your name, the production you are interested in, and a few dates you can make. They will e-mail you back with details. You can also volunteer-usher at their Broadway theater, MTC at the Biltmore. See their listing in the Broadway section for more details.

MCC THEATER
Lucille Lortel Theater
121 Christopher Street (between Hudson and Bleecker Streets)
(212) 924–2817
www.mcctheater.org
Ushers per performance: 3
MCC is a small but popular Off Broadway company that has made a name for itself by producing such plays as the Pulitzer Prize–winning *Wit* and has worked with such actors as Calista Flockhart, Bridget Fonda, Thomas Gibson, Kyra Sedgwick, Marisa Tomei, Allison Janney, and Lili Taylor over its twenty-plus-year history. Make ushering reservations a week or two before performances begin. Slots fill up quickly.

MINT THEATER COMPANY
311 West 43rd Street, third floor (between Eighth and Ninth Avenues)
(212) 315–0231
www.minttheater.org
Ushers per performance: 1–2
This small, well-respected company concentrates on rediscovering lost classics from the nineteenth and twentieth centuries. Recent productions have included *The Voysey Inheritance, House of Mirth,* and *Mr. Pim Passes By*. Ushering slots do get filled quickly; call Monday through Friday noon to 6:00 P.M. two to three weeks before performances begin to be assured of a reservation.

THE NEW GROUP THEATER
410 West 42nd Street (between Ninth and Tenth Avenues)
(212) 244–3380, ext. 301
www.thenewgroup.org
Ushers per performance: 2
A high-profile company with many productions that have won all the

awards and transferred to long runs on Broadway and at major Off Broadway theaters, including *Avenue Q, This Is Our Youth, Ecstasy, Another American Asking and Telling,* and others. Call two weeks in advance for ushering reservations.

NEW WORLD STAGES
340 West 50th Street (between Eighth and Ninth Avenues)
(646) 871–1730
volunteer@newworldstages.com
www.newworldstages.com
Number of ushers: 1–2 per show, per theater
From the ashes of the World Wide Cinema (what used to be every cheap bastard's favorite $2 movie theater) comes a complex of seven state-of-the-art Off Broadway theaters. The theaters are owned and operated by the Dodgers, a producing organization that has been responsible for many of Broadway's biggest hits over the last twenty or so years. Since opening the doors to the theater complex they have played host to such productions as *Altar Boyz, Naked Boys Singin,* and the *Gazillion Bubble Show.* To make an ushering reservation, e-mail them two weeks ahead of the date you want. Check out their ushering rules and procedures on their Web site.

NEW YORK THEATRE WORKSHOP (NYTW)
79 East 4th Street (between Second Avenue and Bowery)
(212) 780–9037, ext. 102
www.nytw.org
Ushers per performance: 6
NYTW produces some of the most daring and artistically challenging productions of any Off Broadway theater; it was the original producer of such Broadway hits as *Rent* and *Dirty Blond.* Ushering slots can be reserved anywhere from the day of a performance to three weeks in advance, depending on the popularity of the show. Be sure to get on their ushering mailing list, and they will send you reminders for each new show. They also throw in free coffee or tea at the concession stand for ushers.

THE PEARL THEATRE COMPANY
Theatre 80
80 St. Marks Place (between First and Second Avenues)
(212) 598–9802
www.pearltheatre.org
Ushers per performance: 4
One of the few true classical repertory companies remaining in New York. Their seasons concentrate on the works of Shakespeare, Chekhov, Coward, the

Greeks, and other Dead European White Men. Their productions are almost never startlingly original, but almost always respectably done. Call one to two weeks in advance for ushering reservations.

PERFORMANCE SPACE 122
150 First Avenue (at East 9th Street)
(212) 477–5829, ext. 304
housemanager@ps122.org
www.ps122.org
Ushers per performance: 2
The longtime home of experimental and cutting-edge theater and dance, P.S. 122 continues to host many well-known and emerging performance artists, including Eric Bogosian, John Leguizamo, and Karen Finley. You never know what you're going to catch there, but it's always daring and innovative. Call or e-mail the week of the performance to book an ushering slot in one of their two theaters.

PLAYWRIGHTS HORIZONS
416 West 42nd Street (between Ninth and Tenth Avenues)
(212) 564–1235
usher@playwrightshorizons.com
www.playwrightshorizons.org
Ushers per performance: 4
Produces a season of new plays and musicals by well-known and up-and-coming playwrights, many of which transfer to larger Off Broadway or Broadway theaters. Past productions have included *Driving Miss Daisy, The Heidi Chronicles, Once on This Island,* and James Joyce's *The Dead*. They maintain a large list of ushers and send out mailings before each show begins performances. You have to be a real go-getter to get one of these coveted ushering slots. First you need to get on their e-mail list by sending them an e-mail (address above) with the words "Add to list" in the subject line. Then they will send out a mass e-mail telling you (and thousands of others) when they will be accepting reservations. On that day, you had better call first thing in the morning, because they usually fill all of their slots within hours.

RATTLESTICK PLAYWRIGHTS THEATRE
224 Waverly Place (off Seventh Avenue at 11th Street)
(212) 627–2556
www.rattlestick.org
Ushers per performance: 1
This up-and-coming Off Broadway theater has begun to build a strong name

for itself producing contemporary playwrights. Past productions have included *Down South, Whale Music,* and *Killers and Other Family.* Call early in the run to snag an ushering slot. They also offer up a schedule of free play readings; check their Web site for details.

SECOND STAGE THEATRE
307 West 43rd Street (at Eighth Avenue)
(212) 787–8302, ext. 216
jschleifer@2st.com
www.2st.com
Ushers per performance: 4
Hailed in past years by the *New York Times* as "the season's most indispensable theater," Second Stage produces a season chock-full of theater heavyweights like August Wilson, Stephen Sondheim, Edward Albee, and many others. To make a reservation, e-mail your full name and requested dates to the above address. They start taking requests three weeks before preview performances begin, and slots can fill up quickly, depending on the popularity of the show.

THE SIGNATURE THEATRE COMPANY
Peter Norton Space
555 West 42nd Street (between Tenth and Eleventh Avenues)
(212) 244–7529
www.signaturetheatre.org
Ushers per performance: 4
Specializes in highly regarded productions focusing each season on the works of a single American playwright. Past seasons have included Arthur Miller, Edward Albee, Maria Irene Fornes, and Sam Shepard. Call at least two weeks in advance. Free coffee, tea, and hot chocolate for ushers!

SOHO PLAYHOUSE
15 Vandam Street (between Spring and Prince Streets)
(212) 691–1555
www.sohoplayhouse.com
Ushers per performance: 1
This theater has been home to such productions as *Killer Joe, Grandma Silvia's Funeral,* and others. Make reservations a few days to a week in advance by calling the box office noon to 7:00 P.M., Tuesday through Saturday.

THEATRE ROW
410 West 42nd Street (between Ninth and Tenth Avenues)
(212) 714–2442
www.theatrerow.org

This space is the home of five state-of-the-art Off Broadway theaters—the Acorn, the Beckett, the Clurman, the Kirk, and the Lion. These spaces are used by many of New York's A-list theater companies, many of whom, though not all, use volunteer ushers. To find out if you can volunteer-usher for a particular show, you need to contact the production company for that show. Call the Theatre Row administrative offices (listed above) to get the contact information for the various companies. For best results you may want to stop by sometime close to showtime and ask about ushering at that specific theater.

THE VINEYARD THEATRE
108 East 15th Street (between Union Square East and Irving Place)
(212) 353–3366, ext. 226 (usher hotline)
housemanager@vineyardtheatre.org
www.vineyardtheatre.org
Ushers per performance: 2
The Vineyard produces and develops new works by many major figures in the American theater. They have brought to life such shows as *Fully Committed*, the Pulitzer Prize–winning *How I Learned to Drive*, and *Three Tall Women*. Make ushering reservations by phone or e-mail one to three weeks in advance.

WOMEN'S PROJECT THEATRE
424 West 55th Street (between Ninth and Tenth Avenues)
Administrative offices: 55 West End Avenue
(212) 765–1706
info@womensproject.org
www.womensproject.org
Ushers per performance: 6
Dedicated to producing and developing the talents of women playwrights, over its twenty-plus-year history this theater has been among the first to work with such artists as Eve Ensler, Maria Irene Fornes, Anna Deavere Smith, Liz Diamond, Tina Landau, and Joyce Carol Oates, among others. Call the office or e-mail them to get on their ushering list. Two weeks before a performance, you'll receive an e-mail that will tell you how to make reservations for that show. Also look for the free series of readings they hold once a year, usually around November.

THE WOOSTER GROUP
The Performing Garage
33 Wooster Street (between Broome and Grand Streets)
(212) 966–3651
www.thewoostergroup.org
Ushers per performance: 2–6

Off the Menu

If there's an Off Broadway show that you're interested in seeing and the theater isn't on this list, just ask at the box office if they use volunteer ushers for that show. There are always new venues popping up, and nontraditional performance spaces being used for new shows. Staff are very much used to answering this question. Nine times out of ten, they will say yes and tell you how to go about making a reservation.

Founded in the early 1970s by Jim Clayburgh, Willem Dafoe, Spalding Gray, and others, this company remains one of the premier experimental theater groups in the world. Their productions regularly tour internationally, but you can see one for free at the Performing Garage where it all started by reserving a slot as a volunteer usher. The ushering slots go fast, so call far in advance to nab one.

YORK THEATRE COMPANY

St. Peter's Church
619 Lexington Avenue (at 54th Street)
(212) 935–5824, ext. 19
www.yorktheatre.org
Ushers per performance: 2

For more than thirty years, York has produced such award-winning musicals as *The Grass Harp, Pacific Overtures, She Loves Me, Company, 110 in the Shade, Sweeney Todd, Carnival,* and *Merrily We Roll Along.* Many of its productions have made the move to Broadway or larger Off Broadway theaters. Call two weeks ahead to make ushering reservations. The theater also presents free staged readings of new musicals on a regular basis. Call or check their Web site for the schedule.

THE ZIPPER THEATER

336 West 37th Street (between Eighth and Ninth Avenues)
(212) 563–0480
www.zippertheater.com
Ushers per performance: 4

This fun and funky theater space located in a converted zipper factory plays host to a variety of no-holds-barred, screw-traditional-theater productions.

Call for ushering reservations anywhere from a couple of days to three weeks in advance, depending on the popularity of the show.

CHEAP SEATS

Truth be told, the following listings are not exactly my idea of bargains. I mean, if you have to put out some actual cash for something, what's the point? But the rest of the world thinks these are good deals, so I'd be remiss if I didn't include this information. Here are a few worthy organizations that can get you good seats in loads of Broadway and Off Broadway theaters and concert halls for a minimum of cash.

AUDIENCE EXTRAS (AE)
61 Lexington Avenue, Suite 1A
(212) 686–1966
www.audienceextras.com

 $85 yearly membership fee, and $30 personal reserve fund toward the $3 service charge per ticket.

PLAY BY PLAY
312 West 36th Street (between Seventh and Eighth Avenues)
(212) 868–7052
www.play-by-play.com

 $99 yearly membership, and $3 service fee per ticket, and a personal reserve fund.

THEATER EXTRAS
(914) 304–4093 or (212) 802–7277
www.theaterextras.com

 $99 annual membership, and $4 service charge per ticket.

THEATERMANIA GOLD CLUB
915 Broadway, Suite 1406
(212) 352–0255, ext. 114
www.theatermania.com/Gold

 $99.00 yearly membership fee, and a $4.50 service charge per ticket.

These four companies exist for the sole purpose of getting living, breathing bodies into the seats of concert halls and theaters around the New York region. When a production needs a crowd—either because critics will be reviewing the production that night, or because it is early in the run and they want a full house to gauge audience response—producers turn to these guys to "paper the house" (translation: fill the seats). The bulk of the tickets offered are for Broadway, Off Broadway, and edgier Off-Off Broadway, theaters, but you can also often snag tickets for classical concerts at such venues as Lincoln Center and Carnegie Hall, as well as major cabaret performances, pop concerts and sporting events (yes, even Mets and Yankees tickets!). Each company operates slightly differently, but here is the basic model that they all follow. You pay a yearly membership fee that ranges between $85 and $99. Once you are a member you have access to their listing of available productions through their Web site, where you can reserve one or two tickets for anything available. They generally offer anywhere from ten to forty offerings at any given time for performances taking place that day or over the next week or two. You will be charged a service fee of $3.00 to $4.50 for each ticket you reserve. Audience Extras and Play By Play will have you maintain a balance in a fund that these service fees are deducted from, while Theater Extras and TheaterMania Gold Club will charge the service charges to your credit card. This is a great way to expose yourself to an amazing array of performances without a whole lot of financial risk. If you use your membership for at least two or three a performances a year, it will easily pay for itself.

TKTS BOOTH
Theater Development Fund (TDF)
Duffy Square (47th Street and Broadway)
South Street Seaport; 186 Front Street (at John Street)
(212) 221–0013
www.tdf.org

Sells tickets for 25, 35, or 50 percent off ticket price plus a $3 service charge per ticket.

"We'll get tickets at the booth" has been the cry of many a spontaneous theatergoer for more than twenty-five years. The TKTS booth sells tickets to Broadway, Off Broadway, music, and dance events the day of the performance at 25, 35, or 50 percent off the ticket price (plus a $3 service charge per ticket). They post the available shows outside the booth on boards, which change throughout the day. They accept payments only in cash or traveler's checks. As a rule, you can be sure you won't find tickets available to the newest, hottest show. The lines can be long, particularly on weekends and holidays. The tickets, however, are for some of the best seats in the theaters. Both locations are open seven days a week.

JUST PLAIN FREE THEATER

AMERICAN ACADEMY OF DRAMATIC ARTS
120 Madison Avenue (between 30th and 31st Streets)
(212) 453–5340
www.aada.org

Some of the most legendary stars of stage and screen have trained at this institution, including Lauren Bacall, Spencer Tracy, John Cassavetes, Grace Kelly, Cecil B. DeMille, Danny DeVito, Colleen Dewhurst, Anne Bancroft, Ron Leibman, Jason Robards Jr., Kirk Douglas, and many others. To date academy alumni have received nominations for more than seventy-two Oscars, sixty Tonys, and 211 Emmys. From September through February the Academy Company—made up of third-year students—presents a season of free productions. Here's a chance to say you saw them when. Click on "Company Plays" on the Web site or call for dates and schedules.

BOOMERANG THEATRE COMPANY
Center Stage/NY
48 West 21st Street, fourth floor (between Fifth and Sixth Avenues)
(212) 501–4069
www.boomerangtheatre.org

This up-and-coming Off-Off Broadway company presents a series of readings of new plays. Also be sure to catch their summer season of free Shakespeare in the parks and public spaces around New York City.

52ND STREET PROJECT
500 West 52nd Street (at Tenth Avenue)
(212) 333-5252

A program through Ensemble Studio Theater that creates short theater pieces by or for the children of Hell's Kitchen in collaboration with professional theater artists. While these may not be Broadway productions, they are surprisingly well put together and offer an evening that is always full of laughter, original music, and a lot of talent (community and professional).

HB PLAYWRIGHTS FOUNDATION
124 Bank Street (between Greenwich and Washington Streets)
(212) 989-7856

Established by acting legends Herbert Berghoff and Uta Hagen in 1965 as an offshoot of their renowned (and low-cost!) acting school, the theater presents four productions a year (always free) and has featured many well-established writers, actors, and directors. In recent years the company has given birth to such productions as *Mrs. Klein, Collected Stories,* and others that have moved to larger pay-for-your-ticket venues. The best way to find out about the performances is to call the office during business hours and ask to be added to their mailing list.

THE JUILLIARD SCHOOL
60 Lincoln Center Plaza (Broadway and 65th Street on plaza level)
(212) 769-7406 (box office)
(212) 799-5000, ext. 251 (drama division)
www.juilliard.edu

 You must call to get on the drama division's mailing list to get their calendar of events.

See tomorrow's stars of stage and screen today. This is considered the preeminent conservatory for actors in the country, and they present a full schedule of productions throughout the school year featuring students at every level of development. Often productions are put together by well-known directors—both faculty members and guest artists. All performances in the fall and early spring are free, though tickets are required and go fast. Call to put your name on the drama division's mailing list to get the calendar of free performances. Every spring they remount all of these productions for a Spring Repertory, but they charge for those tickets ($15). To get the free tickets, line up at the box office on the day they become available, usually two weeks before the performances begin; otherwise you'll probably be sold out of the event. You can also line up an hour before the show to try to get

Standing Room Only

Dying to see that boffo Broadway hit, but you don't have the hundred bucks for the ticket or can't wait the six months until one becomes available? Standing room is what you're looking for. Many, but not all, Broadway theaters sell standing-room tickets. They're available only on the day of the performance and only if the show is completely sold out. It will cost you somewhere between $15 and $25 for the honor of standing to watch the show. The good news is that you'll have a great view: Standing room is directly behind the orchestra seating. And if you get tired, keep your eyes peeled for an empty seat for the second act. Check with the specific box offices for details.

in on a standby basis. Performances by the music division are also free, though not those by the dance and opera departments.

NEW DRAMATISTS

424 West 44th Street (between Ninth and Tenth Avenues)
(212) 757–6960
www.newdramatists.org

New Dramatists is an organization devoted to developing playwrights, both up-and-coming and established, along with their material. They conduct an ongoing series of readings and workshops of new plays, musicals, and screenplays staffed with many leading actors and directors from the New York theater scene. Performances take place throughout the week (Monday through Friday) in the late afternoon or evening. All readings are free, and almost all are open to the public. Check the Web site or call for a calendar of events.

THE NEW SCHOOL FOR DRAMA

151 Bank Street (between Washington Street and the West Side Highway)
(212) 229–5859
www.newschool.edu/academic/drama

From the end of January through May, The New School For Drama presents Random Acts, with graduating MFA (Masters of Fine Arts) students performing in original one acts written by students in the playwrighting program. All performances are free, but reservations are required.

NEW YORK SHAKESPEARE FESTIVAL/ THE PUBLIC THEATER

425 Lafayette Street (at Astor Place)

(212) 260–2400

www.publictheater.org

From the people who bring you Shakespeare in Central Park every summer come other free theater events throughout the year. Every spring and fall they hold a two-week festival of readings and workshops called New Work Now!; many of the pieces presented here have later ended up on their main stage, including the plays *Stop Kiss, References to Salvador Dali Make Me Hot, Topdog/Underdog,* and others. The Public also offers cheap rush tickets to each and every performance on the day of the performance. Check their Web site for the details about these and many other free events that pop up throughout the year.

NEW YORK UNIVERSITY GRADUATE ACTING PROGRAM

721 Broadway (between Waverly and Washington Streets)

111 Second Avenue (between 6th and 7th Streets)

(212) 998–1921

www.gradacting.tisch.nyu.edu

THE CATCH **Only second-year productions are free.**

One of the most respected graduate acting programs in the country has a distinguished alumnus list that boasts the likes of Billy Crudup, Camryn Manheim, Marcia Gay Harden, Barry Bostwick, Tony Kushner, and many others. See full productions of classics and contemporary plays mounted by the second-year students (they charge for the third-year student productions). Tickets are available one week before performances begin and sell out very quickly for these intimate performance spaces. Check the Web site or call for schedule and details.

RATTLESTICK THEATRE COMPANY

224 Waverly Place (off Seventh Avenue at 11th Street)

(212) 627–2556

www.rattlestick.org

Rattlestick annually offers a three-week festival of readings of new plays and works in progress every summer. Call or check their Web site for schedule and details.

THEATREWORKS USA

The Lucille Lortel Theater
121 Christopher Street (between Hudson and Bleecker Streets)
(212) 332–0001
www.theatreworksusa.org

Theatreworks USA is unquestionably the leading producer of professional theater for young audiences. Each year their wonderful productions tour to every corner of the country and reach over four million people. And every summer they present their newest production for free to New York audiences. Not-for-profit groups such as summer camps can reserve blocks of tickets, and individuals need to line up at the theater, where they distribute a limited number of tickets on a first-come, first-served basis. For more information check out their Web site or call the number above.

YORK THEATRE COMPANY

St. Peter's Church
619 Lexington Avenue (at 54th Street)
(212) 935–5824, ext. 19
www.yorktheatre.org

Presents a varied schedule of free staged readings of new musicals at various times throughout the week. Call or check their Web site for schedule and details. Presents free staged readings on new musicals most Monday nights at 7:30 P.M.

FREE WILL(IAM): FREE THEATER IN THE PARKS

SHAKESPEARE IN CENTRAL PARK

New York Shakespeare Festival/The Public Theater
Delacorte Theater
Turtle Pond (midpark at West 81st or East 79th Street)
(212) 539–8750
www.publictheater.org

The granddaddy of all Shakespeare in the Park festivals, now in its sixth decade of free performances in Central Park. They present star-studded productions each summer (at least one of which is always a Shakespeare play). They start handing out the free tickets at 1:00 P.M. each day at the Delacorte in Central Park and from 1:00 to 3:00 P.M. at the Public Theater (425 Lafayette Street between East 4th Street and Astor Place). In recent years they have also started handing out tickets in various locations throughout the five boroughs;

call for details. These tickets are always in demand, so plan to spend a while on line. But don't let that deter you: This event attracts a great cross section of people, and waiting on line is often as much fun, if not more, than the show itself. If you don't have the time to wait, take a chance and stop by the Delacorte box office at 7:30 P.M., when they release many reserved tickets.

Here are some other companies that bring the Bard and other works to a neighborhood near you. All the performances are free, but some of these companies are not shy about passing the hat at the end of the night. Call or check their Web sites for shows, times, and specific locations:

BOOMERANG THEATRE COMPANY, Central Park and other parks; (212) 501–4069; www.boomerangtheatre.org.

CIRCUS AMOK, politically minded circus performances in public parks throughout the five boroughs every June; (718) 486–7432; www.circus amok.org.

CITYPARKS THEATER, various companies present Shakespeare and other productions as well as performance workshops in parks throughout Manhattan and Brooklyn in July and August; (212) 360–8290; www.cityparksfoundation.org.

GORILLA REP, Shakespeare plays that change locations with each scene; Riverside Park just north of 79th Street; www.gorillarep.org.

HUDSON WAREHOUSE, Riverside Park; (212) 560–6579; www.hudsonwarehouse.net.

INWOOD SHAKESPEARE FESTIVAL, Inwood Hill Park and other parks; (917) 918–0394; www.moosehallisf.org.

NEW YORK CLASSICAL THEATRE, West 103rd Street and Central Park West; (212) 252–4531; www.newyorkclassical.org.

SHAKESPEARE IN THE PARK(ING LOT), Ludlow Street (between Delancey and Broome Streets); www.drillingcompany.org.

THEATER FOR THE NEW CITY, political street theater in parks throughout the five boroughs; (212) 254–1109; www.theaterforthenewcity.net.

"I'll open my case, and I might catch a coin, but all ears may listen for free."

—Steve Forbert
"Grand Central Station, March 18, 1977"

MUSIC: OF FREE I SING

EW YORK IS AWASH in free music, from almost any street corner or subway platform to clubs, bars, churches, parks, and concert halls. Any season, any day of the year, you can find the strains of any style of music: classical, rock, jazz, country, folk, experimental, world, ethnic . . . if you can hum it, you can find it somewhere in New York for free. Particularly during the summer months, you can hardly turn around without being enticed into another amazing performance at one of the many free concert series all over the city. This being New York, these venues attract top-name artists whom you'd usually have to pay top dollar to see. And I'm not talking about one great show a summer; this goes on week after week, all summer long. One thing to be aware of when attending free shows at many bars and clubs is they do often have a one-, two-, or more-drink minimum, which could add up to a tidy sum. Check out the prices before you order, too; sometimes even a Coke could cost as much as $5.

ROCK, POP, FOLK, AND ALTERNATIVE

THE BACK FENCE
155 Bleecker Street (at Thompson Street)
(212) 475–9221
www.thebackfenceonline.com

 They charge admission on Saturday night only.

Straw on the floor, free peanuts at the bar, and free classic rock, country, and folk rock six nights a week.

THE BAGGOT INN
82 West 3rd Street (between Thompson and Sullivan Streets)
(212) 477–0622
www.thebaggotinn.com

 No cover or minimum for shows Sunday through Wednesday nights only.

During the week you will find nights of bluegrass jams, acoustic open mike, blues, country, and rock.

DEMPSEY'S PUB
61 Second Avenue (between 3rd and 4th Streets)
(212) 388–0662
www.thebaggotinn.com/dempseys.html

Grab your penny whistle and uilleann pipes and come on down to Dempsey's every Tuesday for a traditional Irish music *seisun* (jam session) at 8:00 P.M. Musicians and listeners welcome.

HANK'S SALOON
46 Third Avenue (at Atlantic Avenue)
Brooklyn
(718) 625–8003
www.hankssaloon.com

This Brooklyn down-home dive saloon is the twang mecca of New York. You will find free live country, rockabilly, and rock music seven nights a week. Don't miss the free barbecue every Sunday and Monday nights, and free pool every Tuesday. Also on Monday you can channel your inner Patsy Cline when they host New York's only country music karaoke night with a live band. No cover, no minimum.

On-the-House Bands

Oh My Rockness, www.ohmyrockness.com, is the go-to Web site for comprehensive listings for every free indie rock show in New York City. These folks cull though hundreds of show listings every week and post them on their Web site for you to check out any-time you want to catch a show. Many of the listings also include in-depth reviews and information on the bands as well as the venues. They also list shows that you have to pay your way into, but if you simply hit the handy-dandy "Free Shows" tab, you can have access to the hundreds of free shows going on every week.

LAKESIDE LOUNGE

162 Avenue B (between 10th and 11th Streets)
(212) 529–8463
www.lakesidelounge.com

A honky-tonk bar with a band in the back room late nights. It's free, but some-times you get what you pay for. They book some good rock bands who try their damnedest to play above the roar of the crowd. No cover, no minimum.

THE LIVING ROOM

154 Ludlow Street (between Stanton and Rivington Streets)
(212) 533–7235
www.livingroomny.com

THE CATCH **One-drink minimum per act, loosely enforced.**

One of the top destinations in New York for an eclectic mix of singer-songwriters, indie-rock, and acoustic music acts every night that attracts a fun and attentive audience. Norah Jones often performed here before she took over the music world, and she still occasionally stops by for an unan-nounced set or two. They will occasionally charge an admission, but the vast majority of performances are free, though they do try to enforce a one-drink minimum per act. They also have a smaller second room upstairs with free music every night.

PADDY REILLY'S MUSIC BAR

519 Second Avenue (at 29th Street)
(212) 686–1210

Free shows/no minimum Sunday through Thursday nights (except some Tuesdays).

The definitive home of Irish music in New York. You'll find everything from Irish rock to traditional Irish music *seisun* on the schedule. Musicians are always welcome to join in on the *seisun*.

PARKSIDE LOUNGE

317 East Houston Street (at Attorney Street)
(212) 673–6270
www.parksidelounge.com

Two-drink minimum that they do try to enforce—but "we're not gonna trow ya out if ya don't drink."

A local bar complete with pool table, pinball games, and a hip jukebox, along with a snazzy back room with live shows every night. You'll find a lot of local rock/alternative/blues bands most nights. They have bluegrass bands that jam every Monday night and comedy throughout the week. Bring your own instrument and join in the fun at the very popular salsa jam every Friday, which starts with free salsa dance classes! Most, though not all, shows are free (except for the two-drink minimum.)

POSTCRYPT COFFEEHOUSE

Columbia University
Basement of St. Paul's Chapel
116th Street and Broadway
(212) 854–1953
www.columbia.edu/cu/postcrypt/coffeehouse

This is one of the great hidden treasures of New York City. Since 1964 every Friday and Saturday night during the school year, this small performance space (only about twenty-five seats) has been filled with the sounds of some of the top names in folk and acoustic music. Past performers have included David Bromberg, Jeff Buckley, Shawn Colvin, Ani DiFranco, John Gorka, Patty Larkin, Lisa Loeb, Ellis Paul, Martin Sexton, Tony Trischka, Suzanne Vega, Jerry Jeff Walker, and Dar Williams. No place in the city presents this music in a more pure form. Here acoustic means *acoustic*—no mikes, no nothing. Always brings in a crowd that is serious about hearing the music. They also serve cheap beer and brownies, but best of all, the popcorn is always free.

THE RED LION

151 Bleecker Street (between Thompson Street and Laguardia Place)
(212) 260–9797
www.redlionnyc.com

 Free shows Sunday through Thursday nights.

A full schedule of rock bands attracts a very young crowd.

JAZZ AND BLUES

ARTHUR'S TAVERN

57 Grove Street (off Seventh Avenue South)
(212) 675–6879
www.arthurstavernnyc.com

 Two-drink minimum per act loosely enforced.

Since 1937 Arthur's Tavern has been serving up a variety of music for every taste: straight-ahead jazz, New Orleans–style jazz, real Chicago blues. On Monday nights for more than forty years, it's been home to the Grove Street Stompers Dixieland jazz band. Stop by any time of night; there's always something going on. Never a cover.

Take a Free Ride!

After a night on the town, Right Rides's mission is to get women home safe. This all-volunteer organization gives free rides home to women on Saturday nights from midnight to 3:00 A.M. (technically Sunday morning). The service is only for women, only on Saturday nights, and they will only take you home. At the moment, Right Rides currently serves thirty-five neighborhoods across the Bronx, Brooklyn, Manhattan, and Queens. To catch a ride home, give them a call at (718) 964–7781 between midnight and 3:00 A.M. any Saturday night, and they will try to have a car to you within twenty minutes. For more information and a detailed map of their service area, check out their Web site, www.rightrides.org.

55 BAR

55 Christopher Street (between Seventh Avenue South and 8th Street)
(212) 929–9883
www.55bar.com

 Early shows on Friday and Saturday nights are always free.

Since 1919 this Prohibition-era dive has been presenting top-of-the-line jazz, funk, and blues. Stop in for the early show any Friday or Saturday night (6:00 to 9:00 P.M.) for a hot set of music with no cover, no minimum, and no attitude. They charge $3 to $5 for their other performances, but there is always free popcorn.

GROOVE

125 MacDougal Street (at West 3rd Street)
(212) 254–9393
www.clubgroovenyc.com

 Free admission only Sunday through Thursday.

Live rhythm and blues, funk, and hip-hop.

PARLOR ENTERTAINMENT

555 Edgecombe Avenue, Studio 3F (between 159th and 160th Streets)
(212) 781–6595
www.parlorentertainment.com

Occasionally you come across one of those events that you feel privileged to have been a part of. Well, that's exactly what goes on every weekend at Ms. Marjorie Eliot's North Harlem apartment. Marjorie graciously welcomes you into her living room, hallway, kitchen, and anyplace else you can find some space to listen to some of the purest, sweetest, swingin'est jazz you will hear anywhere and for any price. And here, of course, there isn't any price. The music begins at 4:00 P.M. on Sunday. Every week Ms. Eliot brings together an ensemble of guest musicians and fifty or more of her closest friends for an afternoon of joyful music. And anyone who attends quickly becomes one of those dear friends. The atmosphere is so warm and comfortable, and the music played so intimately, you'll think you're sitting in a friend's livingroom listening to some of your favorite tunes. Which, in fact, you are.

Underground Music

For years the platforms of the New York City subway system have been the place to hear a varied, eclectic mix of music from all parts of the world played by some of the most talented (and sometimes not-so-talented) musicians around, all playing their hearts out for a handout. And for just as long, the police and MTA wished these folks would stop clogging up the subway's platforms and tunnels. They tried everything from ticketing to arresting offenders to get rid of them. It didn't work. The musicians stayed, and the quarters kept being tossed.

Finally, though, someone smart at the MTA convinced the city to give in to the old adage "If you can't beat 'em, join 'em" and organized the MTA Arts for Transit Music Under New York (MUNY) program. So now you'll find jazz bands, folksingers, didgeridoo players, steel drummers, tap dancers, break-dancers, blues singers, salsa, and, of course, the ever-present Ecuadorian pan flute bands playing throughout the MTA system. MUNY holds auditions every spring at Vanderbilt Hall in Grand Central Station (open to the public) and has twenty-three locations where there are more than 150 performances every week. Some of the most popular sites are Grand Central Terminal, Penn Station, Times Square Station, 42nd Street (Sixth and Eighth Avenue stations), Grand Central Shuttle, Columbus Circle Station, Union Square, and Astor Place. Performances take place throughout the day and into the late night. For more information check out www.mta.info/mta/aft or call (212) 878–7452.

Of course, you'll still find plenty of other musicians littered throughout the system. My personal favorite is singer-songwriter Kathleen Mock (www.mockmusic.com), whose haunting melodies and beautifully resonant voice ring out in stations around the Upper West Side and Williamsburg and Park Slope in Brooklyn. When you're waiting for that late-night train to finally arrive, you'll be glad these folks are there to help you through the long wait.

ST. NICK'S PUB
773 Saint Nicholas Avenue (corner of 149th Street)
(212) 283–9728

 A posted three-drink minimum, but it is basically never enforced.

This nondescript Harlem pub is the home of the city's hottest jam session every Monday night starting at 9:30 P.M. But the swinging doesn't end on Monday; every night of the week some of the best players around take to the stage, including many top-name surprise guest appearances by the likes of Wynton Marsalis, Savioun Glover, Olu Dara, James Carter, and others. There is a sign on the tables saying they charge a cover and a three-drink minimum, but they basically never enforce it.

CLASSICAL MUSIC

BROOKLYN HEIGHTS MUSIC SOCIETY
157 Montague Street (between Henry and Clinton Streets)
info@brooklynsymphonyorchestra.org
www.brooklynheightsorchestra.org

This well-respected community orchestra is made up of a mix of amateur, student, retired, semiprofessional, and professional musicians. They present an array of symphony, orchestral, and chamber concerts in libraries, churches, and temples around Brooklyn. You are also welcome to bring your own bassoon, tuba, or triangle and join in on their open rehearsals every Monday evening. Check their Web site for the schedule or e-mail them for more information. Performances and rehearsals are always free, but they will be happy to accept your donation.

BROOKLYN QUEENS CONSERVATORY OF MUSIC
58 Seventh Avenue (at Lincoln Place)
Park Slope, Brooklyn
(718) 622–3300
42–76 Main Street (at Blossom Avenue)
Flushing, Queens
(718) 461–8910
www.bqcm.org

The conservatory is one of the country's oldest community music schools. They

How Do You Get to Carnegie Hall?

Forget about practicing—just join Norman Seaman's Concert/Theater Club, and he can get you there (and into Lincoln Center, Merkin Hall, and others) for hundreds of concerts a year for free. The Concert/Theater Club is a mom-and-pop organization that has been filling seats at major concert halls and theaters all around the city for more than fifty years. Primarily offering the best seats in the house to classical performances, the club also offers its members the chance to attend the occasional Broadway production, Off Broadway play, and film screenings. One-year memberships to the club will run you $29.95 for single tickets to all events, $39.95 for two tickets to all events, or $49.95 for four tickets to all events. For more information call (212) 330–7932 (daily-offering hotline) or (845) 279–8296. To join, send a check to Norman Seaman's Concert/Theater Club, 322 West 52nd Street, Suite 693, New York, NY 10101.

offer a full schedule of free concerts that run the gamut from children's recitals to professional-level classical and jazz performances. Sometimes there's a charge for guest performers and the larger concerts, but most shows are free.

CARNEGIE HALL NEIGHBORHOOD CONCERT SERIES
Locations throughout the five boroughs
(212) 903–9670
www.carnegiehall.org

For more than twenty-five years, the distinguished hall has presented more than eighty concerts a year (September through April) in neighborhoods throughout the five boroughs in libraries, churches, and community centers. The series presents a mix of classical, jazz, pop, and folk music; all shows are free and open to all. For schedule and location information, call or click on the "Explore & Learn" menu at their Web site.

DONNELL LIBRARY CENTER
20 West 53rd Street (between Fifth and Sixth Avenues)
(212) 621–0618
www.nypl.org

This library presents an extensive calendar of musical performances throughout the week, including classical, jazz, show tunes, opera, and more. All performances are free.

THE INTERCHURCH CENTER
475 Riverside Drive (between 119th and 120th Streets)
(212) 870–2200
www.interchurch-center.org

This interdenominational center for all faiths offers free concerts every Wednesday at 12:05 P.M., September through May. Performances last about thirty minutes; the programs range from string quartets to woodwind ensembles, traditional African folk music to Celtic songs and dances, medieval to jazz, vocal soloist to choir, piano to organ, emerging artists to established professionals.

THE JUILLIARD SCHOOL
60 Lincoln Center Plaza (Broadway and 65th Street on the plaza level)
(212) 769–7406
www.juilliard.edu

 Free tickets go quickly.

See the leading artists of tomorrow, today. This is the preeminent conservatory for classical musicians in the country, and they present a huge array of classical, chamber music, and jazz concerts by students and faculty throughout the year. Most of the performances are free, though some require tickets. To get tickets for these events, stop by the box office on the day they become available; otherwise you may be sold out of the event. You can also line up an hour before the show to try to get in on a standby basis. Venues are throughout Lincoln Center and the Juilliard School, and events are scheduled in the afternoon and evening all week long. Check the Web site or pick up a copy of the performance schedule at the box office. Performances by the drama division are also free, though not those by the dance and opera departments.

MANHATTAN SCHOOL OF MUSIC
120 Claremont Avenue (between 121st Street and Seminary Row)
(212) 749–2802, ext. 4528
www.msmnyc.edu

A full schedule of free classical and jazz concerts by students, faculty, and visiting artists, and master classes.

MANNES COLLEGE OF MUSIC
150 West 85th Street (between Columbus and Amsterdam Avenues)
(212) 496–8524
www.mannes.edu

A full schedule of free orchestral, chamber-music, and jazz concerts through-out the school year.

NYU DEPARTMENT OF MUSIC AND PERFORMING ARTS PROFESSIONS
35 West 4th Street, Suite 777 (at Greene Street)
(212) 998–5424
www.steinhardt.nyu.edu/music

Students and faculty present a full schedule of classical, chamber, jazz, and musical theater concerts along with their calendar of talks and workshops, all free and open to the public.

TRINITY CHURCH
74 Trinity Place (Broadway at Wall Street)
(212) 602–0747
www.trinitywallstreet.org

 THE CATCH **$2 suggested contribution, but nothing required.**

The Concerts at One series offers classical, jazz, and popular music perform-ances every Thursday afternoon. You can also catch lunchtime performances at their sister church nearby, St. Paul's Chapel (Broadway and Fulton Street), every Monday at 1:00 P.M. Both of these national landmarks are steeped in American history and worth a look anytime.

OUTDOOR SUMMER CONCERTS

During the summer months New York is the Mecca, Medina, Jerusalem, and Emerald City of free music. Almost any open green space transforms into a con-cert hall for an amazing array of established stars and cutting-edge performers of practically every genre of music. Many of these venues have become quite popular over the years—which means you should be sure to show up early to claim your space on the lawn or in the stands.

BAM RHYTHM & BLUES FESTIVAL

Metrotech Center (between Flatbush Avenue, Jay, Johnson, and Willoughby Streets)
Downtown Brooklyn
(718) 636–4100
www.bam.org
Thursday at noon, June through August.
Brown-bag it over to Brooklyn for this hot festival of legendary stars. Don't be misled by the name of the festival: In the past the festival has lined up a varied roster of top-name performers such as Dr. John, the Robert Cray Band, Los Lobos, Steel Pulse, Burning Spear, and others.

BRYANT PARK

Sixth Avenue between 41st and 42nd Streets
(212) 768–4242
www.bryantpark.org
Known mostly for the hugely popular film series on Monday nights, the park also hosts a great deal of concerts and performances throughout the summer. You will find the likes of the B52s, Carly Simon, the Beach Boys, and other big-name groups performing in the park for the TV show *Good Morning America*. Also, classical, jazz, and Broadway performances in the afternoon and evening. Check the Web site for the extensive schedule.

CELEBRATE BROOKLYN

Prospect Park Bandshell (Prospect Park West and 9th Street)
Park Slope, Brooklyn
(718) 855–7882, ext. 45
www.celebratebrooklyn.org
June through August.
Brooklyn's popular free series presents a star-studded schedule of everything from free films to spoken word and dance performances, rock, jazz, Latin, folk, and world music.

CENTRAL PARK SUMMERSTAGE

Rumsey Playfield
72nd Street, midpark
(212) 360–2777
www.summerstage.org
June through August.
If New York is the Promised Land of free concerts during the summer, this is the Wailing Wall. The schedule runs the entire length of the summer,

with performances almost every night of the week and a wildly varied schedule that runs the gamut from opera to hip-hop, from world to teeny-bopper pop. You're likely to find names you're familiar with—like Joan Jett, Randy Newman, David Byrne, or the Indigo Girls—and just as likely to be wowed by performers whose names you never would have come across if not for SummerStage's daring programming. There are also evenings devoted to spoken word and dance. Seating is on a first-come, first-served basis; for some of the more popular shows, the line starts hours before the gates open.

COOL MUSIC FOR WARM SUMMER DAYS

1 Battery Park Plaza (between Pearl and Bridge Streets);
Wednesday at 12:30 P.M.

345 Park Avenue (between 51st and 52nd Streets);
Thursday at 12:30 P.M.

(212) 407–2429
www.rudin.com

Local musicians of every sort (Dixieland, folk, rock, classical, and more) entertain the lunchtime crowd every Wednesday (downtown) and Thursday (uptown).

EL MUSEO DEL BARRIO

1230 Fifth Avenue (at 104th Street)
(212) 831–7272
www.elmuseo.org
Thursday at 6:00 P.M., June through August.

Every Thursday evening the museum turns on the heat (and the volume!) with an exhilarating Latin concert series. Spotlighting both local favorites and international stars performing in a surprising variety of styles within the Latin music world, including hip-hop, Cuban surf, rock, reggae, bachata, and, of course, salsa.

FREE CONCERTS IN PARKS

Neighborhood parks throughout Brooklyn, the Bronx, and Manhattan
(212) 360–8290
www.cityparksfoundation.org
June through September.

The undisputed champ of free events, the City Parks Foundation offers over 1,100 free performances throughout the year in parks throughout the five boroughs, with the bulk of the events taking place between June and

September. They offer everything from free concerts, theater, dance, hip-hop, and Latin events; the Charlie Parker Jazz Festival; SummerStage; as well as a huge amount of kids' events. Check out their Web site for a detailed schedule; they are sure to have something fantastic going on practically every day of the summer. And as if that weren't enough, the City Parks Foundation also offers a full schedule of free tennis, golf, and track and field lessons for kids in these parts all summer long.

HARLEM MEER PERFORMANCE FESTIVAL
Charles A. Dana Discovery Center
Central Park (110th Street and Central Park North)
(212) 860–1370
www.centralparknyc.org
Sunday at 4:00 P.M., June through September.
Upper Central Park makes a beautiful backdrop for this free concert series showcasing established and emerging jazz, Latin, dance, and gospel artists.

HARLEM WEEK/HARLEM JAZZ AND MUSIC FESTIVAL
Throughout Harlem and Manhattan
(212) 862–7200
www.harlemdiscover.com
End of July to August.
What started out as a one-day event has grown into a monthlong celebration of African-American life in America. The festival offers many concerts throughout the month in different locations around Harlem and Manhattan, as well as films, lectures, sporting events, street fairs, and more. Most events are free. Check the Web site for this year's schedule.

JAZZMOBILE
154 West 127th Street (between Lenox and Seventh Avenues)
(212) 866–4900 or (212) 866–3616 (concert hotline)
www.jazzmobile.org
Various locations around the five boroughs.
Since 1964, Jazzmobile has been bringing the music to the people by presenting a lineup of world-class musicians in parks, libraries, schools, and street corners all around New York and the surrounding areas. They also offer free Saturday workshops and master classes for students ages seven and up at PS 197 in Harlem, with such artists as Max Roach, Branford Marsalis, and Donald Byrd. Check the Web site for details.

The Best of the Fests

During the summer months the entirety of downtown Manhattan can be summed up by three words and one punctuation mark: It's a festival! From the Hudson River, around Battery Park, up to the South Street Seaport, and everywhere in between, there are literally hundreds and hundreds of free concerts, performances, and events scheduled from June to September as a part of these downtown fests. While many of the specific venues and concert series are listed in this chapter, the scope of these festivals is ever expanding. You owe it to yourself and your ever-contracting entertainment budget to check out their Web sites or nab a copy of their festival guides.

DOWNTOWN NYC RIVER TO RIVER FESTIVAL, *www.rivertorivernyc.org*
HUDSON RIVER FESTIVAL, *www.hudsonriverpark.org*
SEAPORT MUSIC FESTIVAL, *www.seaportmusicfestival.com*

MADISON SQUARE PARK

Between Madison and Fifth Avenues from 23rd to 26th Street
(212) 538–1884
www.madisonsquarepark.org
June to August.

Taking the lead of Bryant Park, Madison Square Park has become a destination for endless free activities in a spectacular green setting during the summer. The free concerts take place on Wednesday evenings and Saturday afternoons during the summer. The Wednesday series includes an eclectic array of well-known artists such as Lucy Kaplansky, James Hunter, and the Regina Carter Quintet, and Saturday afternoons are filled with music from up-and-coming folk and blues performers. The park also hosts a summer reading series with literary heavyweights, children's activities, and many other unique events throughout the year. Check out their Web site for schedules and details.

MARTIN LUTHER KING JR. CONCERT SERIES

Wingate Field (across the street from Kings County Hospital)
Winthrop Street (between Brooklyn and Kingston Avenues)
(718) 469–1912
www.brooklynconcerts.com
Monday, July and August.

Stars of gospel, soul, funk, and jazz perform. Performers have included Mighty Clouds of Joy, Teena Marie, Stephanie Mills, the O'Jays, Chaka Khan, Hezekiah Walker, and the Gap Band.

McCARREN PARK POOL PARTIES
Lorimer Street between Driggs and Bayard Avenues
Williamsburg, Brooklyn
www.thepoolparties.com
(718) 302–5050
Sunday in July and August.
Brooklyn's favorite abandoned pool plays host to a wild and rocking concert series every Sunday during July and August. This indie-rock fest attracts fans from all over the city and beyond and encourages music lovers to join in on the fun, which is by no means limited to the stage. The goings-on include a 30-foot Slip 'n Slide, hula hoops, a dodgeball court, and even water volleyball. The concerts are free, but reservations are encouraged. Check out their Web site for more details and to make reservations.

MET IN THE PARKS
Parks throughout the five boroughs
(212) 362–6000
www.metoperafamily.org
June.
For three weeks in June, the world-renowned Metropolitan Opera Company sheds the pomp and pretense of the opera hall and presents concert performances to the masses in Central Park and other parks throughout the five boroughs. Check the Web site for schedule and locations.

MUSIC AT CASTLE CLINTON
Battery Park
(212) 835–2789
www.rivertorivernyc.com
July 4 and Thursday evenings in July and early August.
The season opens with a large open-air concert in Battery Park on the Fourth of July weekend, drawing thousands of listeners; then the shows move into the smaller space at Castle Clinton. Tickets are required (free, but limited) for the Castle Clinton shows and given out on a first-come, first-served basis at 5:00 P.M. on the day of the show. Past performers have included Crash Test Dummies, Taj Mahal, Mark Cohen, Billy Bragg, Emmylou Harris, Shawn Colvin, and Junior Brown.

NAUMBURG ORCHESTRAL CONCERTS
Naumburg Bandshell, Central Park (midpark at 72nd Street)
info@naumburgconcerts.org
www.naumburgconcerts.org
Tuesday evenings, late June to August.
This may not be the biggest or most well-known outdoor concert series, but having presented free concerts in Central Park since 1905, it is the oldest continuous series of such concerts anywhere in the country. The series regularly includes performances by the New York Chamber Symphony, Empire Brass, and others. Check their Web site for a schedule of concerts.

NEW YORK PHILHARMONIC
Concerts in the Parks
(212) 875–5709
www.nyphil.org
July.
For more than thirty-five years, the Philharmonic has brought millions of people into the parks for what they call "Priceless Music Absolutely Free." With guest musicians and conductors, they present two programs of classical and popular music in city parks throughout the five boroughs and always cap the evening off with a spectacular fireworks display.

RIVER & BLUES
Battery Park City Parks
Robert F. Wagner Jr. Park (at Battery Place)
(212) 267–9700
www.bpcparks.org
Thursday evenings, July and August.
Bring a picnic dinner and enjoy the spectacular sunset views of the lower Hudson while you enjoy these jazz, blues, funk, and fusion performances. Past performers have included Hiram Bullock, Glen Velez, and Howard Fishman.

SEASIDE SUMMER CONCERT SERIES
Asser Levy Park (at West 5th Street and Surf Avenue)
Brighton Beach, Brooklyn
(718) 469–1912
www.brooklynconcerts.com
Thursday evenings, July and August.
Travel out to the heart of Brooklyn and travel back in time to this series that features many of the biggest names in music and comedy from the 1950s, 1960s, 1970s, and 1980s (golden oldies, disco, rock, and stand-up comedy).

In past years they have featured appearances by Gladys Knight, Liza Minnelli, Michael Bolton, Jay Black and the Americans, Todd Rundgren, Pat Benatar, Kenny Rogers, the Temptations, David Brenner, the Village People, and others.

SOUTH STREET SEAPORT
Pier 17 (at Fulton and South Streets)
(212) SEAPORT (732–7678)
www.southstreetseaport.com
Tuesday through Sunday at noon and 5:30 P.M., May through September.
Starting with a huge Cinco de Mayo Festival and running throughout the spring and summer, the South Street Seaport presents lunchtime and after-work concerts in every style of music, from country, folk, and rock to gospel, jazz, and Latin. The performers often include well-known acts as well as up-and-coming artists. Many summer weekends are also filled with full-day music, sports, and other festivals. Any day you can count on running across your fair share of jugglers, mimes, magicians, and other buskers to keep you entertained. Monday is the only day they don't schedule any official programs. Call or check the Web site for up-to-date information.

SUMMER IN THE SQUARE
Union Square (14th to 17th Streets between Park Avenue and University Place)
(212) 460–1208
www.unionsquarenyc.org
Wednesday at 12:30 P.M., June through August.
Stop by the park for a midday, midweek jolt of music. Every week brings something completely different, including jazz, classical, blues, Brazilian, and theater, and free yoga classes, dance performances, and children's shows later in the day. Check their Web site for the weekly schedule.

MUGGER: "Don't make a move. This is a stick-up. Your money or your life! . . . Look, bud, I said your money or your life!"

JACK BENNY: "I'm thinking it over."

FILM: CHEAP SHOTS

NOW THAT WORLD WIDE CINEMAS is a distant memory (what most cheap New Yorkers used to lovingly refer to as "the $3.00 theater") and prices are more than $10.00 a ticket, there has never been a greater need to find places to see movies without spending the moolah. If you've ever been among the throngs of people camped out at Bryant Park on a summer Monday evening, you know what I mean. Well, Bryant Park is only the beginning of the cheap cinema offerings throughout the city. From outdoor screenings under the stars during the summer to bars, libraries, and even theaters throughout the year, here is your list of where to get your fix of free flicks.

FREE MOVIES BY THE WEEK
(YEAR-ROUND)

TIME	MONDAY	TUESDAY	WEDNESDAY	THURSDAY	FRIDAY	SATURDAY	SUNDAY
MULTIPLE SCREENINGS; Call for schedule		French Institute (with membership)					
1:00 P.M.							
1:15 P.M.							
1:30 P.M.	Brighton Beach Library (twice a month) Bay Ridge Library	Sheepshead Bay Library					
2:00 P.M.			St. Agnes Library		58th Street Library	Baychester Library New Dorp Library Sony Wonder (twice a month)	
2:15 P.M.							
2:30 P.M.			Donnell Library				
2:45 P.M.							
3:00 P.M.				Mapleton Library	Yorkville Library (twice a month) Ottendorfer Library (twice a month)		
3:15 P.M.							
3:30 P.M.							
3:45 P.M.							
4:00 P.M.					MoMA (after 4:00 P.M.)		
4:15 P.M.							
4:30 P.M.							
4:45 P.M.							
5:00 P.M.	Wakefield Library			Chatham Square Library (third Thursday)			
5:15 P.M.							
5:30 P.M.							
5:45 P.M.							
6:00 P.M.	Jefferson Market Library			Sony Wonder (every other week)	Central Library (twice a month)		
6:15 P.M.			Instituto Cervantes				
6:30 P.M.			Mid-Manhattan Library		Deutsches Haus (selected weeks)		
7:00 P.M.	Barbès (first and third Monday)	Central Library (twice a month)					
7:15 P.M.							
7:30 P.M.							
7:45 P.M.							
8:00 P.M.		Telephone Bar					
8:15 P.M.							
8:30 P.M.							
8:45 P.M.							
9:00 P.M.							
9:15 P.M.							
9:30 P.M.							
9:45 P.M.							
10:00 P.M.	RiFiFi						

FREE MOVIES BY THE WEEK
(SUMMER)

TIME	MONDAY	TUESDAY	WEDNESDAY	THURSDAY	FRIDAY	SATURDAY	SUNDAY
6:30 P.M.	Monday Movie Series						
7:00 P.M.			Socrates				
7:30 P.M.					Celebrate Brooklyn		
NIGHTFALL	Bryant Park	McCarren Park Pool	Movies under the Stars River Flicks Riverside Park South	Movies with a View	River Flick		Bohemian Hall

FREE FLICKS

ANTHOLOGY FILM ARCHIVE
32 Second Avenue (at 2nd Street)
(212) 505–5181
www.anthologyfilmarchives.org

 You must be an Anthology member.

For those of you on the lookout for something other than what you will find at your local multiplex, Anthology is definitely the place for you. This world-renowned institution specializes in collecting, preserving, and exhibiting American independent, experimental, and avant-garde films and video, as well as some classics from Hollywood and European filmmakers. If you are willing to shell out the $50 yearly membership fee, you are entitled to attend all of their Essential Cinema screenings, which happen at least once a week, for free. Without the membership you would pay $8 for each screening. The membership also gets you into any of their other screenings for $5.

BARBÈS
376 9th Street (corner of Sixth Avenue)
Park Slope, Brooklyn
(718) 965–9177
www.barbesbrooklyn.com
www.brooklynindependent.com
First and third Monday of the month, 7:00 P.M.
This intimate Park Slope performance space hosts an incredibly eclectic variety of shows every week, mostly music, but on the first and third Monday of

the month they turn on the projector for the Brooklyn Independent Film Series. The free series focuses on the kind of films that you are not going to be seeing at your local multiplex, including features, documentaries, and shorts. The filmmakers are often present at the screenings for Q and A's following the films. Every other night you will find a music collection that ranges from Americana and blues to Mexican *bandas,* Venezuelan *joropos,* and Romanian brass bands. Most shows are free, though they do pass the hat!

BRYANT PARK SUMMER FILM FESTIVAL
West 40th to West 41st Streets (between Fifth and Sixth Avenues)
(212) 512–5700
www.bryantpark.org
Monday at nightfall, June through August.
This is the granddaddy of all free film screenings in New York. It has become incredibly popular, and as a result you need to get there mighty early if you have any hope of claiming a piece of the greenery for your own. They start letting people onto the lawn at 5:00 P.M. Since HBO foots the bill for this event, you can be sure you'll get a preview of something coming soon to a friendly cable network near you. There is always a cartoon before the feature, and then you can join the crowd dancing to the HBO trailer just before the film begins (don't ask me why). The features on the huge screen range from cinema classics (*Doctor Zhivago, Rear Window, An American in Paris*) to kitschy favorites (*Viva Las Vegas, The Wild One*).

CASA ITALIANA ZERILLI-MARIMÒ
24 West 12th Street (between Fifth and Sixth Avenues)
(212) 998–8739
www.nyu.edu/pages/casaitaliana
This NYU institution hosts four to five free screenings of classic and contemporary Italian films throughout the school year. The films are just a small part of their full schedule of exhibitions, performances, and talks on all things Italian. All events are free and open to the public.

CELEBRATE BROOKLYN
Prospect Park Bandshell (Prospect Park West and 9th Street)
Park Slope, Brooklyn
(718) 855–7882, ext. 45
www.celebratebrooklyn.org
Most Fridays at 7:30 P.M., July and August.
Brooklyn's popular free series presents everything from free films to spoken-word and dance performances, rock, jazz, Latin, folk, and world music. Classic and silent films are often accompanied by live contemporary music and performers.

CZECH CENTER

1109 Madison Avenue (at 83rd Street)
(212) 288–0830
www.czechcenter.com

Bohemian Hall & Beer Garden
29–19 24th Avenue (at 31st Street)
Astoria
www.bohemianhall.com
Every other Thursday at 7:00 P.M., September to June, at the Czech Center.
Every Sunday at 8:00 P.M., July and August, at the Bohemian Hall.
The Czech Center hosts a series of classic and contemporary Czech films with English subtitles at the Czech Center throughout the year. During the summer the series moves across the river to Astoria at the bastion of all things Czech in New York, the Bohemian Hall & Beer Garden. Kick back, raise a beer, and watch a film.

DEUTSCHES HAUS

42 Washington Mews (near University Place)
(212) 998–8660
www.nyu.edu/deutscheshaus
Selected Fridays at 6:30 P.M., and other times.
This cultural center for all things German regularly holds free film screenings. Recent series have focused on film versions of Kafka's novels, gay films in early German cinema, and the films of Marlene Dietrich, as well as contemporary films from Germany. Most screenings are held on Friday evenings, but there are others scattered throughout the week on their schedule. Often films are accompanied by lectures and live performances. Call or check the Web site for schedule and details.

FRENCH INSTITUTE/ALLIANCE FRANÇAISE

Florence Gould Hall
55 East 59th Street (between Madison and Park Avenues)
(212) 355–6160
www.fiaf.org
Tuesday afternoons and evenings.

THE CATCH   **You must be a French Institute member.**

While not exactly free, for fans of French films this is a pretty worthwhile deal. If you're a member of the French Institute ($90 for a single or $140 for a family), you can attend the weekly Cine Club screenings every Tuesday

Who Wants to Be a Moviemaker?

Do you ever find yourself walking out of a movie thinking I could do better than that? Or do you just know you could be the next Scorsese, if you knew where to start? Well, here's your chance to put your money (or should I say time?) where your mouth is. By volunteering your time at schools and facilities like Film/Video Arts (270 West 96th, Street between Broadway and West End Avenue; 212–222–1770; www.fva.com) or Downtown Community Television Center (87 Lafayette Street, between White and Walker Streets; 212–966–4510; www.dctvny.org), you are able to take classes and use their equipment and facilities free of charge. Both ask for a commitment of approximately sixteen hours a week doing administrative or production work in exchange for the free ride. For more information see the chapter titled "Education: Cents-Less Smarts."

for free (otherwise it costs $9 each week). This usually consists of a double feature, often of recent popular favorites as well as classics and lesser-known films. All films are shown in French with English subtitles.

INSTITUTO CERVANTES
211–15 East 49th Street (between Second and Third Avenues)
(212) 308–7720
www.cervantes.org
Wednesday at 6:15 P.M.

For lovers of Spanish and Latin American films or English-language films that deal with those parts of the world, there is no better destination than the weekly film series put together by the Cervantes Institute. They also offer free panel discussions, lectures, and a great library (see page 190). For more information on other activities, call or check their Web site.

IRIS & B. GERALD CANTOR FILM CENTER AT NYU
36 East 8th Street (between Broadway and University Place)
(212) 998–4100

Every week during the school year, the center holds many screenings of international films, Hollywood hits, and student films. Some events are limited to NYU students; others are free and open to the public. Call or drop by for a schedule.

McCARREN PARK POOL

Lorimer Street between Driggs and Bayard Avenues
Williamsburg, Brooklyn
www.summerscreen.org
www.mccarrenpark.com
Tuesday at 8:00 P.M., July and August.

Everyone in the pool! But this time swap the bathing suit for a big old tub of popcorn. This popular summer film series takes place in the once-abandoned Olympic-size McCarren Park swimming pool every July and August. The night starts off with live music at 7:00 P.M. and the movies roll at 8:00. In the past the series has included such films as *Purple Rain, Bring It On, Bonnie and Clyde,* and *Repo Man.*

MONDAY MOVIE SERIES

All Saints Parish Hall
707 Washington Street (at 7th Street)
Hoboken, New Jersey
summermovies@aol.com
www.allsaintshoboken.com
Monday at 6:30 P.M., July and August.

Just on the other side of the Hudson, you can escape the heat of the city with this series of classic Hollywood films shown in the air-conditioned Parish Hall. They even throw in free seltzer and popcorn.

MOVIES UNDER THE STARS

Pier A Park (1st Street and Frank Sinatra Drive)
Hoboken, New Jersey
(201) 420–2207
www.hobokennj.org
Wednesday at 8:00 or 8:30 P.M., June through August.

For the cost of a ride on the PATH train ($1.50), hop over to Hoboken, where they show many recent hits and blockbusters in this summer series.

MOVIES WITH A VIEW

Empire-Fulton State Park (between the Brooklyn and
Manhattan Bridges)
(718) 802–0603
www.brooklynbridgepark.org
Thursday nights, July and August.

In the shadow of the majestic Brooklyn Bridge, this film series offers up Hollywood and independent films, many of which have been shot in, are about, or are made by people from Brooklyn. The evening always starts off with a live DJ spinning some tunes to set the mood, and they also provide free valet parking for your bicycle.

MUSEUM OF MODERN ART (MoMA)
11 West 53rd Street (between Fifth and Sixth Avenues)
(212) 708–9480
www.moma.org
Free Friday, 4:00–8:00 P.M.

The museum has two movie theaters that are free with admission to the museum—and on Friday afternoons and evenings, that's free, too (well, technically it's "pay what you wish," but . . .). They show classic and contemporary independent and art films. Call for the latest schedule and details.

OCULARIS
Galapagos Art and Performance Space
16 Main Street (between Water and Plymouth Streets)
DUMBO, Brooklyn
(718) 384–4586
www.galapagosartspace.com
www.ocularis.net

Ocularis runs a number of art film series in Williamsburg, Long Island City, and Astoria throughout the year. The screenings are in conjunction with institutions like P.S. 1 Contemporary Art Center, the Asia Society, the African Film Festival, and others. They show documentaries, experimental and avant-garde films, and contemporary and emerging-artist flicks, as well as features from around the world (in other words, you are not going to see *Terminator 3* here). Screenings are often accompanied by live music and dance. Some films are free, others are not; check the Web site for a detailed schedule.

RIFIFI
332 11th Street (between First and Second Avenues)
(212) 677–1027
www.rififinyc.com
Monday at 10:00 P.M.

THE CATCH One-drink minimum (but beer is always cheap!).

The blood and guts flow every Monday night along with Pabst Blue Ribbon. It is always a fun and lively crowd in this comfy coffeehouse-esqe bar/screening room. Each week they schedule such bloody good classics as *Hellraiser, Halloween, Evil Dead, Dawn of the Dead,* and all of their many

Everyone's a Critic

Here's your chance to let Hollywood know what you think of their films. Many major film studios run private screenings of soon-to-be-released films. They're hoping to gauge response, figure out how to market the movie, learn what changes might be needed, or simply see if the movie's any good. There's no way to necessarily get on a list to see these previews, because they want a random sampling of people, but they are constantly going on, and there are ways to increase your chances of getting an invitation.

You'll often find people handing out screening passes in front of multiplexes around New York (particularly Loews Lincoln Square–Broadway between 67th and 68th Streets). If you see someone handing out passes, don't be afraid to approach and ask for one. These folks are paid by the number of people they can get to show up at the screenings. If you promise to show up, they want you. They are usually (though not always) looking for people between the ages of seventeen and thirty-four, but they don't check IDs. And they won't let anyone involved in the entertainment industry into the screenings. If that's you, when they ask what you do for a living, remember to embrace your inner accountant.

sequels. They also have great free comedy shows almost every other night of the week.

RIVER FLICKS

Pier 46, Hudson River and Christopher Street

Pier 54, Hudson River and 14th Street
(212) 732–7467
www.hudsonriverpark.org

Wednesday, dusk at Pier 54 (films for grown-ups).
Friday, dusk at Pier 46 (films for kids).
July and August.
Every Friday night grab the kids and take them down to Hudson River Park for some of the best family films ever put to celluloid. Whether it is animated features like *Shark Tales* or *Shrek,* live-action comedies like *Back to the Future* or *Daddy Day Care,* or classics like *Willy Wonka and the Chocolate Factory* (an annual event!), the whole family is sure to have a great time. Or you can get a sitter for the little ones every Wednesday night and make your way up to Pier 54 to catch some adult films. All right, don't get crazy, these

are all films rated PG-13 or R, like *Fast Times at Ridgemont High, Clerks,* and *Gladiator.* Whenever you decide to go, the films are all free, and even the popcorn is on the house.

RIVERSIDE PARK SOUTH
Pier 1 (Hudson River between 70th Street)
(212) 408–0219
www.riversideparkfund.org
Wednesday evenings at dusk, July and August.
As the development of the Hudson River waterside continues to spread uptown, the free opportunities are following. The newest addition to the riverside, and your weekly calendar of free events, is this park between 65th and 72nd Streets. Grab a blanket and picnic under the stars while you catch a fun selection of cinema classics and Hollywood blockbusters such as *Chicago, Who's Afraid of Virginia Woolf?, Dirty Rotten Scoundrels,* and *Fiddler on the Roof.* The park also hosts a full schedule of other free events every week, including yoga and Pilates classes, concerts, lots of kids' events, and free kayaking.

SOCRATES SCULPTURE PARK'S OUTDOOR CINEMA
32–01 Vernon Boulevard (at Broadway)
Long Island City, Queens
(718) 956–1819
www.socratessculpturepark.org
Wednesday at 7:00 P.M., July and August.
Since the borough of Queens is the most culturally diverse place on the face of the planet, with communities from almost every country in the world, you can say this festival is both a local and an international one. Each week the series chooses a film that represents a community in Queens (Greek, Cuban, Korean, Brazilian, Indian, etc.). They fill out the evening with live music and dance performances from the country and have local restaurants provide the regional cuisine. The performances and film are free, but you will have to pay for the food. Films have included *Zorba the Greek, Buena Vista Social Company, Central Station,* and *House Party.*

SONY WONDER TECHNOLOGY LAB
550 Madison Avenue (at 56th Street)
(212) 833–7858
www.sonywondertechlab.com
Saturday at 2:00 P.M. (twice a month).
They screen recent and some less recent Hollywood favorites (*The Wedding*

Planner, Hitch, House of Flying Daggers, Muppets from Space) on their amazing high-definition screen. They accept reservations the week of the film and give out any remaining tickets at 1:45 P.M. Throughout the week they also offer free screenings geared toward kids age six and younger (*Elmo, Sesame Street,* etc.) followed by fun kid-friendly workshops. Check their Web site or call for the schedule of screenings. Get there early and enjoy the four floors of interactive activities—everything's free.

TELEPHONE BAR & GRILL
149 Second Avenue (between 9th and 10th Streets)
(212) 529–5000
www.telebar.com
Tuesday at 8:00 P.M.

Step into the back room at this English pub for flick every Tuesday night. They show everything from Oscar-winning films to made-for-TV kitsch on their impressive 9½-foot screen. No cover or minimum, but of course they would be happy to sell you a Guinness or two while you enjoy the movie.

BETTER THAN THE BOOK

PUBLIC LIBRARIES
www.nypl.org/branch/events/
www.brooklynpubliclibrary.org

Many public libraries throughout Manhattan, Brooklyn, and the Bronx show regularly scheduled films every week. These films could include black-and-white classics from the 1930s and 1940s, documentaries, foreign films, and recent features. Here's a list of the branches with screenings on a regular basis; call or check the Web sites to confirm schedules.

MANHATTAN BRANCHES

CHATHAM SQUARE LIBRARY, 33 East Broadway (between Catherine and Market Streets); (212) 964–6598; the third Thursday of the month at 5:00 P.M.

DONNELL LIBRARY CENTER, 20 West 53rd Street (between Fifth and Sixth Avenues); (212) 621–0618; Wednesday at 2:30 P.M.

58TH STREET LIBRARY, 127 East 58th Street (between Lexington and Park Avenues); (212) 759–7358; Friday at 2:00 P.M.

JEFFERSON MARKET LIBRARY, 425 Sixth Avenue (at 10th Street); (212) 243–4334; Monday at 6:00 P.M.

MID-MANHATTAN LIBRARY, 455 Fifth Avenue at 40th Street; (212) 340–0849; every Wednesday at 6:30 P.M.

OTTENDORFER BRANCH, 135 Second Avenue (at St. Marks Place), (212) 674–0947; every other Friday at 3:00 P.M.

ST. AGNES LIBRARY, 444 Amsterdam Avenue (between 80th and 81st Streets); (212) 877–4380; Wednesday at 2:00 P.M.

YORKVILLE LIBRARY, 222 East 79th Street (between Second and Third Avenues); (212) 744–5824; Friday at 3:00 P.M. (twice a month).

BROOKLYN BRANCHES

BAY RIDGE, 7223 Ridge Boulevard (at 73rd Street); 718-748-5709; every Monday at 1:30 P.M.

BRIGHTON BEACH, Brighton First Road (near Brighton Beach Avenue); (718) 946–2917; every other Monday at 1:30 P.M.

CENTRAL LIBRARY, Grand Army Plaza (Flatbush Avenue and Eastern Parkway); (718) 230–2100; Friday at 6:00 P.M. (feature films), Tuesday at 7:00 P.M., twice a month (documentaries), and other times; call for schedule.

MAPLETON, 1702 60th Street (at 17th Avenue); (718) 256–2117; Thursday at 3:00 P.M.

SHEEPSHEAD BAY, 2636 East 14th Street (at Avenue Z); (718) 368–1815; Tuesday at 1:30 P.M.

WAKEFIELD BRANCH, 4100 Lowerre Place (at East 229th Street); (718) 652–4663; Monday at 5:00 P.M.

BRONX BRANCHES

BAYCHESTER LIBRARY, 2049 Asch Loop North; (718) 379–6700; call for details.

STATEN ISLAND BRANCHES

NEW DORP BRANCH, 309 New Dorp Lane (at Clawson Street); (718) 351–2977; Saturday at 2:00 P.M.

ALIEN: "On this cable system, we receive over one million channels from the farthest reaches of the galaxy."

BART: "Do you get HBO?"

ALIEN: "No, that would cost extra."

—The Simpsons

TELEVISION TAPINGS: PUBLIC ACCESS

AFTER HOLLYWOOD, NEW YORK is home to the most small-screen shows. While Los Angeles is the place to be if you want to see tapings of sitcoms, the kinds of programs that are based in New York have a mix of everything, including talk shows, game shows, variety shows, comedies, and courtroom shows. It's possible to get tickets to many of these shows the week of the taping, but many of the more popular shows have long waiting lists and require you to request tickets from a couple of months to up to a year in advance. All television tapings are free, but be warned that some do require a substantial commitment of time. The upside is that there's usually a very funny comedian working the crowd trying to keep you entertained while you sit around waiting for the official fun to begin.

The audience is an important part of the show, so they want to keep you lively for when they need you to hoot, holler, and applaud wildly. And one of the best ways they have found to keep you interested is through bribery. Often these shows offer giveaways for the audience. You could receive anything from key chains and T-shirts to Broadway tickets, CDs, and books.

THE COLBERT REPORT
513 West 54th Street (between Tenth and Eleventh Avenues)
(212) 586–2477
www.comedycentral.com/shows/colbert_report
Tape days: Monday through Friday at 7:30 P.M. The *Daily Show*'s Stephen Colbert tackles the issues of the day, and hurts them. Reserve tickets through the Web site, though they do go fast. You can also show up at the studio at 7:00 any night to try for standby tickets.

THE DAILY SHOW WITH JON STEWART
733 Eleventh Avenue (between 51st and 52nd Streets)
(212) 586–2477
www.comedycentral.com
Tape days: Monday through Thursday 5:30–7:30 P.M. (arrive by 4:00). Emmy-winning news satire/comedy talk show. Reserve tickets months ahead through the Web site. You must be at least eighteen years old. You can also try your luck on the day of the show by showing up early and hoping for some no-shows.

EMERIL LIVE
(212) 401–2422
www.foodnetwork.com
"Bam!" It's a cooking show with a live band and celebrity guests. They tape shows at various times throughout the year and only give tickets away through a lottery system. The Food Network runs the ticket lottery once a year or so. Check out their Web site or call periodically, or sign up for their newsletter to find out when to send in an entry.

GOOD MORNING AMERICA
West 44th Street and Broadway
(212) 930–7855
www.abcnews.go.com/GMA
Tape days: Monday through Friday 7:00–9:00 A.M. Hang out with Diane Sawyer and the GMA gang in their Times Square studio as they talk about world events, chat with celebrities, and tell you the best way to clean your dust bunnies. Send for tickets through the Web site about a month in advance.

Plan to arrive at 6:00 A.M.; the show is on the air from 7:00 to 9:00. You can also always join the crowd on the street outside the studio.

JUDGE HATCHETT

National Studios
460 West 42nd Street (between Ninth and Tenth Avenues)
(212) 352–3322 or (866) 283–4362
www.judgehatchett.com
The court is in session Tuesday, Wednesday, and Thursday at 10:30 A.M. and 3:00 P.M.

LATE NIGHT WITH CONAN O'BRIEN

NBC Studio
30 Rockefeller Plaza (49th Street, between Fifth and Sixth Avenues)
(212) 664–3056
www.nbc.com/conan
Tape days: Tuesday through Friday 5:30–6:30 P.M. Join Conan for his late-night wiseass interviews. Call the ticket request line for reservations two to three months in advance. Standby tickets are given out at 9:00 A.M. at the NBC Studio lobby on a first-come, first-served basis. Standby tickets do not guarantee you'll get into the show; it will depend on how many people with reserved tickets fail to show up at the taping later that day.

THE LATE SHOW WITH DAVID LETTERMAN

The Ed Sullivan Theater
1697 Broadway (between 54th and 55th Streets)
New York, NY 10019
(212) 975–1003 (general info)
(212) 247–6497 (standby tickets)
www.lateshowaudience.com
Tape days: Monday through Thursday at 5:30 P.M. (4:15 arrival time), and again on Thursday at 7:00 P.M. (5:00 arrival time). It's the top ten list, viewer mail, Stupid Pet Tricks, Paul, Dave, and you, all together in a very chilly studio (bring a sweater!). For advance tickets, fill out an application at their Web site or in person at the theater (Monday through Friday 9:30 A.M. to 12:30 P.M. or Saturday and Sunday 10:00 A.M. to 6:00 P.M.). They will call you if they have tickets available for the day you requested, but be prepared to answer a David Letterman trivia question when they call (Who runs the Hello Deli? Name a recent Top Ten category? Who is Dave's announcer?) or you are out of luck. Send for tickets at least two months in advance. To get standby tickets on the day of the taping, call the standby phone line at 11:00 A.M. You have to be pretty lucky and persistent to nab one of these rare tickets, but give it a shot; there isn't an in-person standby line.

LIVE WITH REGIS AND KELLY

7 Lincoln Square (at 67th Street and Columbus Avenue)
(212) 456–3054
www.tvplex.go.com/buenavista/regisandkelly

Tape days: Monday through Friday at 9:00 A.M. (arrive at 8:00). Regis tries not to lose it, Kelly tries to understand it, and Gelman tries to keep it all together on this morning chat show. For advance tickets, send a postcard with your name, address, phone number, the date for which you would like tickets, and the number of tickets requested (limit four per person). Send ticket requests to Live Tickets, Ansonia Station, P.O. Box 230777, New York, NY 10023. Requests can take up to a year to be filled. To try for standby tickets on the day of taping, arrive at the studio as early as 7:00 A.M.; tickets are given out on a first-come, first-served basis.

MARTHA

221 West 26th Street (between Seventh and Eighth Avenues)
(917) 438–5999
www.marthastewart.com/martha

Tape days: Tuesday at 10:00 A.M., Wednesday and Thursday at 10:00 A.M. and 2:00 P.M. Martha loosens up the apron strings on her morning talk show, which includes lots of celebrity guests, audience participation, and, of course, a few tips on everything from homemade apple pies to handmade xylophones. The tickets can be hard to come by, and they can be had only through the Web site. Check it often for when new dates are available. For standby tickets the day of, get there two hours before showtime and bring your knitting to work on while you wait on line.

THE MAURY SHOW

New York's Hotel Pennsylvania
401 Seventh Avenue (between 32nd and 33rd Streets)
(212) 547–8421
www.mauryshow.com

Tape days: Wednesday, Thursday, and Friday at 8:30 A.M. (arrive by 8:15 A.M.). Audience-participation talk show. Call for tickets anytime up until the day of taping. If you don't have tickets, they say you can always come to the studio the day of the taping; they'll probably be able to get you in.

THE MONTEL WILLIAMS SHOW

433 West 53rd Street (between Ninth and Tenth Avenues)
(212) 989–8101
www.montelshow.com

Tape days: Wednesday and Thursday at 10:00 A.M., 1:00 P.M., and 4:00 P.M. Audience-participation talk show. Call for tickets anytime up until the day of taping, or fill out a request form on their Web site.

THE PEOPLE'S COURT
401 Fifth Avenue, eighth floor (at 37th Street, between Fifth and Madison Avenues)
(888) 780–8587
tickets@peoplescourt.com
www.peoplescourt.com

Tape days: Tuesday and Wednesday at 10:00 A.M. and 2:00 P.M. (be prepared to stay for three hours). Courtroom reality show. Call or e-mail for tickets any time up until the day of taping.

RACHAEL RAY SHOW
222 East 44th Street (between Second and Third Avenues)
www.rachaelrayshow.com

Tape days: Tuesday, Wednesday, and Thursday at 11:30 a.m. and 4:00 p.m. The perky anti-Martha, Rachael Ray cooks and chums it up with celebrities on her daytime talk show. Tickets are in high demand for the show, so be prepared to wait up to a year for your tickets to show up. To try for tickets, fill out a form at their Web site. To try for day-of-the-show standby tickets, show up at 10:00 A.M. (for the 11:30 show) or 2:30 P.M. (for the 4:00 show), grab a standby voucher, and keep your fingers crossed.

SATURDAY NIGHT LIVE
NBC Studio
30 Rockefeller Plaza (49th Street, between Fifth and Sixth Avenues)
(212) 664–3056
www.nbc.com/snl

Tape days: Saturday, September through June. The original late-night comedy sketch show, with popular guest stars and top-of-the-charts musical guests. They run a lottery every August to give away tickets for the upcoming year of shows. Check the Web site for details. You may have better luck getting standby tickets, which are distributed every Saturday at 7:00 A.M. at the NBC Studio lobby on a first-come, first-served basis. Standby tickets do not guarantee you'll get into the show; it will depend on how many people with reserved tickets fail to show up later for the dress rehearsal at 8:00 P.M. or the live show at 11:30.

T.R.L.

45th Street and Broadway
(212) 398-8549
TRLcasting@mtvstaff.com
www.mtv.com/onair/trl

Tape days: Monday through Thursday at 1:00 P.M. You pick the hits, and they play the videos. Call or e-mail for tickets three months ahead of time. To be a member of the studio audience, you must be at least sixteen years old and no older than twenty-four. For standby tickets on the day of the show, line up at the 44th Street entrance at about 11:30 A.M. If you don't make it into the studio, join the throngs of screaming fans outside on Broadway between 44th and 45th Streets, Monday through Thursday at 1:00 P.M.

THE VIEW

320 West 66th Street (off West End Avenue)
(212) 456-0900
www.abc.go.com/daytime/theview

Tape days: Monday through Friday at 11:00 A.M. (plan to arrive by 9:30 A.M.). Barbara and the gals talk about everything from terrorism to bra sizes. Fill out a ticket request form at the Web site. Tickets will be sent for dates about four to six months from the date they are received. They often have room for you the day of the show, however: Stop by the studio no later than 8:30 A.M. to stand in line. These tickets are distributed on a first-come, first-served basis. You must be at least eighteen years old to attend.

WHO WANTS TO BE A MILLIONAIRE

30 West 67th Street (at Columbus Avenue)
(212) 479-7755
www.millionairetv.com

Tape days: Tuesday and Wednesday at noon and 3:00 P.M. Meredith Vieira is the host with the most (money, that is). Fill out their ticket request form at their Web site. And when you attend a taping, you can also audition to get into the "hot seat" yourself. You must be at least eighteen to attend.

"I've been asked to say a couple of words about my husband, Fang. How about 'short' and 'cheap'?"
—Phyllis Diller

I COULD SAY THAT the price of comedy shows in New York is no laughing matter, but that would be too obvious, so I'll just say the cost of laughing in the city is no joke (sorry, couldn't resist). Suffice it to say, yucks cost bucks (okay, I'm done). But you can have the last laugh by stopping in at one of these free comedy nights. Many feature newcomers taking their first shots at stand-up or are opportunities for more established comics or improv troupes to try out new material—or more likely a combination of the two. The schedules do change from time to time, so be sure to call to confirm information before showing up.

COMEDY BY THE WEEK

TIME	MONDAY	TUESDAY	WEDNESDAY	THURSDAY	FRIDAY	SATURDAY	SUNDAY
3:00 P.M.	New York Comedy Club						
3:30 P.M.							
4:00 P.M.							
4:30 P.M.							
5:00 P.M.							
5:30 P.M.							
6:00 P.M.							
6:30 P.M.							
7:00 P.M.			People's Improv Theater				
7:30 P.M.							
8:00 P.M.			People's Improv Theater				
8:30 P.M.			Youth Hostel				
9:00 P.M.							
9:30 P.M.			People's Improv Theater				Upright Citizens Brigade
10:00 P.M.							
10:30 P.M.							
11:00 P.M.	People's Improv Theater	People's Improv Theater	Upright Citizens Brigade	People's Improv Theater			
11:30 P.M.							
Midnight					Upright Citizens Brigade	Magnet Theater	

MAGNET THEATER
254 West 29th Street (between Seventh and Eighth Avenues)
(212) 244–8824
www.magnettheater.com
Saturday at midnight
Every Saturday the Magnet Theater attracts all kinds of funny folks to their Magnet Mixer, when veteran improvisers join forces with students and any Joe off the street who wants to take part in these one-of-a-kind improv free-for-alls. They also offer free improv classes once a month and other free shows regularly. Check their Web site for the schedule and details.

NEW YORK COMEDY CLUB

241 East 24th Street (between Second and Third Avenues)
(212) 696–5233
www.newyorkcomedyclub.com
Monday at 3:00 P.M.

 "We couldn't possibly charge you to watch the open mike."

Once a week this stand-up club opens its microphone to anyone who has $5 and thinks he's the next Seinfeld. You never know what you're going to see during this show. It might be painful, it might be sad, it might be offensive, and it might even occasionally be funny, but if you want to try your luck, watching is free: There's no charge, and no drink minimum (though you may need a couple of shots of something to make it through).

NEW YORK INTERNATIONAL YOUTH HOSTEL

891 Amsterdam Avenue (between 103rd and 104th Streets)
(212) 932–2300
www.hinewyork.org
Wednesday at 8:30 P.M.

Join the international crowd at New York's very own official youth hostel to yuck it up every Wednesday night, when a parade of up-and-coming stand-up comedians head uptown. The show is free and open to all. The youth hostel also hosts many other events and walking tours throughout the week, and, of course, it is one of the best cheap sleeps in the city, with beds starting at $29 a night. Check out their Web site for more details.

THE PEOPLE'S IMPROV THEATER

154 West 29th Street (between Sixth and Seventh Avenues)
(212) 563–7488
www.thepit-nyc.com
Wednesday at 7:00, 8:00, 9:30, and 11:00 P.M.; Monday, Tuesday, and Thursday at 11:00 P.M.

The People's Improv Theater (aka the PIT) is one of the top spots for improv and sketch comedy in New York, and they top the list of Cheap Bastard–friendly (aka free) shows offered every week. The jackpot of jollies happens every Wednesday night with four free shows starting at 7:00 P.M., when owner and improv master Ali Farahnakian takes to the stage for a full

Time Out for Laughs

Far be it from me to ever recommend laying down some cash for anything, but if you are in the market for free comedy, you may want to fork over a few bucks for a copy of Time Out New York. *In addition to those ongoing free shows listed in this chapter, there are always tons of other shows popping up all over the place. These free shows change venues more often than stand-up comics get heckled, so for the most up-to-date listings for everything around town,* Time Out *can't be beat. Their listings include comedy, theater, film, music, clubs, museums, and much more. They also make a special note of those events that are free. A typical week is likely to have up to 300 free events. Check out their Web site for free access to some but not nearly all of their listings (www.timeoutny.com). The cheapest of you will take a notebook with you and peruse the listings at any of New York's major bookstores; but if you are ready to take the plunge, pick up a copy at any newsstand around the city.*

hour of wackiness, along with some guest performers. At 8:00 and 9:30 P.M. their top improv teams take each other on for an all-out comedy competition, and anyone is welcome to join in on the fun as they top off the evening with an improv jam at 11:00 P.M. There is always a full house for these Wednesday-night shows, so plan on turning up early to grab a seat. The free laughs keep on coming every Monday, Tuesday, and Thursday night at 11:00, when they offer other improv jams and stand-up open mic.

UPRIGHT CITIZENS BRIGADE
307 West 26th Street (at Eighth Avenue)
(212) 366–9176
www.ucbtheater.com
Sunday at 9:30 P.M., Wednesday at 11:00 P.M., and Friday at midnight.
UCB is one of New York's leading comedy improv troupes and the only one that gives it away for free. They host three freewheeling performances every week. Wednesday night is School Night, a late-night set of stand-up comedy hosted by Justin Purnell with guest appearances by some of the city's best comedians (www.ucbschoolnight.com). On Sunday nights, don't miss Asssscat

3000 for improvisation at its purest, with guest performers from such shows as *Saturday Night Live, Late Night with Conan O'Brien, The Daily Show with Jon Stewart,* and others. Every Friday night at midnight they host their outrageous version of an open mic night that includes sketch and stand-up comedy. They don't take reservations for these shows, so get there a couple of hours early to grab tickets. They always have a full house for these shows, and the evening is well worth the effort.

"Dancing: The highest intelligence in the freest body."

—Isadora Duncan

DANCE: FREE EXPRESSION

MAYBE IT'S BECAUSE New Yorkers are always on their feet—racing along the sidewalks, crammed together in the subways, or trudging up a five-story walk-up—but it seems that everyone in New York dances in one way or another. Or perhaps it's the palpable energy of the city that draws dancers from every corner of the planet. Whatever the reason, New York is like a dance itself, and its clubs, public spaces, and studios abound with opportunities for you to strut your stuff without unstuffing your bank account. If you prefer to watch, New York is home to some of the world's leading dance companies and conservatories, so the talent on display at no cost is unrivaled anyplace in the world.

WATCHING IT

CELEBRATE BROOKLYN
Prospect Park Bandshell (Prospect Park West and 9th Street)
Park Slope, Brooklyn
(718) 855–7882, ext. 45
www.brooklynx.org/celebrate
June through August.
Brooklyn's popular free series regularly commissions new works by local and internationally recognized dance companies and presents dance concerts throughout the summer schedule. Their calendar also includes free films, readings, and music of every genre.

CENTRAL PARK SUMMERSTAGE
Midpark (enter at East or West 72nd Street)
(212) 360–2777
www.summerstage.org
June through August.
A complete schedule of free performances throughout the summer, from big names to the cutting edge in music, opera, dance, spoken word, and more. This is a very popular venue; claiming a spot on line early is recommended. Dance performances most Friday evenings.

DANCING IN THE STREETS
545 Eighth Avenue, Suite 8SE (between 37th and 38th Streets)
(212) 625–3505
www.dancinginthestreets.org
Commissions and presents all forms of dance and movement performances throughout the city. All productions are site-specific performances in various parks, open spaces, and indoor spaces. Most performances are free.

THE JOYCE THEATER
175 Eighth Avenue (at 19th Street)
(646) 792–8355
www.joyce.org

 Work as a volunteer usher to see the performances for free.

The leading theater for dance companies, the Joyce plays host to practically every major company from around the country and around the world. Call to set up dates to be a volunteer usher and see the show for free. They begin taking reservations two weeks in advance.

THE KITCHEN
512 West 19th Street (between Tenth and Eleventh Avenues)
(212) 255–5793
usher@thekitchen.org
www.thekitchen.org

 Work as a volunteer usher to see the performances for free.

Although its location has moved farther uptown in recent years, the Kitchen remains firmly downtown in ethos. For the last thirty-plus years, it has been home to such nontraditional, uncategorizable performers as Philip Glass, Laurie Anderson, Bill T. Jones and Arnie Zane, Eric Bogosian, David Byrne with the Talking Heads, Meredith Monk, Brian Eno, John Lurie, Robert Mapplethorpe, Cindy Sherman, and many others. Performances strive to combine music, dance, video, spoken word, and any other forms an artist feels like playing with at the moment. E-mail about two weeks in advance to reserve a spot as a volunteer usher.

LINCOLN CENTER OUT OF DOORS FESTIVAL
65th Street and Broadway
(212) 875–5766
www.lincolncenter.org
Throughout August.
This eclectic performance, music, and dance festival every August features leading modern, ethnic, and cutting-edge dance companies, as well as music from around the world in almost every genre and a great selection of children's performances.

MOVEMENT RESEARCH
Dance Theater Workshop
219 West 19th Street (between Seventh and Eighth Avenues)

Judson Memorial Church
55 Washington Square South
(212) 539–2611 (event hotline)
(212) 598–0551
www.movementresearch.org

Monday at 8:00 P.M. at Judson Memorial Church, September through June. Every other Tuesday at 7:00 P.M. at Dance Theater Workshop, September through June.

Presents free modern, improvisational, and adventurous dance performances every Monday night at Judson Memorial Church and works in progress every other Tuesday at their Open Studio performance at Dance Theater Workshop. Both series are held September through June and attract many of the most highly regarded and up-and-coming downtown dance artists.

NEW YORK UNIVERSITY
Tisch School of the Arts—Graduate Dance School
111 Second Avenue, fifth floor (between Sixth and Seventh Streets)
(212) 998–1982
www.dance.tisch.nyu.edu
October through May.

The graduate dance department offers free contemporary dance performances throughout the school year, often with notable guest choreographers.

DOING IT

CHELSEA MARKET
75 Ninth Avenue (between 15th and 16th Streets)
www.chelseamarket.com

Triangulo School of Argentine Tango
(212) 633–6445
www.tangonyc.com
Saturday 4:00 to 7:00 P.M.

What was once the birthplace of that most American of icons, the Oreo cookie, is transformed into a truly international atmosphere every Saturday afternoon. This gourmet marketplace plays host to a free milonga (tango salon) provided by the Triangulo School of Argentine Tango. When you need to take a break from the dancing, stop in and grab a few free samples at many of the gourmet shops in the market.

CONSULATE GENERAL OF ARGENTINA IN NEW YORK
12 West 56th Street (between Fifth and Sixth Avenues)
(212) 603–0400
www.consarny.com
Tuesday and Wednesday at noon.

If you want to learn how to tango, who better to teach you than the country of Argentina itself. The Consulate General of Argentina holds two free ongoing classes every week on Tuesday and Wednesday for anyone interested in learning how to tango (and if that makes you want to take a trip to Argentina, they don't mind that either).

DANCE TANGO
South Street Seaport, Pier 16 (between the Ambrose and Peking ships); Sunday 7:00–10:00 P.M.
(212) 726–1111
www.dancetango.com
May through September.
Put a rose in your mouth and head down to South Street Seaport for free tango lessons and dancing to live and recorded music under the stars.

DANCING ON THE PLAZA
Charles A. Dana Discovery Center, Central Park
110th Street and Central Park North
(212) 860–1370
www.centralparknyc.org
Thursday at 6:00 P.M., August.
The Harlem Meer makes a stunning backdrop as you dance beneath the stars at this free summer dance series. Each week it's a new style of live music to dance to: swing, salsa, rock and roll, disco, or ballroom. Free lessons begin at 6:00 P.M., live bands at 7:00 P.M.

MIDSUMMER NIGHT SWING AT LINCOLN CENTER
65th Street and Broadway
(212) 875–5766
www.lincolncenter.org
Late June through July.
Yes, you too can be a dancer at Lincoln Center. Beginning in late June and running through July, the plaza at this famed performance center turns into the best dance floor in New York City. Every night they present top names from every sort of dance music, including American regional, Latin, Caribbean, African, ballroom, rhythm and blues, and, of course, swing! You can pay your way onto the official dance floor ($12), which is usually pretty

overcrowded, but the savvier folks spread out on the vast plaza to Savoy shuffle to their heart's content. Dance lessons begin at 6:30 P.M., dancing at 8:00 P.M.

MOONDANCE
Hudson River Park
Pier 54, Hudson River and 14th Street
(212) 533–PARK (7275)
www.hudsonriverpark.org
Sunday evenings, July and August.
Swing, tango, and cha-cha away every Sunday night under the stars with live music from New York's hottest bands. Free lessons begin at 6:30 P.M., and the dancing keeps going until 10:00.

SANDRA CAMERON DANCE CENTER
199 Lafayette Street (between Broome and Kenmore Streets)
(212) 431–1825
www.sandracameron.com
The last Friday of every month.
This popular dance studio offers classes to the masses in swing, salsa, ballroom, and tango. Stop in for one of the monthly guest nights and get a free introductory swing and salsa class, some hot dance performances, and open swing, salsa, and ballroom dance sessions. There's even free wine and cheese!

SO YOU WANT TO BE A DANCER: WORK-STUDY DANCE CLASSES

New York is the place to be if you hope to join those tapping feet on 42nd Street—but it's not a cheap dream to pursue. Group dance classes can cost as much as $15 per hour. But fear not, there are ways for you to make it to the Great White Way without spending such a great green amount. Many of the leading dance studios around New York offer scholarships, internships, or work-study options in exchange for free classes, or to greatly reduce the cost of classes.

BROADWAY DANCE CENTER

322 West 45th Street (between Eighth and Ninth Avenues)
(212) 582-9304
www.broadwaydancecenter.com

 Reduced rate of $5 per class in exchange for work-study hours.

Classes in jazz, ballet, tap, modern, tumbling, and aerobics with leading teachers from Broadway and around the world. They run an extensive work-study program that's open to dancers at any level. Students work in various positions around the studio (front desk, cafe, office, boutique, or cleaning crew). For each work-study hour worked, you earn one class at a discounted rate of $5 instead of the regular rate of $18 per class. No audition is required, but you must apply, interview, and make a four- to six-month commitment to a work-study schedule.

MOVEMENT RESEARCH

Dance Theater Workshop
219 West 19th Street (between Seventh and Eighth Avenues)
(212) 598-0551
(212) 539-2611 (event hotline)
www.movementresearch.org

Movement Research classes are more likely to win you a chance to work on an Off-Off Broadway performance art piece than a part in a Broadway musical. If that's your type of dance, this is absolutely the place for you. They offer a full schedule of classes and workshops in contact improvisation and modern and postmodern techniques, as well as other classes that defy simple definition but combine all kinds of movement influences from around the world. Work-study students are expected to work about ten hours a week in exchange for unlimited free classes. Hours and assignments are flexible and could include registering students for morning or weekend classes, working on the tech crew during performances, running light errands, or distributing flyers. Call to schedule an interview; no audition required.

PERIDANCE

132 Fourth Avenue, second floor (between 12th and 13th Streets)
(212) 505-0886
www.peridance.com

Offers classes in ballet, jazz, tap, yoga, hip-hop, and an emphasis on all forms of modern. They have various work-study positions where you can get a free class for every hour and half you work. Stop by to fill out an application; no audition required.

STEPS ON BROADWAY
2121 Broadway (between 74th and 75th Streets)
(212) 874–2410
www.stepsnyc.com

 $15 registration fee required.

Classes in all styles and levels. They accept all levels of dancers into the work-study program, but you must be committed to training and be willing to work eight to ten hours a week. Work-study students work at the registration desk or in their administrative offices, clean studios, or help prepare for performances. Depending on your specific job, you will be able to take all the classes you want either for free or $3.00 each (regularly $14.50 per class). Call to set up an interview.

THE WEST SIDE DANCE PROJECT
260 West 36th Street, third floor (between Eighth and Ninth Avenues)
(212) 563–6781
www.westsidedanceproject.com

This small dance studio offers classes in jazz, ballet, and tap. They have auditions a couple of times a year for their scholarship program. You don't necessarily need to be a "dancer" to win one of these positions. They look for people who are pursuing careers in the musical theater and are hoping to improve their dance skills. Scholarship winners are required to work one three-hour shift at the front desk a week and must take at least five hours of dance classes a week.

"Money disappears
like magic."
—Arabic Proverb

YOU MIGHT THINK THE closest you can get to seeing a free magic show in New York is watching how quickly people's money disappears when they play three-card monte, but you'd be wrong. There is a thriving world of magic in this city, and even with nothing up your sleeve, you can be entertained by many of the finest magicians in the world without spending a single quarter (not even that one you have hidden behind your ear). Just stop into any of the handful of magician supply shops around the city to be dazzled at the magic counter, or visit during one of their weekly free performances.

FANTASMA MAGIC

421 Seventh Avenue, second floor (33rd Street between Sixth and
Seventh Avenues)
(212) 244–3633
www.fantasmamagic.com
Saturday at 2:00 and 4:00 P.M.

Just wandering through this wonderfully magical store, playing with all the
unusual items, and strolling through the free Houdini Museum could be
enough entertainment for a day. But every Saturday it gets even more entertaining when they offer free magic shows at 2:00 and 4:00 P.M. They also have
plans to offer free magic lessons, juggling lessons, and balloon sculpting
classes in the future. Call for details.

SOCIETY OF AMERICAN MAGICIANS

Goldman Auditorium
1425 Madison Avenue (at 98th Street)
www.geocities.com/samparentassembly
First Friday of the month at 8:00 P.M.

This is the oldest and most prestigious magicians society in the world. Their
monthly meeting brings together an array of talent from those trying to break
into the business to masters of the art. And wherever there are magicians,
there is magic. Once they take care of their secret magician business, they

Old Dogs and New Tricks

*How do you make a burrito disappear? Stop by the downstairs dining
room at Maui Tacos (330 Fifth Avenue, between 32nd and 33rd
Streets; 212–868–9722) any Saturday afternoon from 2:00 to 5:00
P.M. Since 1938 a group of professional and amateur magicians has
been gathering (only recently at Maui Tacos) to perfect new tricks,
exchange ideas, sample some exotic salsas, take full advantage of the
free refills on the sodas, and try to slip something past their hardest
audience—each other. There is no formal show here, just a chance to
see some amazing artists working on their craft in an informal, one-
on-one setting. And the tacos are pretty tasty, too. Over the years, the
group has migrated to various eateries. If you don't find them at Maui
Tacos, call the folks at Tannen's (212–929–4500). They should know
where to find them.*

often open up the meetings to the public with free magic shows. Check their Web site for schedule and information.

TANNEN'S MAGIC STUDIO
45 West 34th Street, Room 608 (between Fifth and Sixth Avenues)
(212) 929–4500
www.tannens.com
Well, they won't tell you how they're done, but everyone behind the counter at Tannen's is a bona fide magician and can show you any trick in the house. And there are thousands of tricks in the place. Of course, the only way to find out the secrets behind the magic is to buy the tricks, but they will demonstrate any one of them for free. There are no shows at this store, but just spend some time around the counter, and you're sure to catch a trick or two.

LIVING IN NEW YORK

> "The remarkable thing about
> my mother is that for thirty
> years she served us nothing
> but leftovers. The original
> meal has never been found."
> —Calvin Trillin

FOOD: ON THE HOUSE

FAST **FOOD, GOURMET FOOD,** exotic food, health food, breads, cakes, wings, hors d'oeuvres, hot dogs, canapés, sushi, Italian, Mexican, Chinese, food, food, food. Anything you desire, it's in New York, and it's better than anywhere else in the world. But for free? Yes indeed. Wander through the many gourmet markets and selected specialty stores around the city, and you'll find a delightful (and filling) selection of samples to chow down on. Make your way to any number of bars and restaurants that set out some grand and some not-so-grand spreads during happy hours. And if you must spend money, you can shop at some fancy joints for pennies, if you know when to go.

HAPPY HOURS

Many bars, pubs, and restaurants around the city offer some kind of free food during happy hours. What you'll find at these places runs the gamut from basic bar food to sumptuous buffets. For the most part you are expected to buy a drink to partake of the eats, but there are usually all kinds of discounts on the drinks as well during happy hours. And hey, if you don't drink or don't feel like footing the bill for a martini, no one says you can't just order a club soda. Be sure to leave the bartender a nice tip though. Yes, in New York, even Cheap Bastards should remember to tip. While I have included here only those places that have a long history of offering free eats, policies do change from time to time.

EAST SIDE

ASHTON'S
208 East 50th Street (at Third Avenue)
(212) 688–8625
There's always something substantial to chow down on during happy hour at this friendly Irish pub. Monday through Friday, 5:00 to 7:00 P.M.

McCORMACK'S PUBLIC HOUSE
365 Third Avenue (between 26th and 27th Streets)
(212) 683–0911
An Irish pub with free food available from 5:00 to 7:00 P.M. every Friday. They usually offer appetizers like skins or wings (though one night they put out some kind of black sausage thing—mmm-mm). Also, they broadcast international rugby games.

NEVADA SMITHS
74 Third Avenue (between 11th and 12th Streets)
(212) 982–2591
www.nevadasmiths.net
Local Irish pub and soccer haven that offers up a buffet of wings and sandwiches every Friday afternoon starting at 5:30 P.M.

ONE FISH TWO FISH
1399 Madison Avenue (at 97th Street)
(212) 369–5677
www.onefishtwofish.com

Stop by this jam-packed uptown seafood restaurant to pick at the appetizers they set out at the bar every Monday through Friday from 4:00 to 6:00 P.M. Though if you really want to dig in, make sure to show up on a Wednesday for ladies' night (half-price drinks for ladies!) or on Thursday evening, when they pull out all the stops with a large buffet of appetizers and other goodies.

PIG 'N WHISTLE ON 3RD
922 Third Avenue (between 55th and 56th Streets)
(212) 688–4646
This low-key Irish pub sets out a small buffet of a couple of tasty selections like chicken fingers, mini pizzas, poppers, or wings. Monday through Friday, 5:30 to 7:30 P.M.

PLAYWRIGHT IRISH PUB
27 West 35th Street (between Fifth and Sixth Avenues)
(212) 268–8868
www.playwrightirishpubnyc.com
Lively Irish pub and horse racing mecca (you can even place your bets from the bar!) sets out a buffet of tasty finger food Monday through Friday from 5:00 to 7:00 P.M.

RODEO BAR
375 Third Avenue (at 27th Street)
(212) 683–6500
www.rodeobar.com
A fun and casual Tex-Mex bar/restaurant with barrels full of freshly roasted peanuts all around. At happy hours (Monday through Friday, 4:00 to 7:00 P.M.) they supply a small buffet of munchies (wings, nachos, potato skins, and the like). On Monday nights kids eat free, and every night they have live rockabilly or country music and never charge a cover. Yee-ha!

ROLF'S
281 Third Avenue (at 22nd Street)
(212) 477–4750
This German restaurant sets out free finger sandwiches at the bar at 6:00 P.M. until they're gone seven nights a week. Be sure to check out the over-the-top Christmas decorations.

TRACY J'S WATERING HOLE
106 East 19th Street (between Park Avenue and Irving Place)
(212) 674–5783
www.tracyjs.com

This small bar packs a big gastronomic wallop by setting out an extensive free buffet every Monday through Friday for the after-work crowd. But you better be quick: The grub is only out from 5:30 to 6:30, and it goes fast.

WEST SIDE

CHANNEL 4
58 West 48th Street (between Fifth and Sixth Avenues)
(212) 819–0095
ww.channel4barnyc.com

This stylish Irish bar and restaurant sets out a nice spread of appetizers—wings, spring rolls, quesadillas—Monday through Friday from 5:00 to 7:00 P.M.

CHARLEY O'S BAR & GRILL & BAR
713 8th Avenue (at 45th Street)
(212) 977–0025

This Broadway-district hangout sets out a small buffet of appetizers Monday through Friday from 3:00 to 6:00 P.M.

D. J. REYNOLDS
351 West 57th Street (between Eighth and Ninth Avenues)
(212) 245–2912

Try your luck at this quiet and friendly Irish pub. Every Thursday and Friday from 5:00 to 8:00 P.M., they set out something different. It might be a hearty snack of wings or chicken nuggets, or you could end up with a substantial meal of steak or chicken marsala over pasta.

KENNEDY'S
327 West 57th Street (between Eighth and Ninth Avenues)
(212) 759–4242

This Irish pub puts out a bit of bar food—wings or meatballs—Monday through Friday, 4:30 to 7:00 P.M. or until it's gone. Good for a nibble, but it probably won't fill you up.

LANGAN'S
150 West 47th Street (between Sixth and Seventh Avenues)
(212) 869-5482

This makes a great pretheater stop. Monday through Friday, 5:00 to 8:00 P.M., you'll find chips and salsa at the bar and a small buffet of bar food, which could include wings, mozzarella sticks, meatballs, or other tasty munchies.

O'FLAHERTY'S ALE HOUSE
334 West 46th Street (between Eighth and Ninth Avenues)
(212) 581-9366 or (212) 246-8928

This theater-district Irish pub satisfies its starving-actor clientele with free shepherd's pie or pasta Monday and Tuesday nights at about 10:30 P.M. Don't worry—you don't have to recite any Shakespeare to partake. They also have free live music seven nights a week (acoustic, rock, and Irish).

O'REILLY'S TOWNHOUSE
21 West 35th Street (between Fifth and Sixth Avenues)
(212) 502-5246

This lively Irish pub with a busy after-work crowd sets out a free buffet of shepherd's pie, pasta, or wings Monday through Friday from 5:00 P.M. "till it's gone."

PETER'S RESTAURANT
182 Columbus Avenue (between 68th and 69th Streets)
(212) 877-4747

This comfortable upscale restaurant treats its upper West Side customers to a sampling of its Asian-influenced American menu at their bar Monday through Friday from 5:00 to 8:00 P.M.

PIG 'N WHISTLE
165 West 47th Street (between Sixth and Seventh Avenues)
(212) 302-0112

Just down the block from Langan's, this makes a great pretheater stop as well. Monday through Friday, 5:00 to 8:00 P.M., chow down on chips and salsa at the bar and a buffet of appetizers.

RUDY'S BAR AND GRILL
627 Ninth Avenue (at West 44th Street)
(212) 974-9169

Look for the Big Pig outside to find the place and "pig out" on the free hot

Sing for Your Supper

Here are a couple of places to stop by and lend a hand or join in on some chanting and get yourself a full meal.

FOOD NOT BOMBS NYC, *Tompkins Square Park; (212) 254–3697; www.abcnorio.org. The artists collective/punk rock club ABC No Rio serves up free vegetarian meals in Tompkins Square Park every Sunday at about 3:30 P.M. This meal is generally meant for the homeless, but they always need volunteers to help in food preparation—and, of course, they'll feed you, too. Stop by ABC No Rio at about 1:00 P.M. to help cook (156 Rivington Street, between Clinton and Suffolk Streets).*

SRI SRI RADHA GOVINDA MANIR, *305 Schermerhorn Street (between Nevins and Bond Streets), Brooklyn; (718) 855–6714; www.radhagovinda.net. This is the main New York Hare Krishna temple; it's very large and well attended. They offer free vegetarian feasts on Sunday nights at about 8:00. All are welcome, and there's no need to shave your head.*

dogs. This is a real neighborhood joint. The franks are always available (1:00 to 10:00 P.M.), but don't try asking for one without ordering a drink first.

THE SUN ROOM
123 West 57th Street (between Sixth and Seventh Avenues)
(212) 664–1589

The saying goes, God works in mysterious ways. Well, one mystery I have no desire to see solved is the Sun Room. Sponsored by the Calvary Baptist Church, this is by all outward appearances your everyday Starbucks-style coffeehouse, complete with cozy couches, reading material, and, of course, coffee and snacks. Now, while you may not be able to get your Caramel Macchiato here, you will save enough money to fill your own coffers because everything in the shop is completely free. *Okay,* you are thinking, *what's the catch? Do I have to listen to a sermon while I sip my coffee?* No, you do not. Born out of the aftermath of September 11, 2001, the cafe strives simply to be a "refuge from the noise." There is no proselytizing going on here, and everyone is welcome to stop in and get a drink, have a nibble, and relax. Of course, if you do have some crisis of faith that a strong cup of joe won't solve, they will be happy to talk it over with you. Otherwise, no catches. Just free coffee, tea, cookies, muffins, and more every Tuesday through Thursday from 11:00 A.M. to 4:00 P.M.

DOWNTOWN, EAST AND WEST VILLAGE

CROCODILE LOUNGE
325 East 14th Street (between First and Second Avenues)
(212) 477-7747
No two words in the English language evoke quite as much joy as the words free pizza, and while it may not be the best pie New York has to offer, the Crocodile Lounge's free pizza certainly does go down well with a mug of cold beer. They will ask you to lay down a few bucks for a drink to get your free, fresh-baked 8-inch pie.

CUCINA DI PESCE
87 East 4th Street (between Second and Third Avenues)
(212) 260–6800
This Italian restaurant sets out free mussels at the bar every day beginning at about 5:00 P.M.

11TH STREET BAR
510 East 11th Street (between Avenues A and B)
(212) 982–3929
Free wings on Friday, 4:00 to 7:00 P.M.

THE THIRSTY SCHOLAR
155 Second Avenue (between 9th and 10th Streets)
(212) 777–6514
They set out a free load of wings, rings, shepherd's pie, or whatever the kitchen happens to have available from about 6:00 P.M. until whenever it's gone. Monday through Friday, 6:00 to 8:00-ish P.M.

TY'S BAR
114 Christopher Street (between Bleecker and Hudson Streets)
(212) 741–9641
On the second Tuesday of every month, get yourself a hearty meal and shake the hand of some of New York's bravest (and gayest) as this gay saloon plays host to the monthly gathering of the gay firemen and EMS organization, Fire-FLAG/EMS. All are welcome. The buffet opens at about 8:30 P.M.

BROOKLYN

THE BRAZEN HEAD
228 Atlantic Avenue (between Court Street and Boerum Place)
Boerum Hill, Brooklyn
(718) 488–0430
www.brazenheadbrooklyn.com

This local Brooklyn bar is heaven for fans of microbrews and darts, and, of course, for Cheap Bastards! Monday nights they serve free wings and things when they welcome dart players of all skill levels from far and wide for an open dart night. Sunday afternoons they roll out the free bagel buffet for your brunching pleasure.

HANK'S SALOON
46 Third Avenue (at Atlantic Avenue)
Brooklyn
(718) 625–8003
www.hankstavern.com

Free live country/rock/rockabilly music Wednesday through Sunday nights at this hard-core Brooklyn dive. On Sunday and Monday nights, don't miss the free barbecue. You never know what they'll be serving up; some weeks it could be a mighty fine spread, others it might be hockey-puck hamburgers and shriveled hot dogs. No cover, no minimum.

FREE SAMPLES: A SAMPLING

New York City is overrun with gourmet markets, farmers' markets, and specialty stores that charge an arm and a leg for anything from a leg of lamb to over-priced olives from around the world. These markets, however, are also gold mines of free samples. You can get a taste of almost anything, from gourmet breads, cakes, and cookies to olive oils, cheeses, and exotic fruits.

AGATA & VALENTINA
1505 First Avenue (at 79th Street)
(212) 452–0690
www.agatavalentina.com

One of New York's premier gourmet markets, they often set out a wide variety of samples of everything from smoothies and cheeses to bread and sometimes even pizzas. But when, oh, when will they set out some tasty tidbits from their incredible-looking desserts and pastries? You will find the best selection of samples on the weekends.

AJI ICHIBAN

37 Mott Street (between Pell and Mosco Streets)
(212) 233–7650

167 Hester Street (between Mott and Elizabeth Streets)
(212) 925–1133

17 East Broadway (between Catherine and Market Streets)
(212) 571–3755

188 Lafayette Street (between Broome and Grand Streets)
(212) 219–4010

This Chinese candy store offers some truly unusual, intensely flavorful delicacies. You'll find signs all over the store encouraging you to try such unusual fare as the dried curry squid, mini roasted crabs, and preserved chili olives. There are tamer selections of chocolates, biscuits, and gummy candies as well.

BAKERY SOUTINE

104 West 70th Street (between Columbus Avenue and Broadway)
(212) 496–1450
www.soutine.com

A lovely neighborhood bakery that always sets out something sweet to nibble on.

BALTHAZAR BOULANGERIE

80 Spring Street (between Crosby Street and Broadway)
(212) 965–1785
www.balthazarbakery.com

THE CATCH   It's not easy to get away without buying something.

Considered one of the best bakeries in the city (and one of the most expensive), Balthazar always offers something to snack on at the register. It's a very small place, so it isn't easy to get away without buying something so you don't look like a Cheap Bastard. If you're willing to brave the stares from behind the counter and from those on line, dive right in—their treats are delicious. But if you are willing to lay down a few bucks, stop by after

Cosi and Toasty

Walk into any of the many Cosi restaurants popping up around New York for a toasty treat. At their sandwich counter you will find a bowl full of ends from the delicious seasoned breads they make for their heaping sandwiches. These hunks of bread are free for the taking, and if you ask nicely, the folks behind the counter will even throw in a side of some tangy dipping sauce. There are more than thirty Cosi locations in New York and more opening up all the time. You are sure to stumble upon one in daily travels, or you can go to their Web site, www.getcosi.com, for an up-to-date list of their locations.

8:00 P.M., when they slice the prices on all baked goods by 40 percent and offer deals on their prepackaged sandwiches and salads.

BLACK HOUND NEW YORK
170 Second Avenue (between 10th and 11th Streets)
(212) 979–9505
www.blackhoundny.com

The delectable treats displayed artistically in the window will beckon you into this fine bakery, but the rich reward are the generous individually wrapped samples of their goods (or should I say goodies!) placed throughout the store. Stop in often!

CHELSEA MARKET
75 Ninth Avenue (between 15th and 16th Streets)
(212) 243–6005
www.chelseamarket.com

The former home of the Nabisco Company and the birthplace of the Oreo cookie has been transformed into a sumptuous marketplace of gourmet shops. Sample breads, brownies, gourmet butters, cookies, and fruit. Selections are particularly abundant on weekends, when you can also sample some fine wines (Friday and Saturday) and even take free dance classes (Saturday). They even supply free high-speed Internet access for those of you who have a laptop equipped for the wireless Web.

ELI'S

1411 Third Avenue (at 80th Street); (212) 717–8100

431 East 91st Street (between York and First Avenues); (212) 987–0885
www.elizabar.com

Stop by these dreamy gourmet markets often to gorge yourself on the generous samples in their bakeries and to ogle at the tantalizing displays. But be warned: While the fresh food is awfully inviting, the prices are ridiculously steep.

GOURMET GARAGE

453 Broome Street (at Mercer Street); (212) 941–5850

117 Seventh Avenue South (at Christopher Street); (212) 414–5910

2567 Broadway (between 96th and 97th Streets); (212) 663–0656

301 East 64th Street (between First and Second Avenues)
(212) 535–6271

1245 Park Avenue (at 96th Street); (212) 348–5850
www.gourmetgarage.com

Sample from the olive bar, cheeses, and other gourmet treats from time to time.

GREENMARKET FARMERS MARKET

Union Square, 17th Street and Broadway
(212) 788–7476
www.cenyc.org

New York has many official farmers' markets (forty throughout the five boroughs), which attract a wide variety of upstate and Long Island farmers to the city to sell their wares. The hands-down best market for samples of everything from heirloom tomatoes and organic apples, beans, and peppers to fresh bread, cakes, and jams is the Union Square market, held every Monday, Wednesday, Friday, and Saturday. Call or check the Web site for information on other markets around the city.

JEFFERSON MARKET

450 Sixth Avenue (between 10th and 11th Streets)
(212) 533–3377

Good bakery, cheese, and deli samples.

MURRAY'S CHEESE SHOP

257 Bleecker Street (at Cornelia, between Sixth and Seventh Avenues); (212) 243–3289

Grand Central Station, 73 Grand Central Terminal (43rd Street at Lexington Avenue); (212) 922–1540
www.murrayscheese.com

Murray's is considered to be one of the finest cheese shops in the world, and you are welcome to sample any cheese in the world at either one of their shops. They often have samples out for you to dip into, but feel free to ask for a bit of anything they have. Their helpful and extraordinarily knowledgeable staff will happily slice off for you a bit of whatever you request. Stop by to meet cheesemakers from all over the world and sample their goods. Check their Web site for an up-to-date schedule of tastings.

THE PENINSULA HOTEL

700 Fifth Avenue (at 55th Street)
(212) 956–2888
www.peninsula.com

This indulgent hotel keeps you healthy and happy with its giveaways. To the left of the front desk, you will always find an inviting bowl of Red Delicious and Granny Smith apples, and to the right a big jar of Lindt chocolate truffles beckons.

POMMES FRITES

123 Second Avenue (between 7th and 8th Streets)
(212) 674–1234
www.pommesfrites.ws

Specializing in "authentic Belgian fries," they offer free samples that consist of about six large fries and your choice of two gourmet dipping sauces. No pressure to buy. A great little snack.

RENAISSANCE NEW YORK HOTEL

714 Seventh Avenue (between 47th and 48th Streets)
(212) 765–7676
www.renaissancehotels.com

Bowls of apples are available in the second-floor lobby, along with some nice comfy chairs. A good place to duck into when you have some time to kill.

TODARO BROS.

555 Second Avenue (between 30th and 31st Streets)
(212) 532–0633
www.todarobros.com

A gourmet market with samples of cheeses, olive oils, bread, and more.

TONNIE'S MINIS

120 West 3rd Street (near McDougal Street)
(212) 473–2002
www.tonniesminis.com

This little cupcake of a shop hands out cupcake shots, the smallest, cutest, tastiest samples of their full-size cupcakes.

TWO LITTLE RED HENS

1652 Second Avenue (between 85th and 86th Streets)
(212) 452–0476

1112 Eighth Avenue (at 11th Street), Park Slope, Brooklyn
(718) 499–8108
www.twolittleredhens.com

Like a little bit of country in the city, this adorable bakery serves up a delicious selection of cakes, cookies, and pastries, and they always have a generous selection of treats out for your sampling pleasure.

UNION MARKET

754–756 Union Street (at Sixth Avenue)
Park Slope, Brooklyn
(718) 230–5152
www.unionmarket.com

This gourmet market in the heart of Park Slope sets out some tasty samples in their deli, and you can always grab an olive or marinated mushroom or two at their olive bar.

VOSGES HAUTE-CHOCOLAT

132 Spring Street (between Wooster and Greene Streets)
(212) 625–2929

1100 Madison Avenue (at 83rd Street)
(212) 717–2929
www.vosgeschocolate.com

You will always find some delicious and exotic chocolates set out on the counter of this wonderfully original chocolate store. The combinations of sweet and spice that they put together somehow manage to melt in your mouth and explode with flavor at the same time.

WHOLE FOODS MARKET

250 Seventh Avenue (at 24th Street)
(212) 924–5969

95 East Houston Street (between Bowery and Chrystie Streets)
(212) 420–1320

4 Union Square South (at Fourth Avenue and 14th Street)
(212) 673–5388

10 Columbus Circle (between 58th and 60th Streets)
(212) 823–9600
www.wholefoodsmarket.com

These health food megamarkets are often, though not always, great destinations to fill up on samples of everything from delicious organic fruits and vegetables to fresh baked goods and exotic teas and coffees. Your best bet is to stop by on the weekend or during lunch hour, but you will almost always find something to nibble on somewhere in the store.

W HOTELS

201 Park Avenue (Union Square at 17th Street); (212) 253–9119

541 Lexington Avenue (at 49th Street); (212) 755–1200

130 East 39th Street (between Lexington and Park Avenues)
(212) 685–1100

120 East 39th Street (between Lexington and Park Avenues)
(212) 686–1600

1567 Broadway (at 47th Street); (212) 930–7400
www.whotels.com

These elegant and funky hotels have amazing lobbies with board games, books, couches, comfy chairs, and overflowing bowls of delicious green apples for you to munch away on.

WILLIAMS-SONOMA

10 Columbus Circle (between 58th and 60th Streets)
(212) 832–9750
www.williams-sonoma.com

The New York flagship location for this purveyor of all things cooking is equipped with a huge kitchen itself. The staff is almost always dishing up something tasty to try. They also hold cooking demonstrations every day at 2:00 P.M. on everything from carving skills to cupcake decoration.

EAT LATE, EAT CHEAP!

Hey, eating late may not be very good for the size of your waist, but it can do wonders for the size of your wallet. If you must spend money—and, of course, I generally do frown on that—then drop by one of these places to eat for half price (after the specified times). These shops, restaurants, gourmet markets, and health food stores all have a policy of cutting their prices at the end of the day to get rid of that day's fresh sandwiches, salads, and other assorted taste delights.

AMISH MARKET
731 Ninth Avenue (between 49th and 50th Streets)
(212) 245–2360
www.amishfinefood.com

This market often slices prices on their precut sandwiches at about 6:00 P.M. on most evenings. The store closes at 10:00 P.M. They don't exactly advertise this, so make sure they don't try to charge you the full price when you get to the register. They also have great olive bars for sampling and occasionally cheeses and desserts for you to taste.

CAFÉ AMRITA
301 West 111th Street (between Eighth and Manhattan Avenues)
(212) 222–0683
www.indiecafes.com

Stop by this relaxed Harlem coffeehouse after 4:30 every day for half-price muffins, scones, and other delicious baked goods.

CAFÉ ANGELIQUE
68 Bleecker Street (between Broadway and Laffayette Street)
(212) 475–3500
www.cafeangelique.com

Delightful little Parisian bakery and cafe slashes the prices in half every night on their sandwiches and pastries from 7:00 until they close at 8:00 P.M.

THE CITY BAKERY
3 West 18th Street (between Fifth and Sixth Avenues)
(212) 366–1414
www.citybakerycatering.com

This gourmet cafe and bakery turns out some of the city's most scrumptious pastries—the problem is a single one of them can easily run you $5. But if you stop by after 3:30 in the afternoon, you might just be lucky enough to snag a whole box of treats (four to six per box) for the ludicrously low price of $5. They don't offer these every day, just when they have a surplus of sweet delights. They often run two-for-one specials late in the day on their artistic tarts. Also, if you are a chocoholic and have never tried their hot chocolate, it is worth spending the money to try it once. The cup is rich enough to warrant its rich price tag—$3.75 with the homemade marshmallow.

FASHION SOUP
124 West 41st Street (between Sixth Avenue and Broadway)
(212) 704–0909
www.fashionsoup.com

As the Campbell's soup commercial goes, "Soup is good food." But these soups are nothing like those watered-down cans of cream of mushroom your mom used to stockpile. These are hearty, tasty, thick, and chunky bowls of soups that fill you up like a meal. Every day there's a new selection of soups and stews with delicious twists on favorites (tomato soup with fennel and artichoke, corn chowder with chicken) or ingenious blends (cream of carrot with ginger, vegetarian mulligatawny). Half-price soups are offered from 3:30 P.M. to closing (about 5:30).

INTEGRAL YOGA NATURAL FOODS
229 West 13th Street (between Seventh and Eighth Avenues)
(212) 243–2642
www.integralyoganaturalfoods.com

A natural food store with an extensive salad bar including all kinds of beans, vegetables, tofu creations, and other green and brown edibles. They sell off generous platters of leftovers from the day at greatly reduced prices ($2.25 for a small and $4.25 for a large) starting at 6:00 P.M. Monday to Friday and at 5:30 on weekends.

NEWS CAFE
107 University Place (between 12th and 13th Streets)
(212) 353–1246

A newsstand/sandwich shop that slashes the prices on its tasty sandwiches, wraps, salads, and baked goods at 7:00 every night. Feel free to sit and read the newspapers and magazines from around the world while eating your cheap dinner (try not to get any dressing on the papers, though). Closes at 10:00 P.M. every night.

TODARO BROS.

555 Second Avenue (between 30th and 31st Streets)
(212) 532–0633
www.todarobros.com

At this gourmet market they sell off their leftover fresh sandwiches for half price from 8:00 to 10:00 P.M. every night.

WILD OATS COMMUNITY MARKET

2421 Broadway (corner of 89th Street)
(212) 874–4000
www.wildoats.com

A health food store that offers 50 percent off at the salad bar as they close it down at about 10:00 P.M.

ZABAR'S

2245 Broadway (between 80th and 81st Streets)
(212) 496–1234 or (800) 697–6301
www.zabars.com

At this world-famous marketplace for gourmet cheeses, deli, coffee, baked goods, and more, they often cut the prices on prepared sandwiches, depending on how much is still left at the end of the day. They make the decision at about 6:00 P.M. They close at 7:30 P.M. Monday through Friday and 8:00 P.M. on Saturday.

"I like best the wine
drunk at the cost
of others."

—Bergen Evans

NOT ONLY DO the wine shops of New York offer you a chance to try some of the finest wines and spirits from around the world, but you can also end up learning a heck of a lot about the fruits of the vine. You'll find two types of wine-tasting situations at stores around the city. One is the local shop that uncorks a bottle or two for customers to try (and hopes you'll buy). The other, more desirable situation is when a vintner or wine distributor brings out an entire line of wines for the public to sample. You get to try more wines, the staff are usually very knowledgeable and eager to teach you about the wines without pushing you to buy anything, and you can usually depend on them bringing something tasty along "to cleanse the palate" between wines. All this can be true about the local shop, but you're just as likely to find a guy with a bottle saying, "Here, try some of this stuff, I hear it's good." Most shops offer a discount on whatever is being tasted that day, so if you're inspired to lay down some cash, this will lighten the blow.

EAST SIDE

AMBASSADOR WINES & SPIRITS
1020 Second Avenue (at 54th Street)
(212) 421–5078
This local shop holds tastings Thursday through Saturday, 4:00 to 8:00 P.M.

BEEKMAN LIQUORS
500 Lexington Avenue (between 47th and 48th Streets)
(212) 759–5857
www.beekmanliquors.com
This sophisticated local shop hosts a full schedule of tastings throughout the week. In addition to the many varieties of wine offered, they often pour various spirits as well. Their events are most consistently held on Thursday and Friday evenings from 4:00 to 7:00 P.M., but check their Web site for many additional chances to imbibe on other evenings.

BEST CELLARS
1291 Lexington Avenue (between 86th and 87th Streets)
(212) 426–4200
www.bestcellars.com
This is a great no-nonsense yet know-it-all place to go to check out some great-tasting wines. The very knowledgeable staff serve up some delightful, inexpensive wines on weekday evenings (5:00 to 8:00); on Saturday (2:00 to 4:00 P.M.) they usually pair the wine with food prepared by local chefs.

CORK & BOTTLE
1158 First Avenue (between 63rd and 64th Streets)
(212) 838–5300
Friday, 5:00 to 7:00 P.M.

CRUSH WINE CO.
153 East 57th Street (between Lexington and Third Avenues)
(212) 980–9463
www.crushwineco.com
Crush may very well be the Holy Grail of wine shops in New York City for anyone interested in tastings. They give you what you want—loads of high-quality wines to taste—when you want it—anytime! Step into the comforts of the tasting room at this sleek and modern shop, and you will always find a diverse selection of six bottles opened and ready for you to gulp down. And it doesn't stop there; they also play host to a variety of larger tastings

SHOP	MONDAY	TUESDAY	WEDNESDAY	THURSDAY	FRIDAY	SATURDAY	SUNDAY
Acker Merrall & Condit Co.						2:00–5:00 P.M.	
Ambassador Wine & Spirits				4:00–8:00 P.M.	4:00–8:00 P.M.	4:00–8:00 P.M.	
Astor Wines & Spirits			6:00–8:00 P.M.	6:00–8:00 P.M.	6:00–8:00 P.M.	3:00–5:00 P.M.	
Beekman Liquors				4:00–7:00 P.M.	4:00–7:00 P.M.		
Best Cellars	5:00–8:00 P.M.	5:00–8:00 P.M.	5:00–8:00 P.M.	5:00–8:00 P.M.	5:00–8:00 P.M.	2:00–4:00 P.M.	
Bierkraft		7:00–8:00 P.M.					
Burgundy Wine Co.	5:00–7:00 P.M.	5:00–7:00 P.M.	5:00–7:00 P.M.	5:00–7:00 P.M.	5:00–7:00 P.M.	11:00 A.M.– 7:00 P.M.	
Candlelight Wines						1:00–5:00 P.M. (SEPT–JUNE)	
Chelsea Wine Vault				4:00–7:00 P.M.	4:00–7:00 P.M.	1:00–5:00 P.M.	1:00–5:00 P.M
Cork & Bottle					5:00–7:00 P.M.		
Crush Wine Company	10:00 A.M.– 9:00 P.M.	10:00 A.M.– 9:00 P.M.	10:00 A.M.– 9:00 P.M.	10:00 A.M.– 9:00 P.M.	10:00 A.M.– 9:00 P.M.	10:00 A.M.– 9:00 P.M.	
Ehrlich Wine and Spirits				5:00–8:00 P.M.	5:00–8:00 P.M.	5:00–8:00 P.M.	
86th Street Corner Wine				4:00–8:00 P.M.	4:00–8:00 P.M.	4:00–8:00 P.M.	
86th Street Wine & Liquor						5:00–8:00 P.M.	
Elizabeth & Vine						5:00–8:00 P.M.	
International Wines & Spirits					4:00–7:00 P.M.	4:00–7:00 P.M.	
Mister Wright Liquors				4:00–7:00 P.M.	4:00–7:00 P.M.	4:00–7:00 P.M.	
Morell & Company						2:00–5:00 P.M.	
Ninth Avenue Vintner					5:00–8:00 P.M.	5:00–8:00 P.M.	
Park East Wines & Spirits						4:00–7:00 P.M.	
Sea Grape Wine & Spirits				5:30–8:30 P.M.			
67 Wines & Spirits		4:00–7:00 P.M.	4:00–7:00 P.M.	4:00–7:00 P.M.	4:00–7:00 P.M.	4:00–7:00 P.M.	
Spirits of Columbus						4:00–7:00 P.M.	
Union Square Wine & Spirits				6:00–8:00 P.M.	6:00–8:00 P.M.	2:00–5:00 P.M.	
Vintage New York						5:00–7:00 P.M. (UPTOWN) 2:00–4:00 P.M. (DOWNTOWN)	
Windsor Court Wine Shop				5:00–8:00 P.M. (SEPT.–MAY)	5:00–8:00 P.M. (SEPT.–MAY)	5:00–8:00 P.M. (SEPT.–MAY)	

and events (some of which are not free), when they crack open even more bottles by specific vineyards or varietals and often include generous spreads of cheese and gourmet food. Check their Web site for a schedule of classes and events.

EHRLICH WINES & SPIRITS
222 Amsterdam Avenue (at 70th Street)
(212) 877–6090
www.ehrlichwines.com
A small corner shop that opens a bottle or two for sampling Thursday, Friday, and Saturday from 5:00 to 8:00 P.M.

86TH STREET WINE & LIQUOR
306 East 86th Street (at Second Avenue)
(212) 396–3535
www.86wine.com
Saturday, 5:00 to 8:00 P.M.

MISTER WRIGHT LIQUORS
1593 Third Avenue (between 89th and 90th Streets)
(212) 722–4564
This large store cracks open a few bottles for tasting on Thursday, Friday, and Saturday from 4:00 to 7:00 P.M. It could be anything from cheap (or shall I say *inexpensive?*) to fine wines.

PARK EAST WINES & SPIRITS
1657 York Avenue (at 87th Street)
(212) 534–2093
Saturday, 4:00 to 7:00 P.M.

UNION SQUARE WINE & SPIRITS
33 Union Square West (between 16th and 17th Streets)
(212) 675–8100
www.unionsquarewines.com
This posh shop is always pouring something wonderful and unusual for you to try. Every week (Thursday and Friday, 6:00 to 8:00 P.M.; Saturday, 2:00 to 5:00 P.M.) they play host to a number of distributors, vintners, and sommeliers from around the city and the world who pour their selections for you to sample in the lavish upstairs salon. From time to time they also collaborate with local restaurants to provide food to match the wines.

Brooklyn Brew

If your tastes are more Michelob then merlot, you will definitely want to hop over the bridge to the borough that once was the home to as many as forty-eight breweries. While many of these are gone, the thirst for beer is still strong in Brooklyn. Bierkraft is a Park Slope gourmet market with a vast selection of beers from every corner of the world (more than 650 brands), and they are not afraid to give it away. Every Tuesday night at 7:00, anyone can stop in for their semiformal beer tastings. No tuxedos required, but a real interest in the art and craft of beer making is. This is a sit-down affair in which a master brewer will lead you through a tasting of five or so handpicked beer and food pairings. You can also stop by anytime to try their house brew of the day. The staff master brewer is known for his batches of unfamiliar beers that can be anything from a Belgian triple to an English mild. Bierkraft is located at 191 Fifth Avenue (between Sacket and Union Streets); (718) 230–7600; www.bierkraft.com.

The Brooklyn Brewery in Williamsburg has brought the fine art of mass-produced beer to Brooklyn, and every Saturday it is on display for all to see. The brewery offers free tours and samples of their brews. For more information see page 217.

And Williamsburg's thriving art galleries, a decidedly more downscale scene than its richer Manhattan counterpart, hand out free bottles of beer at its openings. For a selection of Williamsburg's galleries, see pages 244–45.

WINDSOR COURT WINE SHOP
474 Third Avenue (between 32nd and 33rd Streets)
(212) 779–4422

This local shop pours some wines every Thursday, Friday, and Saturday, 5:00 to 8:00 P.M., September through May.

WEST SIDE

ACKER MERRALL & CONDIT CO.
160 West 72nd Street (between Columbus Avenue and Broadway)
(212) 787–1700 (store)
(212) 875–0222 (wine workshop)
www.ackerstore.com

America's oldest and finest wine shop (if they don't say so themselves) is a great place to head any Saturday from 2:00 to 5:00 P.M. to sample some of their "finest" wines. This is a great chance to learn a few things from their knowledgeable staff or visiting vintners. They also run **The Wine Workshop,** which holds a full schedule of seminars and classes on the finer points of wine. They charge a pretty penny for these workshops, but they do use volunteers as pourers in the classes, which allows you to attend them for free. Call The Wine Workshop to add your name to the list, and they will call you when they have an opening (see page 151 for more information).

BEST CELLARS
2246 Broadway (between 80th and 81st Streets)
(212) 362–8730
www.bestcellars.com

Like its sister shop on the East Side, they offer tastings often accompanied by food prepared by local chefs.

CANDLELIGHT WINES
2315 Broadway (between 83rd and 84th Streets)
(212) 877–7085

A small local store that opens up a couple of bottles and sets out some cheese and crackers on Saturday, 1:00 to 5:00 P.M., September through June.

CHELSEA WINE VAULT
75 Ninth Avenue (between 15th and 16th Streets)
(212) 462–4244
www.chelseawinevault.com

A great wine find located in the Chelsea Market. They offer four full days of tastings, of everything from Beaujolais and bubbly to scotches and other spirits. Stop by Thursday and Friday evenings from 4:00 to 7:00 P.M. and Saturday and Sunday afternoons from 1:00 to 5:00 P.M. Don't miss their once-a-year Open House Anniversay celebration. This is a wonderful event that happens on a Saturday in early November: You'll find more than fifty wines for sampling, free catered hors d'oeuvres, and free introductory wine classes.

Booze Clues

In New York City you barely ever have to pay for a drink because of the multitude of promotions and special events going on at bars every night. The trick is to know where and when to show up to swig a few free cups of cheer. That's where MyOpenBar.com comes in. This Web site bills itself as "Your guide to free booze," and they have a day-by-day listing of every open bar, giveaway, and drink-fest they can find in the city. Some events are completely free, but others do have hefty cover charges—all of the details (along with some acerbic commentary) are clearly spelled out in the listings.

86TH STREET CORNER WINE & LIQUOR COMPANY
536 Columbus Avenue (at 86th Street)
(212) 496–1769
Thursday, Friday, Saturday, 4:00 to 8:00 P.M.

INTERNATIONAL WINES & SPIRITS
2903 Broadway (at 113th Street)
(212) 280–1850
Friday and Saturday, 4:00 to 7:00 P.M.

MORRELL & COMPANY WINE & SPIRITS MERCHANTS
1 Rockefeller Plaza (at 49th Street, between Fifth and Sixth Avenues)
(212) 688–9370
www.morrellwine.com
This fancy (and expensive) wine store brings in distributors to hawk their line of wines every Saturday, 2:00 to 5:00 P.M.

NINTH AVENUE VINTNER
669 Ninth Avenue (between 46th and 47th Streets)
(212) 664–WINE (9463) or (877) 664–9463
A friendly community shop that brings in vintners to show off their wines most Fridays and Saturdays, 5:00 to 8:00 P.M.

Corkscrew U

Don't know your Asti Spumonti from your elderberry wine? Take a class. There are many courses offered throughout the city that will let you expand your choice of wines beyond twist-off or cork. Most of these are one-day seminars on wines from specific regions of the world, but some are in-depth courses exploring every aspect of the wine, from seeds to sipping. And you can take the classes for free by volunteering to be a "pourer" for these classes. Basically all that's involved is showing up for the class an hour or so early, setting out the glasses and class materials for the paying students, pouring the wines that are used in the classes, and staying a little while after the class ends to load the glasses in the dishwasher. While the class is on, you're able to fully participate and taste all the wines used. See the chapter titled "Education: Cents-Less Smarts" for more details on classes at the New School Culinary Arts Program and The Wine Workshop.

67 WINES & SPIRITS
179 Columbus Avenue (at 68th Street)
(212) 724–6767
www.67wine.com

A fine store for fine wines and every bit of wine paraphernalia you could ever imagine. Make your way up to the second-floor kitchen area and get an education in wines by sampling vintages of different countries, regions, types, and styles Tuesday through Saturday, 4:00 to 7:00 P.M. They often have cooking demonstrations or at least something tasty to nibble along with the wines. Check their Web site for a listing of weekly events.

SPIRITS OF COLUMBUS
730 Columbus Avenue (between 95th and 96th Streets)
(212) 865–7070

This local shop offers tastes from a few inexpensive bottles Saturday, 4:00 to 7:00 P.M. They sometimes sample a selection of kosher wines on Friday.

VINTAGE NEW YORK
Uptown, 2492 Broadway (between 92nd and 93rd Streets)
(212) 721–9999

Downtown, 482 Broome Street (between Wooster and Greene Streets)
(212) 226–9463
www.vintagenewyork.com

Every other Saturday from 2:00 to 4:00 P.M. at the downtown store and from 5:00 to 7:00 P.M. at the uptown store, it is your chance to "Meet Your (Wine) Maker." This series of events features New York State vintners and their fine wines. At all other times, this store charges for its samples, but you can also always stop in to sample some delicious New York cheese and chocolates. Check their Web site for the schedule of events.

DOWNTOWN EAST

ASTOR WINES & SPIRITS
399 Lafayette Street (at East Fourth Street)
(212) 674–7500
www.astoruncorked.com

New York's largest wine store offers tastings grouped by region or type, giving you the opportunity to try everything from Dom Perignon to the wines of New Zealand and South Africa; from moderately priced to fine wines. The friendly staff offer samples in a no-pressure-to-buy atmosphere. Be sure to cleanse your palate with the gourmet breads and cheeses that often accompany the wines. Wednesday, Thursday, and Friday, 6:00 to 8:00 P.M., Saturday, 3:00 to 5:00 P.M. Check the Web site for a calendar of events.

ELIZABETH & VINE
253 Elizabeth Street (between Houston and Prince Streets)
(212) 941–7943

This tiny shop offers samples from a few bottles along with cheese and crackers. Saturday, 5:00 to 8:00 P.M.

BURGUNDY WINE COMPANY

143 West 26th Street (between Sixth and Seventh Avenues)

(212) 691–9092

www.burgundywinecompany.com

The folks at this specialty shop like their Burgundy, and they also like to share it. You can stop in any day they are open, and you will have a chance to sample a bottle or two of their favorite wines. They crack open a bottle for you to sip every night from 5:00 to 7:00 P.M. and on Saturday from 11:00 A.M. to 7:00 P.M. They make a point of making Wednesday evenings a particularly good night to stop in, mostly because they want a good excuse to goof off from work. They always have at least three bottles open, some cheese, and often some live jazz to get you in the mood.

SEA GRAPE WINE & SPIRITS

512 Hudson Street (between Christopher and West 10th Streets)

(212) 463–7688

www.seagrapewines.com

Thursday, 5:30 to 8:30 P.M.

"You'd be surprised
how much it costs
to look this cheap."
—Dolly Parton

HAIR, BEAUTY, AND MASSAGE: FREE-STYLE

JUST BECAUSE YOUR bank account is running low doesn't mean you can't look and feel like a million bucks. In fact, looking good and feeling good can look and feel a whole lot better the less you pay to get that way. And in New York anything you need or want done can be had for nothing or very little: haircuts, coloring, highlights, facials, makeovers, manicures, and massage. The most common places to look for free or cheap services are salons with training programs, beauty and barbering schools, and manufacturers testing new products.

PRODUCT TESTING CENTERS

Here's your chance to be the first on your block to try out the newest products that some of the leading hair care manufacturers are developing. These companies are in the final stages of testing these items and want your opinion. Fear not: These creams, colors, mousses, and gels have all gone through a battery of tests already and are safe for you to use. In other words, you won't end up with a head full of green hair (unless, of course, that's what you want). You should know, though, that they won't be able to customize colors for your hair. You will be able to choose your colors, but they must be selected from the standard set of colors prepared for the shelves of any local store.

CLAIROL PRODUCT EVALUATION SALON
345 Park Avenue, lobby (between 51st and 52nd Streets)
(646) 885–4200 or (646) 885–4201

The services they offer and the products they test include hair coloring, highlights, relaxers, conditioners, styling mousses, and gels. All services are free and performed by licensed and skilled stylists. You must stop by first to apply—Monday through Thursday from 9:30 to 11:00 A.M. or 1:30 to 4:00 P.M. All men and women age eighteen or older may participate. The services they provide at any given time depend on the products being tested. The most common and consistent service offered is hair coloring. Once you're accepted onto the models' panel, you're welcome to come back in once a month for treatments.

L'ORÉAL TECHNICAL CENTER
575 Fifth Avenue, second floor (at 47th Street)
(212) 984–4008

Women must have shoulder-length or shorter hair (but not too short).

This is the product evaluation salon for all L'Oréal coloring and hair care products. Stop by Monday through Thursday 10:00 A.M. to 4:00 P.M. for an evaluation and patch test. If they accept you into the program, they will color your hair every four weeks. They occasionally use men as well (long hair not necessary) but primarily seek women.

Don't Be THAT Cheap!

While these may be students, and you may be getting your hair done for free or at a very low price, this is still New York, so don't forget to tip! The fact is, as students these stylists probably aren't being paid. They may even be paying to do this work for you. A Cheap Bastard can still be a nice bastard.

REDKEN TESTING CENTER
15 Mercer Street (between Grand and Canal Streets)
(212) 885–1317
www.redken.com/hairmodel

They test all the new Redken products in development and can offer you quite a few fantastic services in the process. They offer coloring services, blow-outs, as well as perms and straightening. Stop by any Wednesday or Thursday afternoon from 2:00 to 4:00 P.M. for an evaluation. Then they will set you up for an appointment. Once you get a treatment, you can set up follow-up appointments every five weeks.

HAIR SALONS

These are some of the most exclusive (and expensive) salons in the city, and they all have training programs for fully licensed hairstylists who are receiving further instruction in specific styles or techniques. This makes it a low-risk situation: You can feel reasonably confident you won't end up with an accidental Mohawk at these salons. The only catch is that you are sometimes required to spend two to three hours at the salon when you are modeling for a class. Many of the salons that offer free services can be picky about whom they use as models; women are generally used more than men, and longer hair gets you an appointment quicker than shorter hair. All the salons listed below offer free cuts and/or colorings.

BUMBLE & BUMBLE

146 East 56th Street (between Lexington and Madison Avenues)
415 West 13th Street, sixth floor (between Greenwich and
Washington Streets)
(917) 606–5091 (hair model information)
(212) 521–6500 (appointments with apprentices)
(888) 528–6253
www.bbumodelproject.com

 For free cuts and styling, models must have long enough hair to have at least 2 to 3 inches cut off.

This salon has a large training program. To get a free cut or style, you'll need to be chosen as a model for one of their professional seminars held on a regular basis. To apply to be a model, fill out their preevaluation form on their Web site or show up to their model call every Monday evening from 5:30 to 6:30 P.M. You can qualify as a cut model, style model, or color model (though you can only be a color model once you have been a cut model). They are looking for models who are willing to see a real change in their style—no trims here. You can even earn Hairmiles—a "frequent styler club" where you can earn points and prizes for coming back for more appointments once you have been approved as a model. If you aren't chosen as a model, you can still schedule a low-price cut or color from a staff apprentice for $10 to $20 on Monday from 10:00 A.M. to 4:00 P.M.

CROPS FOR GIRLS

154 Orchard Street (between Stanton and Rivington Streets)
(212) 677–2772
www.cropsforgirls.com

 To get a free cut, you have to go from long hair to very short or let Michael do whatever he wants with your hair.

This salon specializes in short haircuts for women. It may be funky, it may be conservative; you never know what it may end up being. But you know it will be very short and Michael Giovan, the owner, will cut it himself. Call to make an appointment. If you are not quite willing to let Michael have his way with your hair, you can always pay for a cut and have it your way since his rates are darn reasonable (especially the $30 student discount!). Women only.

Fancy Places at Not-So-Fancy Prices

These salons all run training programs and charge reduced rates for stylish cuts given by their students. These appointments are generally easier to get than the free ones:

CARSTEN INSTITUTE, *41 Union Square West (Broadway and Fifth Avenue); (212) 675–4884; Tuesday through Saturday from 8:30 A.M. to 1:30 P.M.; $17 cuts; $35 color.*

CUTLER SALON, *115 East 57th Street (between Park and Lexington Avenues); (212) 308–3838; 465 West Broadway (between Prince and Houston Streets); (212) 674–2210; Tuesday, Wednesday, and Thursday; $10. They hold trainings twice a year, where they offer free cuts to hair models. Check their Web site for times (www.cutlersalon.com).*

MINARDI BEAUTY FOCUS, *29 East 61st Street, fifth floor (between Fifth and Madison Avenues); (212) 308–1711; Wednesday afternoons; $25 cut and style (also use models for coloring classes some Monday nights—free coloring, but you must stay for the entire five-hour class).*

MIWA ALEX HAIR SALON, *24 East 22nd Street (between Broadway and Park Avenue); (212) 228–4422; Tuesday mornings; $25.*

PARLOR, *102 Avenue B (between 6th and 7th Streets); (212) 673–5520; www.parlorhairsalon.com; Monday 9:30 A.M. to 3:00 P.M.; $15 cuts and style.*

PAUL LABRECQUE SALON, *171 East 65th Street (at Third Avenue); (212) 595–0099; Monday; $25 for cuts; coloring and highlights also available, but pricey.*

THE REDKEN EXCHANGE, *565 Fifth Avenue (between 46th and 47th Streets); (212) 984–4703; www.redkensalon.com. Stop by Thursday at noon for a consultation, and they'll schedule you for a color and/or cut by a professional learning new techniques. It could take two weeks to a month to get an appointment. $15 for services. Occasionally offer free services to test new products.*

SALON ISHI, *70 East 55th Street (between Madison and Park Avenues); (212) 888–4744; Wednesday evenings; $15 for cuts or color.*

SCOTT J. SALONS & SPAS, *242 East 86th Street (between Second and Third Avenues); every Wednesday morning; 257 Columbus Avenue (at 72nd Street); some Wednesday mornings; (212) 769–0107; $10 cuts/$20 color.*

SHIGE KOSUDA SALON, *141 East 55th Street (between Lexington and Third Avenues); (212) 759–2397; Tuesday and Wednesday; $10.*

VIDAL SASSOON, *90 Fifth Avenue (between 14th and 15th Streets); (212) 229–2200; 730 Fifth Avenue (at 56th Street); (212) 535–9200; show up at 6:00 P.M. on Wednesday for a consultation, and they will schedule an appointment for you the following week; $20–$40 (depending on how far into the program the student is).*

YOUNGHEE SALON, *64 North Moore Street (between Greenwich and Hudson); (212) 334–3770; www.youngheesalon.com; Wednesday; $15.*

DRAMATICS NYC

158 East 23rd Street (between Third and Lexington Avenues)
(212) 460–5709
www.dramaticsnyc.com

Show up any Monday at 10:30 A.M., and maybe you will be picked by one of the instructors for a free cut. This small chain of New York salons caters to a young, energetic, and on-the-go crowd, and they train all of the new stylists for their salons at this location. If you do not get picked for that class, they will call you back for another class.

FACE STATION

855 Lexington Avenue (between 64th and 65th Streets)
(212) 249–8866
www.facestation.com

This bustling upper East Side salon offers free cuts and colors by their assistants most weekdays from 10:00 A.M. to 7:00 P.M. Give them a call a few days ahead to schedule an appointment.

JEFFREY STEIN SALON

685 Third Avenue (at 43rd Street); (212) 557–0005

1336 Third Avenue (at 76th Street); (212) 772–7717

Jeffrey Stein has seven salons around the city, but these two offer free cuts for hair models on Wednesday mornings (43rd Street) and on Tuesday (76th Street). They offer cuts to men and women, depending on what skills and styles they're working on. Call one to two weeks in advance to set up an appointment.

MATRIX GLOBAL ACADEMY

435 Hudson Street (between Leroy and Morton Streets)
(917) 606–9500
www.matrix.com/globalacademy

This huge and stylish salon is a training facility owned and operated by Matrix, the supplier of endless products to every salon from Super Cuts to the super-high-end salons. The academy trains licensed and experienced hair stylists in the latest products, techniques, and styles. They use models during their training events, giving you a chance to get free coloring services (they will also trim and style your hair as well). To be a model, you need to stop by and fill out a short application, and they will take a picture of you. They will call you when they can schedule an appointment for you.

OSCAR BOND SALON SPA
42 Wooster Street (between Grand and Broome Streets)
(212) 334–3777
www.oscarbondsalon.com

Slick Soho style is served up at this salon. Stop by Monday through Thursday from 10:00 A.M. to 4:00 P.M. and let them know you are interested in being a hair model. They will give your hair the once-over and let you know if they have a class coming up that they can use you in. If they use you in the class, all the services are free.

RICCARDO MAGGIORE SALON
18 West 56th Street, second floor (between Fifth and Sixth Avenues)
(212) 586–6482
www.riccardomaggiore.com

Class models get free cuts and/or coloring during the Tuesday classes. Call to put your name on the list.

SALON DE QUARTIER
1032 Second Avenue (between 54th and 55th Streets)
(212) 688–5460

206 Smith Street (between Butler and Baltic Streets)
Cobble Hill, Brooklyn
(718) 246–7244
www.salondequartier.com

High-energy salon offers free cuts by assistants whenever they hold classes (about once a month at the Brooklyn location and every now and then at the Manhattan salon). Call or stop by to leave your name, and they will call you when they are scheduling appointments.

SALON ZIBA
200 West 57th Street (between Broadway and Seventh Avenue)
(212) 767–0577
www.salonziba.com

They hold separate cut and color trainings once a month. Call to put your name on the list, and they will call you when they need a model for the classes, which are generally held on weekday mornings. The appointments for cuts are free and include wash, cut, style, and blow-dry, but they do charge $10 for the color appointments ($15 for highlights), which do not include a blow-dry. Also, they are very strict about appointment times. Be there on time or you are out of luck.

TONY & GUY HAIRDRESSING ACADEMY (TIGI)

673 Madison Avenue, second floor (at 61st Street)
(212) 702–9771 or (800) 256–8585

Hair stylists come from all over the country to take part in the classes and continuing education at this hotshot salon. Thursday, Friday, and Saturday services can cost you up to $300, but if you are able to nab an appointment during their class hours Sunday through Wednesday, not only is your service free, but they will even throw in three free products. Stop by on Friday at 6:00 P.M. for a consultation, and they will set up an appointment for you in the next week or two if they can use you in one of the classes. All appointment times are in the morning. They are looking for men and women who are willing to make a "noticeable change" in their styles or colors, so no "a little off the top" here. Once you are registered with them, you can call back for more appointments every month or so. These stylists are all experienced professionals, so you can pretty much depend on quality services here.

BEAUTY SCHOOLS

These schools are training folks to sit for their state licensing exams, so the amount of experience and skill fluctuates greatly from student to student. You do take on some risk of a coif catastrophe when you put your head in their hands. In fact, they usually have you sign a release to this effect before you get your haircut. The students are supervised, but the level of supervision varies from place to place. The better you describe what you'd like done, the happier you'll be with your results.

AMERICAN BARBER SCHOOL

252 West 29th Street (between Seventh and Eighth Avenues)
(212) 290–2289

THE CATCH A low fee is charged for work done by students.

They offer haircuts for $5, but you might get lucky and find their "flyer guy" handing out flyers for even cheaper cuts at 29th Street and Eighth Avenue. Stop by anytime Monday through Friday from 9:00 A.M. to 6:30 P.M. for a cut.

ATLAS BARBER SCHOOL
34 Third Avenue (between 9th and 10th Streets)
(212) 475–1360

 They charge a fee for services performed by students.

This must be the minor-league farm system for Astor Place Haircutters (world renowned for their quick clipper cuts at $12 a snip). If you're in the market for one of those maybe neat, maybe funky, anything-you-can-do-with-a-clipper-in-ten-minutes-cuts, this is the place for you. It will run you $5 a buzz.

AVEDA INSTITUTE
233 Spring Street (between Sixth Avenue and Varick Street)
(212) 807–1492
www.aveda.com

 They charge a fee for services performed by students.

This upscale beauty school offers hair, facial, and spa services by students using Aveda's organic products. Prices are a bit steeper than at other beauty schools, but still pretty cheap by New York standards (haircut $20; coloring $25 to $60). You can also be a model for Aveda classes and receive services for free. Call (212) 367–0339 for details. It is best to try to book appointments four to six weeks in advance.

CHRISTINE VALMY INTERNATIONAL SCHOOL FOR ESTHETICS
437 Fifth Avenue, second floor (between 38th and 39th Streets)
(212) 779–7800
www.christinevalmy.com

 They charge fees for services provided by students.

Many of the students who train here go on to work at some of the most exclusive (and expensive) spas in New York, but while they are in school it won't cost you much to let them poke and prod at your face. A one-hour facial will run you $27 during the day, $38 evenings and Saturdays.

LEARNING INSTITUTE FOR BEAUTY SCIENCES
22 West 34th Street (between Fifth and Sixth Avenues)
(212) 967–1717

38–15 Broadway (at Steinway Street), Astoria, Queens
(718) 726–8383

2384 86th Street (at Twenty-fourth Avenue), Bay Ridge, Brooklyn
(718) 373–2400
www.libsbeautyschool.com

 They charge a low fee for services performed by students.

Okay, this place isn't too swanky, and the cuts won't be cutting edge, but if you're in the market for a basic cut, style, color, or manicure, it certainly is cheap. Their most consistent clientele are old ladies and recently released convicts, which makes for a very interesting waiting room! The fees are $6 for a shampoo and cut, manicure $4, and lip, chin, or eyebrow wax $4. All work is performed by students.

NEW YORK INTERNATIONAL BEAUTY SCHOOL
500 Eighth Avenue (between 35th and 36th Streets)
(212) 868–7171
www.nyibs.com

 They charge a low fee for services performed by students.

The Beauty School salon offers cut-rate services starting at $4. Senior students perform such services as styling, cuts, perms, coloring, and hair relaxing while being supervised by licensed instructors. Stop by Monday through Thursday from 9:00 A.M. to 2:00 P.M., Friday until noon, and Saturday until 1:00 P.M.

MASSAGE

QUINTESSENCE REIKI
Spring Wellness
636 Broadway (at Bleecker Street)
(917) 570–8013 or (212) 388–9817
reikimaster.michael@gmail.com

This is not your Uncle Ike's idea of a massage. Reiki works with the energy of the universe (rei) and the body's energy (chi); the practitioners only lightly touch you during a session. The results can be surprisingly relaxing, calming, and healing. Lead by Reiki master Michael Stoltz, Quintessence holds free "Healing Circles" the first and third Wednesday of each month from 7:00 to 9:00 P.M., which consists of a guided meditation, a short hands-on session (so to speak) lasting between ten to twenty minutes, and a question-and-answer discussion about the practice.

THE SWEDISH INSTITUTE FOR MASSAGE THERAPY
226 West 26th Street (between Seventh and Eighth Avenues)
(212) 924–5900
www.swedishinstitute.com

 They charge low fees for massage therapy performed by students.

If you want a free massage, you'll have to start dating a massage therapist, and even then it's not a sure thing (we've all seen the *Seinfeld* episode). So when you need some good cheap hands-on massage, check out the P. H. Ling Clinic at the Swedish Institute. They have two options for low-cost massage. The Stress Reduction Clinic is open to all (but slots fill up quickly) and offers a package of six relaxing and refreshing massages for $150. You register for a series of six one-hour massages, and each week you will receive either a Swedish or Shiatsu session (based on therapist availability). No preferences for modality are taken; you take what you're given from week to week. The Therapeutic Massage Clinic is available to those who have a prescription from a doctor or chiropractor for treatment on a specific injury or condition. You must register for a package of twelve one-hour massages for $250. This series consists of twelve consecutive weekly sessions. Each patient will receive both Eastern (Shiatsu) and Western (Swedish, sports massage, or the like) treatments throughout the twelve weeks. The work is performed by students in their final semester and supervised by faculty. Both clinics are

Rugs, a Blender, and a Makeover

Whenever you're in need of some professional beauty assistance, stop by any makeup counter at the finer department stores and have a pro do the work for you. Try the counters at the following stores:

MACY'S, *151 West 34th Street (at Sixth Avenue); (212) 695–4400.*

BERGDORF GOODMAN, *754 Fifth Avenue (at 58th Street); (212) 753–7300.*

SAKS FIFTH AVENUE, *611 Fifth Avenue (at 50th Street); (212) 753–4000.*

LORD & TAYLOR, *424 Fifth Avenue (at 38th Street); (212) 391–3344.*

BLOOMINGDALE'S, *1000 Third Avenue (between 59th and 60th Streets); (212) 705–2000.*

All of the above offer free makeovers using their oh-so-pricey products. Of course, the hope is that you will then buy a load of $43 mascara, $59 lipsticks, and $94 skin-cleansing citrus retonifier—but that's up to you.

offered three times a year and are very popular; applying for a slot as early as possible is advised.

MAKEUP

IL MAKIAGE MAKE-UP CLUB
174 Hudson Street
(917) 364–3472
www.ilmakiage.com
Be a model for one of their afternoon makeup classes, and you not only get a makeover for nothing but also up to $25 worth of makeup for free. The classes are held Sunday through Wednesday.

NYBS CREATIVE ARTS
  7 West 45th Street, second floor (between Fifth and Sixth Avenues)
  (212) 245–6371
  www.nybsca.com
This makeup school with a primarily Japanese student body is always looking for models for class (of any ethnicity). You may even get paid for your time. Call to set up an interview. Classes held in the afternoon, Monday through Friday.

REAL ESTATE: THIS LAND IS YOUR LAND

Y

ES, APARTMENTS IN New York are just as ridiculously expensive as you've heard they are. With studio apartments the size of a closet going for more than $1,000 a month considered to be a steal—if you can find one—the price of four walls and a bed has really made living in Manhattan almost impossible. But even while the rents were continuing to skyrocket, I managed to find myself a spacious studio apartment in a desirable neighborhood for the unbelievable rent of $560 a month (and it just went up from $521). You might think I'm lucky, but I contend that all it takes for anyone to get such a deal is lots of patience and perseverance. There are thousands of apartments like this all around the five boroughs (and, yes, plenty in Manhattan) through the Mitchell-Lama and 80/20 programs. And these places can be yours without any exorbitant broker's fee, "key fee," or huge deposit.

All that's generally required to move in is the first month's rent and one month's rent as security. The secret is getting your name on as many waiting lists as you can for older buildings, and putting in as many applications as you can for new developments. This won't solve your apartment needs in the short term, though. Unfortunately, it can take between one and ten years for your name to come up (I waited three years), but don't let that stop you from putting your name on lists. Even if you're going through the I-don't-even-know-if-I'll-still-be-in-New-York-in-three-years syndrome, put your name on the lists. If you're still here, and you probably will be, you'll be happy you did. If you aren't, they'll just call the next lucky Cheap Bastard.

LOW-RENT, NO-FEE APARTMENTS

NEW YORK CITY HOUSING DEVELOPMENT CORPORATION
110 William Street (between John and Fulton Streets)
(212) 227–5500 (administrative office)
(212) 863–5610 (affordable housing hotline)
www.nychdc.com

 Each building has various maximum income eligibility restrictions.

Everywhere you look in the city, there is a new building going up, and chances are that building is part of some program through the Housing Development Corporation (HDC) that makes it possible for us Cheap Bastards to get into some of the hottest real estate on the planet. The HDC has any number of programs to get you into these buildings, with such fun names as LAMP, New HOP, Mixed Income, 80/20, Taxable 80/20, New HOP 80/20, and CO-OPS (yes, you can even buy a co-op!), and they seem to be coming up with new programs (and catchy names) every day. But all the programs operate under the same basic premise: The HDC gives the developers certain tax breaks and low-interest loans if they make a portion of the apartments in the swanky new building available to low- and middle-income people (at low- and middle-level rents!). Each building and program has its own income restrictions (some of them up to as much as $141,800 for a family of four), and there are heaps of paperwork and interviews that you need to go

At Your Service

Can't afford any New York City rents? Can't afford to raise a family in New York? Well then, how about raising a family and living in a penthouse duplex on Central Park West? Yes, it can be done. Get a position as a live-in nanny, butler, cook, or personal assistant to the upper crust of New York society and live way beyond your means.

The most common live-in job (particularly for women) is as a nanny. Besides room and board, nannies are paid between $400 and $800 a week for their child care duties and some light housekeeping responsibilities (though some families try to push that part of the job description to the limit). Agencies and families are looking for at least a one-year commitment and some experience. The best way to look for a nanny position is through word of mouth, but there's no shortage of agencies to place you as well. Any reputable agency will not charge you a fee; any fees are paid by the families. Here are a few good places to start your search:

PROFESSIONAL NANNIES INSTITUTE, *501 Fifth Avenue, Suite 908; (212) 692–9510; www.profnannies.com.*

A CHOICE NANNY, *850 Seventh Avenue, Suite 706; (212) 246–5437; www.achoicenanny.com.*

NANNIES PLUS, *(845) 469–5130 or (866) 492–1039; www.nanniesplus.com.*

THE NANNY AUTHORITY, *(973) 466–2669; www.nannyauthority.com.*

NY NANNY CENTER, *250 West 57th Street; (212) 265–3354; www.nynanny.com.*

FAMILY EXTENSIONS, *(203) 966–9944 or (800) 932–2736; www.familyextensions.com.*

If taking care of somebody else's kids isn't your idea of a good time, there are many other live-in positions you can apply for. The rich and famous need you to do everything from cook for them to clean for them, teach their children, keep track of their personal calendars, and attend to their private aircraft. If your calling is to be a majordomo, valet, chauffeur, or housekeeper, try these agencies:

LIFESTYLE RESOURCES, *23 West 36th Street, Suite 4B (between Fifth and Sixth Avenues); (212) 947–9792; www.sterlinglifestyle.com.*

DOMESTIC PLACEMENT NETWORK, *(805) 640–3608 or (877) 206–5262; www.dpnonline.com.*

BEST DOMESTIC SERVICES OF NEW YORK CITY, *10 East 39th Street, Suite 1118; (212) 683–3060; www.bestdomestic.com.*

through. The good news is, once you are in, you are in. You do not need to maintain a low income to remain in the apartments. They list all of the buildings currently accepting applications and those who will soon be accepting applications on their Web site. The competition can be pretty stiff for these apartments, so it is a good idea to apply to a number of buildings at one time. The time between application and move-in date can be anywhere from a few months to a few years.

HOUSING PARTNERSHIP DEVELOPMENT CORPORATION
450 Seventh Avenue, Suite 2401 (between 34th and 35th Streets)
(646) 217–3370
www.housingpartnership.com

THE CATCH Must meet income requirements and limitations to qualify.

This is a chance to own a new home or condo in neighborhoods around the city with small down payments (as low as 5 percent) and many tax exemptions and incentives—and maybe even no closing costs. The mission of the NYCP's New Homes/Neighborhood Builders program is to increase home-ownership opportunities for moderate-income families who are priced out of the conventional real estate market. If you qualify, you can become the owner of a brand-new condo, single-family, or multifamily home. These homes or buildings are built from the ground up by reputable architects and contractors, come complete with many amenities, and are heavily subsidized by the city. There are developments in all five boroughs in such neighborhoods as Fort Green, Harlem, Coney Island, Bedford Stuyvesant, Williamsburg, Crown Heights, Hunts Point, and others. Check out the Web site for a list of current projects.

MITCHELL-LAMA HOUSING COMPANIES

CITY-SPONSORED DEVELOPMENTS

Department of Housing Preservation and Development
100 Gold Street (between Frankfurt and Spruce Streets,
near the Brooklyn Bridge)
(212) 863–6500 (city-sponsored Mitchell-Lama)
(212) 863–5610 (affordable housing hotline)
www.nyc.gov

STATE-SPONSORED DEVELOPMENTS

NYS Department of Housing and Community Renewal (DHCR)
25 Beaver Street (between Broad and New Streets)
(212) 480–7343
www.dhcr.state.ny.us/ohm/ohm.htm

Applicants must meet income requirements, and waiting lists can be long.

There are 132 city-sponsored buildings and 269 state-sponsored buildings in the Mitchell-Lama program (many in the five boroughs), with a total of more than 110,000 units throughout the system. This program was created in the 1950s to provide affordable housing for low- and moderate-income families. The apartments in these buildings are larger than the average shoe boxes most New Yorkers call home, there are no broker's fees, and the rents are amazingly low. Get the lists of buildings with open waiting lists through the Web sites or call. You must apply to each building separately; there is no centralized waiting list. The waits could be anywhere from one to ten years, so apply early and to many buildings. The income requirements vary, depending on the building and the size of your household. Once you have an apartment, though, you are not required to maintain a low income level. You will need to submit your income tax forms to the building management each year, which adjusts your rent yearly according to state-mandated levels. Once you have exceeded a certain prescribed level of income, you'll be required to pay "market value"—still ridiculously cheap. Market value rents (the maximum you will pay) range from studio apartments for $521 to three-bedroom apartments with a terrace for $997 (these do vary somewhat from building to building).

"Children are poor
man's riches."

—English proverb

NEW YORK IS an amazing place for kids, and not just for those who can afford to go to the Manhattan Day School. Yes, at times it may seem like there are so many places to go, sights to see, things to do— and ways to drop a load of cash—that New York doesn't feel very kid-friendly for a parent's wallet. Fear not. There are classes, movies, fun and games, readings, even health insurance, and tons of other fun and useful things for kids without Mom and Dad having to stop at the ATM. During the week, you can fill out any day's schedule with the endless free after-school programs. And on weekends there is never a shortage of creative fun for the whole family in the major parks, museums, and other institutions throughout the city.

Dial-a-Teacher

Can't find the capital of Uzbekistan? Stumped by the square root of the hypotenuse? Or just want to check that you spelled Crispus Attucks correctly? Then call up a teacher and get some help. The Dial-a-Teacher program, run by the United Federation of Teachers, has been helping out baffled students and parents for more than twenty years by fielding more than 2,000 calls a week. A staff of forty-five teachers fluent in Spanish, French, Haitian Creole, Italian, Greek, Hebrew, Chinese, and, yes, English stand at the ready to help you with your homework in any subject Monday through Thursday, 4:00 to 7:00 P.M., throughout the school year.

These folks won't just give you the answers to your questions; since these are all qualified teachers you're talking to, they will strive to reteach the ideas behind the questions, making sure you understand the answers. And if you have already finished your homework, they will be happy to check your work with you. Dial-a-Teacher also offers a battery of workshops for parents during the day or in the evening designed to make parents more aware of what their children are learning and teach them how to help their children more effectively at home.

Dial-a-Teacher can arrange to hold workshops at local schools or at their Manhattan headquarters. If you attend workshops at the Dial-a-Teacher offices, they will send a bus to pick you up, take you home, and even serve you breakfast and lunch! And yes, all help and workshops are free of charge. For homework assistance call (212) 777–3380. To find out more about workshops, call (212) 598–9205 or click on "parents" at the Web site www.uft.org.

AFTER-SCHOOL PROGRAMS

BEACON SCHOOLS
80 locations throughout the five boroughs
The NYC Department of Youth and Community Development
156 William Street (between Ann and Beekman Streets)
(212) 788–6754
www.nyc.gov/dycd

Don't ever say New York City didn't give you anything! The eighty Beacon School programs are a gift to every student and parent in New York City. Spread throughout every school district in the five boroughs, the programs offer extensive after-school, evening, and weekend programs that are basically free day camp for students of all ages. Each program's activities vary, but they all generally include time for homework help and tutoring as well as lots of fun structured activities. Activities might include arts and crafts, sports, drama, music, dance, music, photography, martial arts, and computer classes as well as vocational training and health classes. Some classes and activities are offered to adults as well. Registration is required for all programs, but everything is free, even the snacks! To find the locations in your neighborhood, check the Web site.

NEW YORK CITY RECREATION CENTERS
42 locations throughout the five boroughs
(See Appendix D for locations)
Dial 311 or (212) NEW–YORK (from outside New York City)
www.nycgovparks.org

At every one of New York City's Public Recreation Centers, you will find a variety of after-school programs (Monday through Friday, 3:00 to 6:00 P.M.) for children ages six to fourteen. The programs at each location vary depending on the center's facilities and staffing, but all strive to incorporate the "Straight A's: Athletics, Arts, and Academics." The schedules could include swim programs, sports instruction, computer classes, Internet access, homework help, arts and crafts, and classes in literacy, performing arts, visual arts, and much more. For schedules and more information, check with the local recreation centers.

ARTS AND CRAFTS

THE ART SHACK
Hudson River Park
Hudson River at Chambers Street
(212) 766–1104
www.manhattanyouth.org

Spend a great afternoon creating all types of projects (painting, drawing, sculpting . . .) with fun teachers and fresh air. All materials are supplied. Weather permitting, Saturday and Sunday, noon to 5:00 P.M., May through September.

CHORISTERS
St. John's In The Village
224 Waverly Place (between Perry and West 11th Streets)
(212) 243–6192
www.stjvny.org

Every Monday afternoon children of all religions and backgrounds gather together in the parish hall of St. John's In The Village to take part in this free music and voice-training program. The curriculum of this very serious program focuses on reading music, sight singing, ear training, and musician-ship while learning the music of a wide variety of classical styles and periods (no contemporary or children's music here). Auditions are required, and once you are accepted into the program you must commit to a full schedule of classes (every Monday afternoon) and performances (one Sunday a month). While this is a church-run program, it is not a religious program at all.

COOPER-HEWITT, NATIONAL DESIGN MUSEUM
2 East 91st Street (at Fifth Avenue)
(212) 849–8353
www.cooperhewitt.org

THE CATCH You must be a New York City high school student.

Through a program called Design Directions, high school students interested in any aspect of design (fashion, industrial, graphic, media, film, interior, architecture, urban planning, and so forth) connect with the vast professional resources in New York City. Programs include daylong workshops, after-school programs, design studio visits, and precollege preparation (college visits; application and portfolio workshops). All classes are free and open to all on a first-come, first-served basis.

FOOLS CO. INC.'S NEW YORK SCHOOL FOR PERFORMING ARTS
Various locations around Manhattan
(212) 307–6000
foolsco@nyc.rr.com
www.foolsco.org

THE CATCH You must be between sixteen and twenty-one years old.

For almost twenty years Jill Russell has been training young adults in all aspects of the performing arts through the Artsworker Apprentice program; free weekly workshops in performance, movement, masks, puppetry, voice and diction, and more, open to all with the desire to learn. No audition or previous experience is needed, but preregistration is required. Call or e-mail for more information.

JAZZMOBILE

PS 197
135th Street and Fifth Avenue
(212) 866–4900 (administrative office); (212) 866–3616 (hotline)
www.jazzmobile.org

 A one-time $80 registration fee is required.

Since 1969 Jazzmobile has been offering free Saturday music workshops and master classes for students age seven and older at PS 197 in Harlem with such musicians as Max Roach, Branford Marsalis, and Donald Byrd. Students need to have at least some basic music knowledge to participate, and they must register and have their skill evaluated to determine if they fit into the beginning, intermediate, or advanced classes. The classes run from November through March, and a one-time registration fee of $80 is required. In summer they also bring a lineup of world-class musicians to the parks, libraries, schools, and street corners of New York City and the surrounding areas. Check the Web site for details.

THE MUSEUM OF MODERN ART (MoMA)

Education Department
11 West 53rd Street (between Fifth and Sixth Avenues)
(212) 708–9828 (high school programs)
(212) 708–9807 (family programs)
www.moma.org

MoMA is an absolute wonderland of free arts activities for everyone from toddlers to teens. The museum offers lively tours and special activities specifically targeted to this young audience (ages four through fourteen), as well as films, discussions with artists, and workshops. All of these family activities are scheduled on the weekends and include free admission to the museum for up to two adults and three children. Many of the programs offer tickets on a first-come, first-served basis at the museum the day of the event; others do require preregistration. For high schoolers the museum offers a number of eight-week and sixteen-week courses every year, which might include drawing, printmaking, or curatorial and museum work. Every Friday night starting at 4:45 P.M., high school students are invited to chow down on some free pizza and watch a great selection of classic, contemporary, and experimental films. Preregistration is required for the courses, but you can just show up for the movies. Check out the Web site for details.

NEW YORK UNIVERSITY PROGRAM IN
EDUCATIONAL THEATRE

Press Annex, 82 Washington Square East, Room 23 (at Washington Place)

(212) 998-5868

www.nyu.edu/education/music/edtheatre

 $110 materials fee.

Thirteen- to eighteen-year-old budding thespians take part in a free five-week intensive summer program called "Looking for Shakespeare." Throughout the session, students will work with a host of theater professionals to shape an original play based on the Bard's themes but taken directly from the participants' own lives. While working on the play, the performers receive coaching in playwrighting, improvisation, acting, voice, and movement, culminating in a fully staged production for the public. Participants must interview and audition for the program, but no experience is necessary, just enthusiasm and energy.

PROSPECT PARK AUDUBON CENTER

Lincoln Road and Central Drive in Prospect Park

(718) 287-3400

www.prospectparkaudubon.org

Nestled in the wilds of Brooklyn's sprawling Prospect Park, the Audubon Center offers a full roster of free activities for all nature-loving kids, from toddlers to teens. Wednesday afternoons kids ages nine through thirteen can drop by and join the Green Team to learn about the natural wonders of the park and how to help conserve them. Friday afternoons the Nestlings (ages three through five) have a fun afternoon full of storytelling, music, and crafts. And on the weekends you will always find special programs as well as regular crafts classes and bird-watching and nature tours for kids of all ages. Some programs require registration, but all are free. Call or check out the Web site for schedule and information.

THE PUBLIC THEATER'S SHAKESPEARE LAB JR.

425 Lafayette Street (between East 4th Street and Astor Place)

(212) 539-8621

www.publictheater.org

One of New York's preeminent and leading purveyors of the Bard's work opens its doors to students for an intensive week of workshops and theater training. Students work on Shakespeare with professional actors, learn about the backstage workings of a professional theater, attend a performance at the Delacorte Theater in Central Park, and get a chance to perform themselves. The workshops are open to students entering the tenth grade and above. No audition is required, but you must register. Workshops run for one week throughout the month of August and are filled on a first-come, first-served basis.

THE WOOSTER GROUP
The Performing Garage
33 Wooster Street (between Broome and Grand Streets)
(212) 966–9796
www.thewoostergroup.org

 You must be a twelve- to seventeen-year-old New York City student.

This edgy, experimental theater company offers a free three-week summer institute. Students get experience working alongside professional artists like company members Willem Dafoe and Kate Valk, as well as developing performance skills and creating original work. No prior experience is required; call for an application.

FILMS

MUSEUM OF MODERN ART (MoMA)
11 West 53rd Street (between Fifth and Sixth Avenues)
(212) 708–9828 (Friday Night at the Movies
for High School Students)
(212) 708–9805 (family programs)
www.moma.org
The education department at MoMA presents Friday Night at the Movies for High School Students, a series of six classic and contemporary films in the spring and fall. Each series consists of films grouped under an intriguing theme (for instance, the irresistible villain: *Dr. Jekyll and Mr. Hyde, Psycho,* and *The Usual Suspects*) and is followed by talks with the film department curators of the museum. Hey, they even throw in free pizza and soda. No tickets or reservations are required—just show up! On Saturday and Sunday mornings the museum invites you to bring down the young'uns for special tours, activities, and screenings. They have special programs for four-year-olds, five- to ten-year-olds, and eleven- to fourteen-year-olds. Some programs require preregistration (and fill up quickly!), and others are first-come,

first-served on the day of the event. All of these programs include free admission to the museum for up to two adults and three children. Check the Web site for details.

RIVER FLICKS
Pier 46, Hudson River and Christopher Street (films for kids)
Pier 54, Hudson River and 14th Street (films for grown-ups)
(212) 627–2020
(212) 732–7467
www.hudsonriverpark.org
Great family-friendly films (all rated G or PG) screen on Pier 46 every Friday at about 8:00 P.M. (or when it gets dark) in July and August. In past seasons films have included *Mary Poppins, Little Shop of Horrors, Willy Wonka and the Chocolate Factory, Harry Potter,* and *Chicken Run.* They also present another series of films for grown-ups every Wednesday night at Pier 54. They set up some chairs on the pier for your comfort, and there's also plenty of room for you to bring a blanket and picnic under the stars while you watch. Of course, no movie is complete without the popcorn—and it's free, too.

FILMS AT PUBLIC LIBRARIES

Many public libraries throughout the city have regularly scheduled films and videos for children between the ages of three and ten every week. These programs usually run anywhere from thirty minutes to a couple of hours and consist of a few short films that could include vintage Disney cartoons, films of children's books, and rare children's classics as well as occasional feature-length films. For more details check out the library Web sites: www.nypl.org (for the Bronx, Staten Island, and Manhattan), www.brooklynpubliclibrary.org, or www.queenslibrary.org. Below is a list of the branches with screenings for children every week. These schedules do change from time to time. Be sure to call the branch to confirm schedules.

MANHATTAN BRANCHES

AGUILAR LIBRARY, 174 East 110th Street (between Third and Lexington Avenues); (212) 534–2930; Tuesday at 4:00 P.M.

BLOOMINGDALE BRANCH, 150 West 100th Street (between Columbus Avenue and Broadway); (212) 222–8030; call for schedule.

Busting Blockbuster

Forget about spending almost $5 to rent videos at Blockbuster or any local video store. Most local libraries have a large collection of children's videos and DVDs. Disney, cartoons, educational and full-length features, classics, and new releases—you'll find plenty on the shelves to please all tastes. You can borrow tapes for a week (three days in Queens). Watch out for the late fees, though: $1 per day at the NYPL, $2 per day in Brooklyn, and a whopping $3 per day in Queens.

COLUMBUS LIBRARY, 742 Tenth Avenue (between 50th and 51st Streets); (212) 586-5098; call for schedule.

JEFFERSON MARKET LIBRARY, 425 Avenue of the Americas (at 10th Street); (212) 243-4334; Tuesday at 3:30 P.M.

96TH STREET LIBRARY, 112 East 96th Street (between Park and Lexington Avenues); (212) 289-0908; Wednesday at 10:30 A.M.

125TH STREET BRANCH, 224 East 125th Street (between Second and Third Avenues); (212) 534-5050; call for schedule.

ST. AGNES LIBRARY, 444 Amsterdam Avenue (between 81st and 82nd Streets); (212) 877-4380; Thursday at 4:00 P.M.

YORKVILLE BRANCH LIBRARY, 222 East 79th Street (between Lexington and Third Avenues); (212) 744-5824; Wednesday at 4:00 P.M.

BRONX BRANCHES

BRONX LIBRARY CENTER, 10 East Kingsbridge Road (between Jerome and Morris Avenues); (718) 579-4244; Wednesday at 2:00 P.M.

FORDHAM LIBRARY CENTER, 2556 Bainbridge Avenue (at Fordham Road); (718) 579-4244; Wednesday at 3:30 P.M.

GRAND CONCOURSE LIBRARY, 155 East 173rd Street (at Selwyn Avenue); (718) 583-6611; Friday at 4:00 P.M.

MELROSE LIBRARY, 910 Morris Avenue (at East 162nd Street); (718) 588–0110; Tuesday at 4:00 P.M.

MORRISANIA LIBRARY, 610 East 169th Street (at Franklin Avenue); (718) 589–9268; Thursday at 3:30 P.M.

PELHAM BAY BRANCH, 3060 Middletown Road (at Jarvis Street); (718) 792–6744; call for schedule.

TREMONT BRANCH, 1866 Washington Avenue (at 176th Street); (718) 299–5177; Wednesday at 3:00 P.M.

WEST CHESTER SQUARE LIBRARY, 2521 Glebe Avenue (at St. Peter's Avenue); (718) 863–0436; Friday at 3:30 P.M.

BROOKLYN BRANCHES

BAY RIDGE, Ridge Boulevard at 73rd Street; (718) 748–5709; Friday at 3:30 P.M.

BROWER PARK, St. Marks Avenue near Nostrand Avenue; (718) 773–7208; Monday at 2:00 P.M.

CENTRAL LIBRARY, Grand Army Plaza (at Flatbush Avenue and Eastern Parkway); (718) 230–2100; Saturday at 11:00 A.M., films for the whole family.

CONEY ISLAND, Mermaid Avenue near West 19th Street; (718) 265–3880; call for schedule.

FLATBUSH, Linden Boulevard near Flatbush Avenue; (718) 865–0813; call for schedule.

KINGS BAY, Nostrand Avenue near Avenue W; (718) 368–1709; Monday at 3:00 P.M.

MARCY, Dekalb Avenue near Nostrand Avenue; (718) 935–0032; call for schedule.

NEW LOTS LIBRARY, New Lots Avenue and Barbey Street; (718) 649–0311; call for schedule.

QUEENS BRANCHES

CENTRAL LIBRARY, 89–11 Merrick Boulevard (between Eighty-ninth and Ninetieth Avenues); (718) 990–0700; Wednesday at 10:30 A.M. (summer only).

FLUSHING LIBRARY, 41–17 Main Street; (718) 661–1200; Friday at 10:30 A.M. (summer only).

QUEENS VILLAGE, 94–11 217th Street (between Jamaica and Hillside Avenues); (718) 776–6800; Friday at 3:30 P.M.

STATEN ISLAND BRANCHES

STAPLETON, 132 Canal Street (at Wright Street); (718) 727–0427; Friday at 3:30 P.M.

SPORTS AND GAMES

BATTERY PARK CITY PARKS
Rockefeller Park House (Hudson River and Chambers Street)
(212) 267–2020
www.bpcparks.org or www.hudsonriverfestival.com
The schedule is chock-full of regularly scheduled activities for kids from toddlers to teens (and plenty for adults as well!). Starting in May and running through October, their weekly schedule includes everything from soccer, in-line-skating lessons, and gardening to drawing classes, concerts, and family dances. Check their detailed Web sites for schedule and locations.

BIG CITY FISHING
Pier 26 (Hudson River at North Moore Street)

Pier 46 (Hudson River at Christopher Street)

Pier 64 (Hudson River and 24th Street)

Pier 84 (Hudson River and 44th Street)

Pier 95 (Hudson River at 56th Street)
(212) 533–PARK (7275)
www.hudsonriverpark.org
New York City and fishing? Not two things you would think go together. Well, the Hudson River is the cleanest it has been for almost a hundred years and the fish are abundant, so come on down and cast a line. The fishing is open to all, but mostly it's children who do the casting. If you're big enough to hold a rod, you're welcome to participate in this catch-and-release fishing. All equipment, bait, and instructions are provided free of charge. Weekends from Memorial Day through Labor Day and weekdays in July and August.

THE CENTER FOR ANTI-VIOLENCE EDUCATION

421 Fifth Avenue, second floor (between 7th and 8th Streets)
Park Slope, Brooklyn
(718) 788–1775
www.cae-bklyn.org

 THE CATCH Free for fourteen- to nineteen-year-old girls only.

Sign up for a free self-defense course or an after-school karate class for teen girls. The self-defense course lasts for five weeks and is offered five times a year; the karate class is taught throughout the school year. The form of karate they teach (Goju) uses a lot of spiritual and meditative exercises (along with the usual kicks, chops, and *hii-yaas!*) to build the girls' inner strength as well as outer. They also offer low-cost/sliding-scale classes for younger children (girls and boys) and adults.

THE CHARLES A. DANA DISCOVERY CENTER

Central Park at 110th Street and Lenox Avenue
(212) 860–1370
www.centralparknyc.org

Sitting majestically on the Harlem Meer at the north end of the park, the Dana Discovery Center offers a variety of free family programs and hands-on exhibits throughout the year. From April through October stop by any Tuesday through Sunday from 10:00 A.M. to 4:00 P.M. and the center will provide you with poles, unbarbed hooks, bait, and instruction booklets for you to while away the hours with some catch-and-release fishing. The Dana Center also offers a variety of educational programs, nature exhibits, jazz concerts (see page 38), and swing dancing on the plaza (see page 70).

CITY PARKS YOUTH TENNIS, TRACK & FIELD, AND GOLF

Locations throughout the five boroughs
(718) 760–6999
www.cityparksfoundation.org

Each year thousands of kids who hope to be the next Tiger Woods or Andre Agassi take to the city parks to participate in one of the most extensive youth training programs anywhere in the world. Children ages five through sixteen can take part in three separate programs supported by the City Parks Foundation and receive free lessons in tennis, track and field, and golf. Each program varies slightly, but lessons, equipment, and tournaments are free. Sometimes the kids even have a chance to meet and learn from stars of the games.

LASKER RINK
Central Park (110th Street and Lenox Avenue)
(212) 348–4867
www.centralparknyc.org

 $5.00 registration fee required for each six-week session.

Two six-week sessions of (almost) free ice-skating lessons are available for children age eight to seventeen between January and March on Tuesday from 4:00 to 6:00 P.M. To take part you must preregister at the North Meadow recreation center (midpark at 97th Street) and lay down your $5 registration fee for each six-week session. Skate rentals are provided free of charge. And, those registered for the classes have free entry into the rink any other time throughout the week, though you will have to pay for your skate rental ($4.75).

LEARN TO PLAY . . . SOCCER, BASEBALL, LACROSSE, BASKETBALL, BASEBALL
City recreation centers and parks throughout the five boroughs
(212) 360–3300
www.nycparks.org
These separate programs run by the City Parks Department offer girls and boys age thirteen and younger (and sometimes fourteen-year-olds) the chance not only to learn the basics of any of these sports but also to play and compete with other children throughout the city. Free and open to all, these leagues go on at different times of year and provide children with all the skills and equipment they need to enjoy the games. Call for schedules and locations.

LEARN TO SWIM PROGRAM
City pools and recreation centers throughout the five boroughs
(212) 360–3300
www.cityparksfoundation.org or www.nycparks.org
Everybody in the pool! Free swimming instruction for children ages three through fourteen is available during the summer at all thirty-three city-run outdoor pools, and lessons continue throughout the year at city-run indoor pools and recreation centers. Recreation center memberships for children younger than age thirteen are free; for fourteen- to seventeen-year-olds it costs $5 to $10. (For more information on other city recreation center offerings, see the chapter titled "Fitness, Fun, and Games: Cheap Thrills." For complete listings of recreation center locations, see Appendix D.)

HEALTH INSURANCE

CHILD HEALTH PLUS
Mayor's Office for Health Insurance Access
Human Resources Administration
330 West 34th Street (between Ninth and Tenth Avenues)
(800) 698–4543
www.nyc.gov/healthstat

This is free or low-cost health insurance available to New York City residents up to age eighteen. The cost of enrolling depends on your income and the size of your family. It's free for anyone whose income is below a certain level; if your income is higher, you may have to pay $9 or $15 per month per child. If your income is too high to qualify for these subsidized rates (around $50,000 a year for a family of four), you can still take part in the program, but you will have to pay full price for the plan (steep, but not thoroughly purse popping at about $150 a month). This is comprehensive coverage (including medical, vision, and dental) and a pretty amazing deal even if you aren't qualified to receive it for free.

MUSEUMS

BELVEDERE CASTLE/HENRY LUCE NATURE OBSERVATORY
Central Park (enter at West 81st or East 79th Streets)
(212) 772–0210
www.centralparknyc.org
Hours: Tuesday through Sunday, 10:00 A.M.–5:00 P.M.

Besides being a castle built high on a hill (a pretty desirable destination for any kid or adult), this is also the home of a nature observatory complete with your fair share of frogs, turtles, and birds and lots of hands-on exhibits. The urban park rangers who run the observatory also run guided tours (free!) on weekends. And if you prefer to explore the wilds of the park on your own, you can borrow a free Birding Kit from them. The kit is filled with useful stuff like a pair of binoculars, a field guide, a sketch pad, and colored pencils. Check out the Web site for tour schedule and details.

BROOKLYN CHILDREN'S MUSEUM
145 Brooklyn Avenue (between St. Marks and Prospect Streets)
(718) 735–4400
www.brooklynkids.org
Free hours: Every Saturday and Sunday, 11:00 A.M.–noon. Also, during the summer, Friday, 5:00–7:00 P.M.
For more than a hundred years, the world's first children's museum has been entertaining and enlightening kids with a mixture of hands-on exhibits and performances and an extensive collection of cultural objects and natural-history specimens. They fling the doors wide open for free entry every weekend for the early birds (11:00 A.M. to noon). During the summer their Free Fridays (5:00 to 7:00 P.M.) are not to be missed: In addition to full access to the museum, they always offer great musical performances for young and old alike on their rooftop.

LEFFERT'S HOMESTEAD
Prospect Park (near Flatbush Avenue and Empire Boulevard)
(718) 789–2822
www.prospectpark.org
Hours: Thursday through Sunday, noon–6:00 P.M.; extended hours during the summer months.
This is one of the few surviving Dutch Colonial farmhouses in Brooklyn, and possibly the only children's historic house museum in the country. The house gives children a chance to explore American history and experience everyday life as it was in the little farming village of Flatbush through hands-on exhibits, storytelling, seasonal celebrations, and craft workshops. Activities are free and open to all.

SONY WONDER TECHNOLOGY LAB
550 Madison Avenue (at 56th Street)
(212) 833–8100
www.sonywondertechlab.com
Hours: Tuesday through Saturday, 10:00 A.M.–5:00 P.M.; Sunday, noon–5:00 P.M.
Start your visit off by meeting B. B. Wonderbot, the talking, all-knowing robot, and wind your way through four floors of interactive fun. Then walk out with your very own "Certificate of Achievement in the Advanced Program in Communication Technology." This is a very popular site; you're advised to make reservations by calling the above number at least a week in advance. They accept reservations only Tuesday through Friday from 8:00 A.M. to 2:00 P.M. You can get in without a reservation, but it could be a long wait in line. Also, don't miss a chance to attend their children's film screenings once a month in their

amazing high-definition theater. Films for grown-ups are shown on Saturday afternoons twice a month.

STORES FOR THE FUN OF IT

There are a few stores around the city that are too amazingly fun to miss. Of course, the danger here is that you'll be tempted, pressured, or whined into spending some actual money. If you can think of these as incredible interactive museums (without gift shops!), then you'll have a great time playing with their "exhibits."

F.A.O. SCHWARZ
767 Fifth Avenue (at 58th Street)
(212) 644–9400
www.fao.com

They have crowned themselves "The Ultimate Toy Store"—and they live up to the billing. Three huge floors of the newest, biggest, best, most state-of-the-art (and most expensive!) toys and games to be found anywhere in the world, and almost all of them are available for you to play with. Plenty of costumed characters, roving magicians, and ridiculously friendly staff make any visit a fun and memorable one.

HALLOWEEN ADVENTURE
104 Fourth Avenue (at 11th Street)
(212) 673–4546
www.halloweenadventure.com

Make a day of walking around this store, playing with all the unusual novelty items and gags, trying on the wild costumes, masks, and hats. And for an extra little treat of tricks, head downstairs to the magic department, where they are always demonstrating some amazing magic tricks, or maybe even see a whole magic show at their theater, where they offer free magic shows throughout the year (except during October).

NBA STORE
666 Fifth Avenue (at 52nd Street)
(212) 515–6221
www.nba.com/nycstore

If you're a basketball fan, this place is a slam dunk. Of course, you'll find every piece of NBA and WNBA paraphernalia you could imagine, but you don't need to buy a thing to have a great time. Lots of free video games, basketball carnival games, and even a full-size cushioned basketball court make the spot worth a visit. They also host a full schedule of special events, including in-store appearances and workshops by basketball greats and concerts. Check the Web site for a schedule of special events.

NEW YORK DOLL HOSPITAL
787 Lexington Avenue (between 61st and 62nd Streets)
(212) 838–7527

This trauma center for teddy bears and other cuddlies in critical condition is unlike any shop you've been in before. If you're prepared for piles of decapitated dolls, unstuffed animals, and just some of the oddest and rarest (and most different-looking) dolls anywhere, then stop by to see who has checked in recently. The doctor on call is sure to be the third-generation owner Irving Chais, a seemingly curmudgeonly fellow who turns kindhearted when kids come by to visit his patients.

NINTENDO WORLD
10 Rockefeller Plaza (48th Street, between Fifth and Sixth Avenues)
(646) 459–0800
www.nintendoworldstore.com

You and your kids will definitely make the "Wii" sound at this video game wonderland. Spread out over two levels, this store offers over 10,000 square feet of hands-on gaming entertainment. You can try out every game and system Nintendo has to offer, including the latest games for the Wii, DS, and Game Boy, as well as classics like Super Mario Brothers and Pokemon, at their more than fifty interactive game stations. Warning: Plan to spend plenty of time here, because it may be hard to drag yourself, eh . . . I mean your kids away from the games.

STORYTELLING

BANK STREET BOOKSTORE
610 West 112th Street (at Broadway)
(212) 678–1654
www.bankstreet.edu/bookstore/

Considered one of the best bookstores for and about children in the city. Every week you'll find many author readings, musical performances, and costumed characters for children, as well as discussions and presentations for

Playtime!

From the countries that brought you Lego and Brio comes a chance to bring your children (age five and younger) for an informal playtime every Saturday, noon to 5:00 P.M. (except during the summer), in the Heimbolt Family Children's Learning Center at the Scandinavia House. Lots of toys to play with (coincidentally, Lego and Brio), Scandinavian costumes, storybooks in the Scandinavian languages (and English), and even a stage. Children, parents, and caregivers from all backgrounds are welcome. The Scandinavia House is located at 58 Park Avenue (between 37th and 38th Streets). For more information call (212) 879–9779 or check the Web site www.scandinavia house.org.

parents. Events are scheduled at various times throughout the week. Call or check their Web site for details. Almost all events are free, though some require reservations.

BARNES & NOBLE BOOKSELLERS
www.barnesandnoble.com

At every Barnes & Noble superstore, you'll find lots of free readings every week for kids and adults. At these locations you'll find story times where B&N staff, authors, costumed characters, and other guest readers gather children around to hear a book or a story. Of course, the kind folks at Barnes & Noble wouldn't mind if you decided to buy the book, but that's up to you. Call stores or check their Web site to confirm dates and times.

EAST SIDE

ASTOR PLACE, 4 Astor Place (between Broadway and Lafayette); (212) 420–1322; Monday at 4:30 P.M.

240 EAST 86TH STREET (between Second and Third Avenues); (212) 794–1962; Saturday at 11:00 A.M.

UNION SQUARE, 33 East 17th Street (between Park Avenue and Broadway); (212) 253–0810; Sunday at 2:30 P.M.

GREENWICH VILLAGE, 396 Avenue of the Americas (at 8th Street); (212) 674–8780; Wednesday at 3:00 P.M.

2289 BROADWAY (at 82nd Street); (212) 362–8835; Sunday at 11:00 A.M.

BROOKLYN HEIGHTS, 106 Court Street (at State Street); (718) 246–4996; Tuesday and Saturday at 11:00 A.M.

PARK SLOPE, 267 Seventh Avenue (at 6th Street); (718) 832–9066; Tuesday at 11:00 A.M.

BAYSIDE, 23–80 Bell Boulevard (at Northern Boulevard); (718) 224–1083; Monday at 11:00 A.M.

FRESH MEADOWS, 176–60 Union Turnpike (at Utopia Parkway); (718) 380–4340; Tuesday at 10:00 A.M.

FOREST HILLS, 70-00 Austin Street (between 69th Road and Continental Avenue); (718) 793–1395; call for schedule.

BAY PLAZA, 290 Baychester Avenue; (718) 862–3945; Tuesday and Thursday at 6:00 P.M.

2245 RICHMOND AVENUE (between Nome and Travis Streets); (718) 982–6983; Tuesday at 10:30 A.M.

BOOKS OF WONDER
16 West 18th Street (between Fifth and Sixth Avenues)
(212) 989–3270
www.booksofwonder.com
Every Sunday at noon.
This is a literary wonderland for kids and one of the few remaining independent bookstores in the city devoted solely to children's books. They host an overflowing schedule of readings and events (almost all free) that varies

from week to week. You can join them every Sunday for story time: Staff members read their favorite classic and contemporary children's stories.

CITYPARKS KIDS
Various parks throughout the five boroughs
(212) 360–8290
www.cityparksfoundation.org or www.nycparks.org
May through August.
Forget about the hassle of getting on a train or in a car to entertain the kids—CityParks Kids brings the fun to you. Throughout the summer, this program schedules a series of performances (storytellers, children's theater, puppet shows) in large and small public parks throughout the five boroughs. Call or check their Web site for locations and schedules.

HANS CHRISTIAN ANDERSEN STATUE
Central Park
Enter at 72nd Street and Fifth Avenue
www.hcastorycenter.org
Saturday, 11:00 A.M.–noon, June through September (rain or shine).
This is storytelling at its purest: No reading, just master storytellers recounting tales from around the world (and, of course, featuring many by Mr. H. C. Andersen himself). Once the weather turns cooler, the storytelling moves to the comfortable confines of the Scandinavia House (58 Park Avenue between 37th and 38th Streets) on the second Saturday of each month at 11:00 A.M. (from October through May). For more information on the Scandinavia House schedule, call (212) 879–9779 or check the Web site www.scandinavia house.org. The stories are appropriate for children age five and older.

LOGOS BOOKSTORE
1575 York Avenue (between 83rd and 84th Streets)
(212) 517–7292
www.logosbookstorenyc.com
Monday at 3:00 P.M.
Join the wonderfully energetic staff storyteller Devorah Hankin every Monday afternoon at 3:00 P.M. for story time. Devorah picks out a few of her favorite new and classic children's stories and shares them with the little ones for a delightful afternoon.

NEW YORK PUBLIC LIBRARY
www.nypl.org/branch/events/
Almost every branch of the NYPL has a children's section with regularly scheduled readings for kids at least once a week. Many—such as the Donnell Library

(20 West 53rd Street, between Fifth and Sixth Avenues; 212–621–0618)— have lots of special classes and workshops in everything from poetry to cat's cradles. For more details pick up a copy of the monthly *Events for Children and Young Adults* catalogs at any branch or check out the library's Web site. (For branch locations see Appendix C.)

NYU PROGRAM IN EDUCATIONAL THEATRE
Provincetown Playhouse
133 MacDougal Street (between West 3rd Street and Washington Square South)
(212) 998–5868
www.nyu.edu/education/music/edtheatre
Sunday at 3:00 P.M.

A popular series of professional storytellers from around the country and around the world. The program also presents a couple of free theater productions for children and young adults each year in the Black Box Theater. Call for schedule and details.

THE SCHOLASTIC STORE
557 Broadway (between Prince and Spring Streets)
(212) 343–6166
www.scholastic.com/sohostore

Drop by this colorful, energetic store almost anytime, and you'll find something going on for you to enjoy. Every month the people who brought you Clifford the Big Red Dog and Harry Potter put together a full schedule of special events and hands-on activities, including author signings, celebrity appearances, craft workshops, and, of course, regular story times (Tuesday and Thursday at 11:00 A.M.). Check the Web site or drop by the store for the schedule of events.

"We haven't the money,
so we've got to think."

—Lord Rutherford

FROM IVY LEAGUE colleges to technical schools, from GED to Ph.D., from continuing education to just-for-fun classes, if you can think of it (and even if you can't), you can learn it in New York. Many classes are offered completely free of charge and with no catch, while others can be had for nothing (or next to nothing) if you're willing to volunteer your time instead of paying. When volunteering, you're put to work in administrative offices, studios, or classrooms, and your work hours are exchanged for classroom hours. You will find the math for these exchanges spelled out in each listing, but always check with the school to confirm these details. The economics of these work-study programs can change over time.

ARTS

CHAMBERS POTTERY

153 Chambers Street, second floor (between Church Street and West Broadway)
(212) 619–7302
www.chamberspottery.com

 Work-study in exchange for free classes. The math: 3 hours of work = 1 hour of free class time.

This small Tribeca pottery studio offers classes for children and adults. A limited amount of space is available for work-study students.

DIEU DONNE PAPERMILL

433 Broome Street (between Broadway and Crosby Street)
(212) 226–0573
(877) DD–PAPER (toll-free outside New York only)
www.dieudonne.org

 Internship/work-study program. The math: 8 hours of work = 1 hour of studio time, plus after 6 to 8 weeks of work you can take a class for free.

This is the place to go in New York to learn everything about the art of hand paper making. This studio, gallery, and mill in Soho is a very small operation, so interns often get the chance to work in the studio assisting masters of the art, as well as performing all the usual glamorous intern duties (cleaning, filing, running errands, etc.). You will need to commit to working one full day a week (11:00 A.M. to 6:00 P.M.), and they would like you to stay for at least six months.

DOWNTOWN COMMUNITY TV CENTER (DCTV)

87 Lafayette Street (between White and Walker Streets)
(212) 966–4510
www.dctvny.org

 Interns work sixteen hours a week in exchange for free classes and equipment and facilities rental.

Learn the creative and technical skills you need to produce your own television programs. DCTV offers interns the use of top-of-the-line equipment and studios and classes in every aspect of television production, in exchange for time spent working in their offices or on their cable TV productions.

DOWNTOWN THIRD THURSDAY
Various historic locations around downtown
(212) 835-2789
www.downtownny.com

 Free admission, but reservations are required.

You are cordially invited into some of the most exclusive and eye-popping locations throughout downtown to hear some of the most informed authors and historians tell you what they know. This delightful lecture series runs the third Thursday of every month from January to May. The public gains access to some hidden architectural gems, both classic and modern, and gets to hear talks by some of New York's smartest folks on the issues, history, and architecture of the downtown area. Reservations are required, but all events are free.

FILM/VIDEO ARTS
462 Broadway, Suite 520 (at Grand Street)
(212) 941-8787
www.fva.com

 Interns work sixteen hours a week in exchange for free classes and equipment and facilities rental.

Michael Moore, the producer and director of the documentaries *Roger and Me, Bowling for Columbine, Fahrenheit 9/11, Sicko,* and *The Awful Truth* on Bravo—and an F/VA alumnus—says this about F/VA: "Film/Video Arts puts this art form in the hands of people who really aren't supposed to be doing it because it is really such an expensive process. What Film/Video Arts has done is to say, 'Money should not be in the way of getting these resources in the hands of people whose stories we should hear.'" F/VA provides state-of-the-art facilities, equipment, and a full schedule of classes for film and video production to all for low rates, but for interns it's all free.

GREENWICH HOUSE POTTERY

16 Jones Street (between Bleecker and West 4th Streets)
(212) 242–4106
www.greenwichhousepottery.com

 Work-study assistants work in the office, gallery, library, studio, or classes in exchange for free or reduced-rate pottery classes.

A full schedule of pottery classes for children, teens, and adults. Greenwich House also has a very fluid and somewhat negotiable work-study program. Students can work in a variety of positions for one to eight hours a week to be a part of the program. Depending on what skills you have and the job you take on, you can get anywhere from $100 off tuition to full tuition plus free firing time and twenty-four-hour access to the studio.

INSTITUTE FOR FINE ARTS AT NYU

The James B. Duke House
1 East 78th Street (at Fifth Avenue)
www.nyu.edu/gsas/dept/fineart/

Though they don't like to advertise it, every Friday at 4:00 P.M. during the school year the institute invites the public to the elegant and monumental halls of the Duke mansion to attend the Silberberg Lectures in the Fine Arts. This is a series of lectures by leading scholars from institutions around the country. The lectures are aimed at the institute's grad students, so this is pretty serious stuff. For more information and a schedule of lecturers, check out their Web site.

THE JAZZ MUSEUM IN HARLEM

Harlem School for the Arts
645 St. Nicholas Avenue (at 145th Street)
(212) 348–8300
www.jazzmuseuminharlem.org

Outside of its birthplace of New Orleans, no place has nurtured and had as much of an impact on jazz music's development as Harlem. This museum (which is more of a concept than an actual brick-and-mortar museum) takes on the mission of educating and enlightening audiences about jazz's storied past, vital present, and evolving future, especially as it relates to Harlem. They offer a full schedule of free courses and lectures throughout the year. Jazz For Curious Listeners is a hands-on exploration of various aspects of jazz history, techniques, and its personalities. These courses, held on Tuesday evenings (two to three sessions per course), are led by museum director

Loren Schoenberg and guest lecturers. Harlem Speaks is a bimonthly lecture series with leading jazz musicians and others devoted to "keeping the flame of jazz alive in Harlem." They also present many free concerts throughout the year. Check out their Web site for a schedule and details. Seating for classes is limited, and registration is required.

MANHATTAN NEIGHBORHOOD NETWORK (MNN)
537 West 59th Street (between Tenth and Eleventh Avenues)
(212) 757–2670
www.mnn.org

 You must be a resident of Manhattan and agree to produce a program for public access TV.

These organizations administer public access for cable TV services in Manhattan and Queens. The federally mandated obligation of cable TV is that they must provide a channel for all residents to exercise their First Amendment right of freedom of expression. They provide training on production equipment (video production, studio production, editing, audio, basic lighting, digital video and editing, and so on) as well as equipment for programs aired on public access TV. Classes and equipment are also provided in each of the other four boroughs, but there's a small fee charged for classes and materials that runs between $50 and $100 per class. (Contact Queens Public Television [QPTV], 718–886–8160, www.qptv.org; Brooklyn Community Access Television [BCAT], 718–935–1122, www.brooklynx.org/bcat; Staten Island Community Television, 718–727–1414, www.sictv.org; or BronxNet, 718–960–1180, www.bronxnet.org.)

URBAN GLASS
647 Fulton Street (entrance on Rockwell, between DeKalb and Fulton Streets)
Brooklyn
(718) 625–3685
www.urbanglass.org

 Studio and office volunteers are "paid" at a rate of $7.50 an hour. This amount is applied to the cost of any class.

This is New York's only glass-art studio open to the general public. They offer classes in glassblowing, neon, lamp working, casting, and anything else that has to do with glass. The classes can be very expensive ($600 for beginning glassblowing), so it can take a while to gain enough hours to work off the class. The good news is that many of your volunteer hours can be spent in the studio. So you can get a lot of useful hands-on experience while you work (and you may even pick up a few great bits of discarded glass art while tooling around). The bad news is that it gets awfully hot in the studio; dress appropriately.

FOOD AND WINE

THE NATURAL GOURMET INSTITUTE FOR FOOD AND HEALTH
48 West 21st Street, second floor (between Fifth and Sixth Avenues)
(212) 645–5170
www.naturalgourmetschool.com

 Work as a kitchen assistant or in their office to audit classes.

Slice and dice, scrub the pots, and—*Bam!*—you can become the next Emeril (but healthier—the school offers classes in "Health Supportive Cooking"). They have a full schedule of classes to satisfy everyone from the novice cook to the most experienced chef. All classes are vegetarian and have a holistic healing bent. The classes range from basic cooking how-tos like "Knife Skills," "Snack Attack: Healthier 'Junk' Food," and "Choosing Safe Foods" to healthful vegetarian and ethnic specialties like "Dazzling Vegan Desserts," "The Miracle of Miso," and "Authentic Indian Buffet." Kitchen assistants begin working at 5:00 P.M., an hour before the classes begin, preparing ingredients and the kitchen; participate in and nibble their way through the classes; and clean up the kitchen after the class is over.

NEW SCHOOL CULINARY ARTS PROGRAM
131 West 23rd Street (between Sixth and Seventh Avenues)
(212) 255–4141
www.nsu.newschool.edu/culinary

 Work as a kitchen assistant to audit classes or as a work-study office assistant in exchange for classes. Office assistant math: 3 hours of work = 1 hour of class.

The kitchen assistant program is similar to the one at the Natural Gourmet

Institute, except the classes are not limited to vegetarian subjects and can be much more indulgent. The schedule includes classes in basic techniques ("How to Boil Water," "Introduction to French Cooking," and "Creative Hors d'Oeuvres"), light and vegetarian cooking ("Low-Fat Sauces," "Light Italian Cooking," and "Cooking for the Way We Eat Today"), holiday cooking and baking ("The Hanukkah Feast," "For Pumpkin Lovers Only," and "Czech Christmas Cookies"), desserts ("Introduction to Cake Decorating," "Strudel Workshop," and "New Chocolate Desserts"). Kitchen assistants do not participate in the classes they work; they only observe. Work-study students are able to take part in classes. Everyone gets to feast on the results of the class work.

WILLIAMS-SONOMA
10 Columbus Circle (between 58th and 60th Streets)
(212) 823-9750
www.williams-sonoma.com
The New York flagship location of this high-end purveyor of everything kitchen hosts daily cooking demonstrations every day at 2:00 P.M. While it's not a hands-on cooking class, you will definitely pick up some useful tips and skills from their highly trained full-time kitchen staff that you can put to use in your own low-end kitchenette. The demonstrations include such subjects as "Knife Skills," "Cupcake & Cookie Decorations," "Braising," "Bread Baking," and many seasonal themes. Stop by the store to pick up a copy of their monthly schedule of demonstrations. If you can't make it for the demos, stop by anytime to try the tempting samples the kitchen is always churning out.

THE WINE WORKSHOP
160 West 72nd Street (between Columbus Avenue and Broadway)
(212) 875-0222
www.ackerwines.com/workshop
As part of Acker Merral Wine Store, "America's oldest and finest wine shop" (if they don't say so themselves), the Workshop offers a full schedule of classes on wines. Prices range from $85 to $1,000 a class, but you can get in on these for nothing as a pourer. Pourers may not always get the chance to actually taste the pricey wines they are pouring for the paying students; this depends on the number of people in the class. If there is room, pourers are welcome to drink up. Of course, volunteer pourers must be prepared to show up early to help set up, pitch in during the class, and stay after to help clean up. Call the workshop to add your name to the list, and they will call you when they have an opening in a class. You can also stop by the store any Saturday afternoon (2:00 to 5:00 P.M.) to sample some of their fine wines (they will do all the pouring then).

MIND

APPLE STORE

767 Fifth Avenue (between 58th and 59th Streets)
(212) 336–1440
www.apple.com/retail/fifthavenue

103 Prince Street (at Greene Street)
(212) 226–3126
www.apple.com/retail/soho

If you are an Apple computer person, these two stores will be heaven for you. The stores are more like community clubs with a jam-packed schedule of free workshops and performances. Every day they have classes on everything from digital photography and music to business applications and podcasting and more. In the evenings, both stores have a regular schedule of in-store performances every month by well-known musicians.

BROOKLYN PUBLIC LIBRARY'S BUSINESS LIBRARY

280 Cadman Plaza West (between Tillary and Pierrepont Streets)
(718) 623–7000
www.biz.brooklynpubliclibrary.org

THE CATCH   "You should only be successful and make us proud."

An abundance of classes and workshops are offered throughout the year targeted toward entrepreneurs, small-business owners, students, small investors, and anyone interested in Brooklyn business. Some highlights include an entrepreneur series, a business fair in May and June, and the "Made in Brooklyn" breakfast series (Yes! Including a free continental breakfast) highlighting specific industries in Brooklyn, from music and film to Key lime pies and Caribbean beef patties. They also play host to the SCORE program, in which small-business start-ups get personalized mentoring from established and retired business owners. Free Internet access is available as well.

THE COOPER UNION FOR THE ADVANCEMENT OF SCIENCE AND ART

Cooper Square (8th Street between Bowery and Third Avenues)
(212) 353–4120
www.cooper.edu

THE CATCH   Brains, brains, talent, and brains, plus a $65 application fee.

Libraries with Class!

At branches of the New York Public Library (www.nypl.org), Brooklyn Public Library (www.brooklynpubliclibrary.org), and Queens Public Library (www.queenslibrary.org), you will find literally thousands of free classes, lectures, and workshops in everything imaginable offered throughout the year. Here is just a sampling of classes. For details and schedules stop into any branch or check the Web sites.

The Art of Breathing and Relaxation
The Art of Public Speaking
Arts and Crafts
Ballroom Dancing
Basic and Intermediate Internet
Basic Mouse Skills
Bead Making Workshop
Become a Stamp Collector
The Big Apple on the Big Screen
Book Discussions
Breaking the Rules Again: Teens Writing Poetry
Bridge Club
Cantonese Program for Parents
Career Exploration Inventory
Checking and Credit 101 Workshop
Citizenship Preparation Workshop in Mandarin
College and You
Computers for Seniors
Conserving Home Energy
Create a Quilt
Create Your Own Photo Album
Create Your Own Shadow Puppet
Crocheting Class
Dance with a Mexican Touch

Doing Business in Taiwan
Drum Clinic
E-mail Basics
ESOL Class
Estate Planning
Fashion Design for Teens
401(k) Rollover
GED Class
Get Connected to Consumer Health Information
Great Ideas Forum
Health Information on the Internet
The History of Greenwich Village
How to Do a Term Paper
How to Read the NYC Subway Map
Illustrated Bookmaking
Internet Search Strategies
Introduction to Computers
Introduction to Excel
Introduction to PowerPoint
Introduction to Word
Investing: How to Research Companies and Industries
Jewelry Making
Job and Résumé Resources Online
Knitting Classes for Beginners
Knitting Club

Learning about the Rights of Immigrants
Makeup Tips and Techniques
Making Your Assets Last
Open Mike Night
Origami
Picture Book Hour
Poetry Writing Workshop
Polish Your Résumé!
So You Want to Be a Songwriter
Sorting through the Life Insurance Maze
Stay C.O.O.L. Under Fire: Dealing with Difficult People
Staywell Exercise for Older Adults
Success in Math
Tai Chi for Seniors
Telescope Moon Watching
Toddler Time
Understanding the 2001 Tax Relief Act
Using MS Word for Your Newsletter
Using Music in Literacy and ESOL
Voice-Over Workshop: How to Break into the Lucrative World of Voice-Overs
Watercolor Class
Work for the U.S. Postal Service
The Write Stuff: A Writing Workshop for Adults

Every one of the 900 students at this top college of art, architecture, and engineering attends completely tuition-free. They do have to cover their own room, board, books, and student fees (totaling about $1,500 a year), but the $30,000 tuition bill is on the house. It shouldn't surprise you that the competition to get into this premier school is pretty stiff. Each year about 2,600 men and women from around the world apply for Cooper Union, and only about 300 are accepted. Gentlemen, start your slide rulers.

EGLISE FRANÇAIS DU ST-ESPRIT

109 East 60th Street (between Park and Lexington Avenues)
(212) 838–5680
www.stespritnyc.net

Free beginning and intermediate French classes are taught every Sunday from 10:00 to 11:00 A.M. These are very small and intimate classes (they have room for no more than ten students per class). They run from September through December and January through June.

ENGLISH CLASSES FOR SPEAKERS OF OTHER LANGUAGES

New York Public Library
Various branches in Manhattan, the Bronx, and Staten Island
(212) 340–0918
www.nypl.org

Beginner and intermediate English classes are offered three times a year (fall, winter, and spring). Space is limited, and registration is required. Check the Web site for branch locations and class schedules.

HENRY GEORGE SCHOOL OF SOCIAL SCIENCE

121 East 30th Street (between Park and Lexington Avenues)
(212) 889–8020
www.henrygeorgeschool.org

Free adult education classes that deal with the hidden factors at work in the economy. Classes include "Progress and Poverty" and "Applied Economics and Economic Science." The classes meet once a week for ten weeks; preregistration is required. They also offer free film forums and upper-level courses such as "Current Events," "The Genesis of Modern Economics," and "Money and Banking." All courses and forums are offered in Spanish as well.

HOUSING EDUCATION PROGRAM
NYC Department of Housing Preservation and Development
100 Gold Street, Room 6C
(212) 863–8830
www.nyc.gov/hpd

 You must be a New York City resident or property owner.

Get a Job, Get a Degree

New York is home to many top-ranked universities and countless other colleges and technical schools throughout the five boroughs. Like any business, these schools need a large support staff to keep the doors open and the students happy—and that's where you come in. From office assistants and administrative staff to maintenance and mailroom clerks, almost all of these jobs include the fringe benefit of free or seriously reduced tuition for classes at these and affiliated schools. So instead of paying $30,000 a year for that graduate degree, why not have them pay you for your time? Forget about paying $10,000 to become a computer systems analyst; you can take advantage of the system to get it for nothing. Salaries at the schools vary, but you probably won't be making the kind of money you can retire on. Still, this extra benefit can make it a very profitable position. Here are some places to start your search:

COLUMBIA UNIVERSITY, *475 Riverside Drive, Room 1901 (between 119th and 120th Streets); (212) 870–2425; www.columbia.edu/cu/jobs.*

NEW YORK UNIVERSITY, *7 East 12th Street, first floor (at Fifth Avenue); (212) 998–1250; www.nyu.edu/hr.*

WWW.HIGHEREDJOBS.COM

This city-run program offers a comprehensive set of courses to help home-owners learn how to keep their properties in good fiscal and physical health. Classes include "Basic and Advanced Building Management," "Building Finances," "Tenant Relations," "Building Maintenance," and others. Courses are generally offered three to five times a year, but many fill up quickly; early registration is recommended.

SMALL BUSINESS DEVELOPMENT CENTER (SBDC)

Pace University, 163 William Street, sixteenth floor (Ann and Beeckman Streets); (212) 618–6655

Baruch College, 55 Lexington Avenue (at 24th Street); (646) 312–4790
www.nyssbdc.org

Ready to start your own business but haven't got a clue what to do? Well, you are going to want to get to know the folks at these SBDCs. Basically, this is your uncle in the business who is going to help you do it right. These centers (two of eighteen throughout the state) are sponsored by the federal government, New York State, and the local universities. They are there to help you through every step of the start-up process and will continue to offer assistance for as long as you're in business, with one-on-one coaching and workshops in everything from business plan development and financial planning to marketing strategies and management. There is never a charge for any of their counseling services, and most classes and workshops are free as well.

BIKRAM YOGA NYC

797 Eighth Avenue, fourth floor (between West 48th and West 49th Streets)
(212) 245–2525
www.bikramyoganyc.com
Friday at 11:30 A.M., pay-what-you-wish class.

Work the front desk for five hours a week for unlimited free classes.

Bikram has become the hottest craze in yoga, in more ways than one. This popular yoga studio literally turns the heat up to more than one hundred degrees for its ninety-minute classes, guaranteeing you will be dripping and exhausted from this vigorous workout. This can be an addictive and expensive habit, with each class running $20. Of course, there is a way to stretch your dollars here. Every Friday at 11:30 A.M., they offer a pay-what-you-wish class where anyone can show up and pay as little as they want for the class. All proceeds from that weekly class go to benefit the AIDS organization Equity Fights AIDS. And if one class a week doesn't satisfy your need for sweat, you can sign up to work one five-hour shift a week at the desk for unlimited free classes. Students are required to take classes for a few months before they can take part in the work-study program. They have three other studios around the city where you can do your work-study, but you have to fill out an application and interview at this location.

DIAS Y FLORES
520–522 East 13th Street (between Avenues A and B)
(212) 260–9344
www.greenthumbnyc.org/events.html
This community garden offers free yoga, tai chi, and drawing classes during the summer months. All supplies for the drawing classes are provided free, but bring your own yoga mats and towel for the others. Class offerings vary from summer to summer; call for schedules and details. The Green Thumb Web site (listed above) is also a great resource for free happenings in community gardens all around the city.

HIGH VIBE HEALTH & HEALING
138 East Third Street (between First Avenue and Avenue A)
(212) 777–6645
www.highvibe.com
This "living food" and health supplements store offers free classes on such subjects as fasting, family nutrition, essential oil treatments, and gallbladder and liver detox. They also hold raw food preparation workshops, but they charge for those.

LULULEMON ATHLETICA
1928 Broadway (at 64th Street)
(212) 712–1767
www.lululemon.com

Once a week this top-of-the-line yoga apparel store pushes the clothing racks aside and turns the shop into a yoga studio. They offer a free yoga class every Sunday from 8:00 to 9:00 P.M. The classes change from week to week but are always led by instructors from some of New York's chichi-est gyms and yoga studios, including Clay, Reebok Sports Club, Bikram Yoga NYC, Exhale Spa, and others.

THE OHASHI INSTITUTE

147 West 25th Street, sixth floor (between Sixth and Seventh Avenues)
(646) 486–1187 or (800) 810–4190
www.ohashiatsu.org

 Work-study students may work in the office, on the cleaning crew, or on special projects in exchange for credit toward classes. The math: 1 hour of work = $10 credit toward class for the first year, $12 thereafter.

Ohashi offers a six-level curriculum on its own style of shiatsu massage (Ohashiatsu) that can be taken by both professionals and laypeople. Ohashiatsu is a stretching, relaxing, and energizing acupressure type of massage that works with the Eastern healing philosophies of chi (energy) and the meridians (energy channels) of the body.

SPIRIT

THE ASIAN CLASSICS INSTITUTE/
THREE JEWELS COMMUNITY CENTER

61 Fourth Avenue (between 9th and 10th Streets)
(212) 475–7752 or (212) 475–6650
www.world-view.org

The institute offers general-interest and teacher-training courses in Tibetan Buddhism, meditation, and Tibetan language, all free of charge. The general-interest courses are drop-in classes open to all, and the formal study teacher-training courses are open to those "willing to make a serious commitment to their studies." These courses have attendance requirements, homework assignments, and tests. The Three Jewels Community Center offers free meditation classes, free coffee and tea, free Internet access, and a free lending library.

FALUN DAFA

Central Park (59th Street and Central Park West) and many other sites throughout the city
(212) 978-9511 or (877) FALUN-99
www.falun-ny.net

THE CATCH None (as long as you aren't in China)

From the folks who brought you tai chi comes a new, very old traditional Chinese exercise, Falun Dafa (or Falun Gong). It's a practice that aims to improve mental and physical well-being through a series of easy-to-learn exercises, meditation, and development of "one's Heart/Mind Nature." And from the folks who brought you Tiananmen Square comes a whole new wave of oppression. This is the group that has gained a lot of attention recently by being banned in China and has seen brutal suppression of its practitioners by the Chinese government. So there must be something to it. They offer free introductory classes as well as weekly group practices.

MANHATTAN JEWISH EXPERIENCE (MJE)

131 West 86th Street (between Columbus and Amsterdam Avenues)

5 East 62nd Street (between Fifth and Madison Avenues)
(212) 787-9533
www.jewishexperience.org

If you're like me and all you remember about Hebrew school as a kid was falling asleep, then here's your chance to try it again. The big difference is that this time you'll stay awake and maybe even enjoy it. MJE offers a full schedule of basic courses for free, including the Monday Night Lounge, which includes a sushi dinner and interesting discussions of how current issues (sexuality, free will, business and medical ethics) relate to the ancient religion, followed by music and dessert. They also offer free basic Learn to Read Hebrew classes (and intermediate and advanced courses for $5 a class). Classes are fun, unintimidating, interactive, and geared for all Jews, particularly those with little or no background in Judaism. These classes are not meant to recruit Jews into a particular sect, but to help you gain a deeper understanding of the age-old traditions and how they fit into modern life. Plus, it's not a bad place to meet a nice Jewish girl or guy and make your mother happy. They also have a full program of intermediate and advanced courses and lectures for which they do charge a small fee ($5 per class). Hey, they even set out some free soft drinks and noshes.

THE OPEN CENTER
83 Spring Street (between Broadway and Lafayette Street)
(212) 219–2527, ext. 117
www.opencenter.org

 Volunteer four hours a week for unlimited free classes (depending on availability).

They offer a huge array of classes and workshops in holistic learning and living. There are classes in everything from feng shui, reflexology, belly dancing, and salsa aerobics to Taoism, Kabbalah, tantric sex, and herbalism. You can also find ongoing yoga and meditation classes here, as well as a number of certification programs. They treat their volunteers with great respect and support. If you're interested in alternative learning, this is the place for you.

SHAMBHALA CENTER OF NEW YORK
118 West 22nd Street, sixth floor (between Sixth and Seventh Avenues)
(212) 675–6544
www.ny.shambhala.org

 Three free classes each week (donations requested, but not required). Work-study is also available for other classes. The math: 1 hour work = $10 class credit.

The Shambhala Center offers a full schedule of classes and lectures on all forms of meditation, yoga, and Buddhist and Eastern practices. Each week they hold two "Learn to Meditate" classes (Wednesday at 6:00 P.M. and Sunday at noon) and an "Open Dharma Gathering" (Tuesday at 7:00 P.M.), which includes a guided meditation and lectures by noted teachers. Both of these classes are on a donation basis. You can also take part in their work-study program to take any of their classes for free. Each hour of work nets you $10 credit toward classes.

"Always laugh when you can. It is cheap medicine."

—Lord Byron

HEALTH AND MEDICAL: LIVE FREE OR DIE

NEW YORK SURELY ranks among the most expensive places to stay healthy. From ordinary checkups to health insurance, getting sick here will cost you. The good news is, New York is also one of the major centers for medical schools and clinical studies, which provide many opportunities for free and low-cost care, often with cutting-edge treatments (excuse the pun). New York is also a center for bleeding-heart liberals, so in this town big government still plays some role in providing services to those in need of low-cost health care through the extensive Health & Hospitals Corporation system and at some community clinics.

TO YOUR HEALTH: FREE CLINICS

In a day and age when medical costs are sky-high and the cost of health insurance is just as stratospheric, it would seem to be just a fantasy that such a thing as a free clinic still exists, right? Well, stop dreaming and start dialing to get yourself an appointment, because it really does, and not just one but two are right here in New York City. These two clinics, one in Manhattan and one in the Bronx, provide free medical care, health education, and social work services to anyone who is uninsured and older than age nineteen. Both clinics are open only on Saturday mornings and are staffed by the medical students and physicians from NYU Medical School in Manhattan and the Albert Einstein College of Medicine in the Bronx.

ECHO FREE CLINIC
Walton Family Health Center
1894 Walton Avenue (at East 177th Street)
Bronx
(718) 583–3060 or (800) 836–1316
www.echo-clinic.org

To make an appointment, call between 9:00 A.M. and 4:45 P.M. Monday through Friday. Appointments are usually about two months from the day you call. The clinic does take a limited number of walk-ins, but you should be prepared to wait a while.

NYC FREE CLINIC
The Institute for Urban Family Health
16 East 16th Street, third floor (between Fifth and Madison Avenues)
(917) 544–0735
http://endeavor.med.nyu.edu/freeclinic/

Appointments made by calling and leaving a message with the very specific information they request on their voice mail. No walk-ins are accepted.

WHATEVER AILS YOU: CLINICAL STUDIES

Medical centers throughout New York run clinical trials for almost any condition imaginable, from cancer to acne, from athlete's foot to weight loss. People

Guinea Pigs: Student Clinics

Calling all brave souls with sore feet, aching muscles, off-balance polarity, and clogged chi: Students at alternative health schools throughout the city are waiting to rub, prick, and stretch you back to health. All over New York there are schools for everything from acupuncture and herbal medicine to polarity therapy and shiatsu. Many of these schools have clinics attached to them where they offer low-cost (and sometimes free) appointments to the public, on whom the students try out their new skills. It may seem a bit scary to let a newbie acupuncturist loose on you with his needles, but rest assured that these are all advanced students, and they're always watched over by professionals. Here is a list of schools and the services they offer:

AYURVEDA'S BEAUTY CARE SPA & BIOTICARE HOLISTIC CENTER, *99 University Place, fifth floor (between 11th and 12th Streets); (212) 529–3300; www.ayurvedasbeautycare.com; free Ayurveda nutritional counseling is offered at various times throughout the year. They also plan to start offering free or low-cost facials and other skin-care services from students soon. Check their Web site or call for schedule and details.*

THE OPEN CENTER, *83 Spring Street (between Broadway and Lafayette Street); (212) 219–2527, ext 116; www.theopencenter .org; free reiki, reflexology, and polarity-therapy sessions. Call to put your name on the list of available clients, and a student will call you when they need a warm body to attend a class or to practice on.*

PACIFIC COLLEGE OF ORIENTAL MEDICINE & ACUPUNCTURE, *915 Broadway (between 20th and 21st Streets); (212) 982–4600; www.pacificcollege.edu; low-cost acupuncture and herbal medicine.*

THE SWEDISH INSTITUTE, *226 West 26th Street (between Seventh and Eighth Avenues); (212) 924–5900; www.swedishinstitute.edu; massage, $150 for six one-hour sessions or $250 for twelve one-hour sessions; acupuncture, $325 for a consultation plus twelve sessions.*

TRI-STATE COLLEGE OF ACUPUNCTURE, *80 Eighth Avenue (at 14th Street); (212) 242–2254 for acupuncture, (212) 242–4307 for herbal medicine; www.tsca.edu; $30 for acupuncture appointments; $20 for herbal medicine appointments (plus the cost of herbs, about $15).*

are always needed to participate in these studies, and all medication and care are provided free of charge—in fact, you can even get paid for participating in many of these studies.

COLUMBIA-PRESBYTERIAN MEDICAL CENTER
Department of Dermatology
161 Fort Washington Avenue, Room 750 (between 165th and 168th Streets)
(212) 305–6953
www.columbiaclinicaltrials.org

Pick a Study, Any Study

To find a study for a particular condition, check out these Web sites:

NATIONAL DATABASES

CENTER WATCH, *a friendly consolidated listing by category; www.centerwatch.com.*

NATIONAL CANCER INSTITUTE, *a searchable database for clinical trials throughout the country for all forms of cancer; www.cancer.gov/clinicaltrials.*

AIDS CLINICAL TRIAL INFORMATION SERVICE, *(800) 874–2572; www.aidsinfo.nih.gov.*

VERITAS MEDICINE, *a database of clinical studies by condition; www.veritasmedicine.com.*

NATIONAL INSTITUTES OF HEALTH, *a national database of conditions and studies for clinical trials in everything from Acidosis to Zellweger Syndrome; www.clinicaltrials.gov.*

NATIONAL CENTER FOR COMPLEMENTARY AND ALTERNATIVE MEDICINE, *which has studies throughout the country funded by the National Institute for Health using every kind of alternative therapy, from acupressure to yoga; www.nccam.nih.gov.*

NEW YORK MEDICAL CENTERS

BETH ISRAEL MEDICAL CENTER, *www.wehealny.org/studies.*

NYU MEDICAL CENTER, *www.med.nyu.edu/clinicaltrials.*

NYU AIDS CLINICAL TRIALS UNIT, *(212) 263–6565; www.hivinfosource.org.*

Constantly organizing new trials for medication and treatment of various skin conditions, including acne, toe fungus, wounds, and more. Treatment and medication are free, and compensation is provided.

NEW YORK HEADACHE CENTER
30 East 76th Street, second floor (at Madison Avenue)
(212) 794–3550
www.nyheadache.com
Conducts clinical trials on different medication and treatments for migraines and other types of headaches. All research-related examinations and treatments are free, and financial compensation is often provided.

HHC TO THE RESCUE

New York City Health & Hospitals Corporation (HHC) was created to provide comprehensive medical care to all people "regardless of their ability" to pay. The corporation consists of eleven acute-care hospitals, six diagnostic and treatment centers, four long-term-care facilities, and more than eighty community health clinics. HHC also operates MetroPlus Health Plan, a health maintenance organization (HMO) for Medicaid recipients. You can expect waits to be a bit longer for all appointments and at emergency rooms at these facilities than at private hospitals, but sit tight and they'll get to you. For more information check the Web site www.nyc.gov/hhc or call (212) 788–3321.

MANHATTAN

BELLEVUE HOSPITAL CENTER, 462 First Avenue (at 27th Street); (212) 562–4141.
COLER-GOLDWATER MEMORIAL HOSPITAL,
  1 Main Street (Coler); (212) 848–6000.
  900 Main Street (Goldwater); (212) 318–8000.
  Roosevelt Island

GOUVERNEUR NURSING FACILITY AND DIAGNOSTIC & TREATMENT CENTER, 227 Madison Street (between Jefferson and Clinton Streets); (212) 238–7000.

HARLEM HOSPITAL CENTER, 506 Lenox Avenue (at 135th Street); (212) 939–1000.

METROPOLITAN HOSPITAL CENTER, 1901 First Avenue (97th Street, between First and Second Avenues); (212) 423–6262.

RENAISSANCE DIAGNOSTIC & TREATMENT CENTER, 215 West 125th Street (between Seventh and Eighth Avenues); (212) 932–6500.

THE BRONX

JACOBI MEDICAL CENTER, 1400 Pelham Parkway South (at Eastchester Road); (718) 918–5000.

LINCOLN MEDICAL AND MENTAL HEALTH CENTER, 234 East 149th Street (between Park and Morris Avenues, near the Grand Concourse); (718) 579–5000.

MORRISANIA DIAGNOSTIC & TREATMENT CENTER, 1225 Gerard Avenue (between East 167th and East 168th Streets); (718) 960–2777.

NORTH CENTRAL BRONX HOSPITAL, 3424 Kossuth Avenue (210th Street, between Gunhill and Jerome Avenues); (718) 519–5000.

SEGUNDO RUIZ BELVIS DIAGNOSTIC & TREATMENT CENTER, 545 East 142nd Street (between Brock and St. Anns Avenues); (718) 579–4000.

BROOKLYN

CONEY ISLAND HOSPITAL, 2601 Ocean Parkway (between Avenue Z and Shore Parkway); (718) 616–3000.

CUMBERLAND DIAGNOSTIC & TREATMENT CENTER, 100 North Portland Avenue (between Park and Myrtle Avenues); (718) 260–7500.

DR. SUSAN SMITH McKINNEY NURSING AND REHABILITATION CENTER, 594 Albany Avenue (at Rutland Road); (718) 245–7000.

EAST NEW YORK DIAGNOSTIC & TREATMENT CENTER, 2094 Pitkin Avenue (between Pennsylvania and New Jersey Avenues); (718) 240–0400.

KINGS COUNTY HOSPITAL CENTER, 451 Clarkson Avenue (between Albany and New York Avenues); (718) 245–3131.

WOODHULL MEDICAL AND MENTAL HEALTH CENTER, 760 Broadway (at Flushing Avenue); (718) 963–8000.

QUEENS

ELMHURST HOSPITAL CENTER, 79–01 Broadway (at 79th Street); (718) 334–4000.

QUEENS HOSPITAL CENTER, 82–70 164th Street (at the Grand Central Parkway); (718) 883–3000.

STATEN ISLAND

SEA VIEW HOSPITAL REHABILITATION CENTER AND HOME, 460 Brielle Avenue (Bradley and Rockland Avenues); (718) 317–3000.

DEPRESSION/MENTAL HEALTH STUDIES AND CLINICAL TRIALS

A number of hospitals and research centers throughout New York conduct ongoing clinical studies of depression and medications for mental illnesses such as Prozac, Zoloft, Wellbutrin, and others. If you qualify for a study, they can provide you with up to one year of free medication and medical care. All studies are supervised and monitored by doctors and psychiatrists adhering to strict clinical testing protocols, some of which could involve the use of a placebo.

MOUNT SINAI MEDICAL CENTER, Compulsive, Impulsive and Anxiety Disorders Clinic, 99th Street and Madison Avenue; (212) 241–3116; www.mssm.edu/psychiatry/ciadp.

NEUROPSYCH RESEARCH ASSOCIATES, 1236 Park Avenue (at 96th Street); (212) 722–6604.

NEW YORK PRESBYTERIAN/CORNELL MEDICAL CENTER, Depression Treatment Study Program, 525 East 68th Street (at York Avenue); (212) 746–5705.

NEW YORK PSYCHIATRIC INSTITUTE, Depression Evaluation Service, 1051 Riverside Drive, Suite 3300; (212) 543–5734; www.depression nyc.org.

ST. LUKE'S/ROOSEVELT HOSPITAL, Mood Disorders Research Program, 910 Ninth Avenue (at 58th Street); (212) 523–7666; www.weheal ny.org/psych.

STD CLINICS

There are eleven city-run STD (sexually transmitted disease) clinics located throughout the five boroughs that provide free testing and treatment for all common STDs. They also provide anonymous and confidential HIV testing and counseling. Of course, you can also get free condoms at all locations. These clinics all operate on a take-a-number-and-wait-on-line basis, so you can never predict how long the wait will be. Most clinics are open Monday through Friday from 8:30 A.M. to 4:00 P.M. and some offer Saturday hours, but always call to check hours and services before heading down to one of these clinics. For more information call the hotline at (212) 427–5120 or check the Web site www.nyc.gov/health.

MANHATTAN

CENTRAL HARLEM STD CLINIC, 2238 Fifth Avenue (at 137th Street); (212) 690–1760.

CHELSEA STD CLINIC, 303 Ninth Avenue (at 28th Street); (212) 239–1718 or (212) 239–0843.

EAST HARLEM STD CLINIC, 158 East 115th Street (off Lexington Avenue); (212) 360–5962.

RIVERSIDE STD CLINIC, 160 West 100th Street (between Columbus and Amsterdam Avenues); (212) 865–7757.

THE BRONX

MORRISANIA STD CLINIC, 1309 Fulton Avenue (at East 169th Street, off Third Avenue); (718) 579–7714.

BROOKLYN

BUSHWICK CLINIC, 335 Central Avenue (between Linden and Grove Streets); (718) 573–4820 or (718) 573–4823.

FORT GREENE STD CLINIC, 295 Flatbush Avenue Extension, fifth floor (at Willoughby Street); (718) 643–4133.

QUEENS

CORONA STD CLINIC, 34–33 Junction Boulevard (between Roosevelt and Northern Avenues); (718) 476–7815.

Safety First: Free Condoms

A Cheap Bastard can be a sexy bastard, but there's no reason you can't also be a safe bastard. Here is a list of places to pick up your free condoms.

NYC CONDOM, *locations throughout the five boroughs; www.nyc condom.org. New York City is no stranger to tall, erect structures— think the Empire State Building, the Chrysler Building—but now the city has taken its knack for extreme phallic symbols to the next level by branding its very own condom. The NYC Condom is distributed for free in hundreds of locations throughout the city. Check out the Web site for the location near you.*

GAY MEN'S HEALTH CRISIS (GMHC), *119 West 24th Street (between Sixth and Seventh Avenues). Provides a huge amount of free services for people with AIDS and everything you need for AIDS prevention, including condoms-a-plenty. Check out the front desks on the fourth and seventh floors. For more information on other services they provide, call (212) 807–6655 or (800) AIDS–NYC, or check the Web site www.gmhc.org.*

THE LESBIAN, GAY, BISEXUAL & TRANSGENDER COMMUNITY CENTER, *208 West 13th Street (between Seventh and Eighth Avenues). The renovated center is home to a full schedule of weekly meetings, support groups, workshops, and social activities, many of which are free. You'll also find the free Pat Parker/Vito Russo Library, and there are always free condoms available at the front desk. For more information on the schedule and activities, call (212) 620–7310, or check the Web site www.gaycenter.org.*

JAMAICA STD CLINIC, 90–37 Parsons Boulevard, first floor (off Jamaica Avenue); (718) 262–5572.

ROCKAWAY STD CLINIC, 67–19 Rockaway Boulevard (at Beach 67th Street); (718) 945–7150.

STATEN ISLAND

RICHMOND STD CLINIC, 51 Stuyvesant Place (at Wall Street); (718) 420–4994 or (718) 420–4995.

> "I cannot afford to waste my time making money."
>
> —Jean Louis Agassiz

FITNESS, FUN, AND GAMES: CHEAP THRILLS

FREE TIME IS a precious commodity in New York, whether you're visiting or you live here. And no place offers more extravagant ways to drop a load of cash when you're able to break away from the hustle and bustle of life in the big city. But wait! There are also tons of things to do and places to go to wind down without breaking the bank. Here are some suggestions for great destinations, recreational activities, and other ways to take it easy for free in New York City. From kayaking along the Hudson to in-line skating lessons in Central Park and a refreshing dip in any of the many public pools throughout the city, New York City really gives you a chance to enjoy your free time. The schedules change from time to time, so be sure to call and confirm all information before showing up.

PARK IT HERE! PARKS OFFERING A VARIETY OF ACTIVITIES

BATTERY PARK CITY PARKS
Hudson River (from Chambers to Vesey Streets)
(212) 267-9700
www.bpcparks.org

This delightful park offers a real windfall of free fun-and-games activities that include volleyball, chess, backgammon, concerts, and in-line skating lessons. You can also borrow a wide variety of recreational supplies like Frisbees, basketballs, jump ropes, board games, and more from the Park House at Rockefeller Park (at Chambers Street; bring a photo ID). They even have a couple of free pool tables available near the Park House. Other programs they run throughout the season include a drumming circle, fishing, bird-watching, family dances, lots of children's programs, walking tours, concerts, and on and on. Check out the Web site for more information, or get a copy of their most recent calendar; they add new activities every season.

BRYANT PARK
Sixth Avenue (between 40th and 42nd Streets)
(212) 768-4242
www.bryantpark.org

This oasis at the dead center of the frenetic midtown bustle is awash with free activities and entertainment throughout the year. During the warmer months its beautiful lawn is the perfect destination for a quick lunchtime snooze or after-work picnic, as long as it is not crammed with throngs attending one of their many high-profile and star-studded free events. Such events include the early morning *Good Morning America* Concerts, the HBO Monday-night film series, Broadway and dance performances, and many others. They also offer free Pétanque lessons (pronounced *pay-TONK*), which is basically the French version of boccie with smaller balls (fill in your own joke here). Stop by the free reading room to borrow a book, newspaper, or magazine while lounging around. And in the wintertime they roll up the lawn and bring out the Pond—a state-of-the-art ice-skating rink where the skating is all free (though you will have to pay a steep $7.50 if you need to rent skates).

CENTRAL PARK
59th Street to 110th Street (between Fifth Avenue and
Central Park West)
(212) 310-6600
www.centralparknyc.org

Whole books have been written about this oasis of natural splendor amid the concrete jungle, and there are many entries in this one about specific destinations for free goings-on. Here's a quick rundown of some of the park's free delights: walking tours; in-line skating lessons; tango, salsa, and swing dance; nature exhibits; the Conservatory Gardens; fishing and birding; borrowed sports equipment from the North Meadow Recreation Center; art galleries; theater; concerts; and much more. To get information about anything going on in the park, check the Web site or stop by one of the park's three visitor centers: Belvedere Castle (midpark at 79th Street; 212–772–0210), the Dairy (midpark at 65th Street; 212–794–6564), and the Charles A. Dana Discovery Center (inside the park at 110th Street and Lenox Avenue; 212–860–1370).

GOVERNORS ISLAND
New York Harbor
(212) 440–2202
www.govisland.com

After over 200 years as a military facility, this island in the center of New York Harbor has now been turned into a public park and national monument with a fantastic selection of free offerings during the summer. The gratis goodies start off with free ferry rides to and from the island from downtown Manhattan and also include guided tours of the island, concerts, exhibitions, lectures, many family-friendly activities, and breathtaking views of New York and the Statue of Liberty. Check out the Web site or call for the ferry schedule and event lineups.

HUDSON RIVER PARK
Harris Street to 59th Street (at the Hudson River)
(212) 627–2020
www.hudsonriverpark.org

Making the link between Battery Park City Park up to Riverside Park, the Hudson River Park is the greatest addition to New York's recreation landscape since 700 swampy acres in the center of Manhattan were made into a humble little park. Once an industrial wasteland, the West Side waterfront is now a major destination for bicyclists and skaters, who can now traverse the entire length of Manhattan. During the summer months it is one of the major epicenters of free fun in New York City. Some of the many free offerings include movies, swing dancing, arts and crafts activities for the kids, Ping-Pong, catch-and-release fishing, open-air professional boxing matches, and concerts. Free kayaking is available at Pier 40 (at Houston Street) and at Pier 96 at 56th Street and you can roll around the ramps of the state-of-the-art skate park (at Franklin Street), visit a water-park playground on Pier 51 (at Jane Street), and enjoy lots of lush lawns for relaxing and tossing a Frisbee around. The park is still in the building stage and every year brings new activities, facilities, and free fun to the West Side.

RIVERSIDE PARK

Hudson River between 62nd and 155th Street
(212) 870–3070 or 311
www.riversideparkfund.org or www.nyc.gov/parks

Riverside Park picks up where the Hudson River Park leaves off to complete the glorious waterfront park that runs practically the entire length of Manhattan. The park's bike and running trails connect, giving you the chance to ride from the South Ferry to the George Washington Bridge, and in between there are endless opportunities for free fun every step of the way. Riverside Park has a full schedule of free events every summer in Riverside Park South (between 62nd and 72nd Streets) that includes films, music and dance performances, and children's events, as well as weekly yoga and Pilates classes. The downtown boathouse has an outpost uptown at 72nd Street for you to enjoy some free kayaking. The remainder of the park is awash in other amenities like public tennis courts, ball fields, a bird sanctuary, a public skate park, gardens, monuments, spectacular views of the Hudson River, and loads of free events thoughout the year.

RECREATION CENTERS

New York City Department of Parks and Recreation runs forty-two recreation centers throughout the five boroughs, and for the price of $75 a year (yes, a year!) you have access to every single one of them. Now, to be totally honest, some of these are not exactly state-of-the-art facilities, but they do have much of the same equipment you'd find at the high-price gyms around town (Nautilus machines, Lifecycles, free weights, dumbbells, et cetera). Some also offer a full schedule of classes (aerobics, yoga, tai chi, boxing, and more), and some even have indoor and outdoor pools (you won't find that at many of the more expensive clubs around town!). Many of the centers also have extensive programs for children and seniors, and all have free after-school programs for kids ages eight through thirteen. The computer resource facilities at many of the centers offer classes and instruction on the Internet and computer programs.

Some of the adult classes charge a small fee in addition to the membership.

For information check the Web site www.nycgovparks.org and click on "Things to Do," or call 311 (see Appendix D for recreation center locations).

SKATING, BIKING, AND RUNNING

BIKE NEW YORK
Recycle-A-Bicycle Training Center
5th Street and Forty-sixth Avenue
Long Island City, Queens
(212) 932–BIKE (2553)
www.bikenewyork.org

 A $20 refundable deposit is required to register for a class.

Whether you are new to navigating New York traffic on your bike or getting back on that bike after years away, you will benefit from taking Bike New York's Savvy Cyclist class. The free one-day class provides the essential knowledge and skills you need to know how to adjust, repair, and ride your bike like an experienced pro. The class is offered on Saturday once a month from March through November. While the class is totally free, they do require a $20 refundable deposit to hold your place in the class. Bike New York also offers other free classes for adults and kids, including classes on commuting with your bike and teaching children how to ride a bike.

BRYANT PARK SKATING RINK
Sixth Avenue (between 40th and 42nd Street)
(212) 768–4242
www.bryantpark.org

 Skating is free, but they charge for skate rentals.

Bryant Park is not just a great place for freebies in the summer anymore. From

late October through January, Bryant Park is converted into a winter wonderland with a full-size state-of-the-art ice-skating rink open to the public
for free all week long. On the weekends the lines do get long and the ice can
be crowded, but the setting is truly a glorious one. If you have your own ice
skates, bring them along, or else you will have to pay about $7 to rent skates.
Check out the Web site for the schedule and special events including performances and fun theme nights.

EMPIRE SKATE CLUB OF NEW YORK
   (212) 774–1774
   www.empireskate.org
This is a membership organization that welcomes all skaters to join in a number of group skates every week. The Tuesday Night Skate (meets at Blades West,
156 West 72nd Street, between Columbus and Amsterdam Avenues, at 8:00 P.M.)
is for high-intermediate and advanced skaters. The Thursday Evening Roll (con-
venes at the Columbus Circle entrance to Central Park at 59th Street at 6:45
P.M.) is for all levels. The Sunday Morning Skate (also meets at the Columbus
Circle entrance to Central Park at 59th Street, at 11:00 A.M.) is open to all levels. All skates are canceled in the case of rain or wet streets; call to confirm.

NIKETOWN RUNNING CLUB
   6 East 57th Street (between Fifth and Madison Avenues)
   (212) 891–6453
   http://niketown.nike.com/niketown/info/event_locator.jsp
   Tuesday and Thursday at 6:30 P.M. and Saturday at 9:00 A.M.
This is one of those freebies that seems just too good to be true, but trust
me, it is for real. Three times a week Niketown hosts a group run for any and
all runners of all levels and abilities, and it is absolutely free. Tuesday and
Thursday nights at 6:30 and Saturday mornings at 9:00 runners gather at the
store on 57th Street and head into the park for organized runs. The session
starts off with a group stretch, and then runners can choose between three
different courses that range between 3 and 6 miles. Along the way, the
running-savvy Nike staff coach you through the runs and cheer you on as you
cross the finish line. You can then head back to the store to top the experience off with another quick group stretch, and then gorge yourself on the
free bagels, fruit, pastries, and bottled water. And if you are heading there
from work, you can even check your belongings . . . for free! Obviously, they
would not mind if you eventually bought a pair of their pricey running shoes,
so they always have plenty on hand for you to try on and even sample during your run.

SKY RINK AT CHELSEA PIERS
Pier 61 (23rd Street and the Hudson River)
(212) 336–6100
www.chelseapiers.com

THE CATCH   Skating is free, but they charge for skate rentals.

If you are looking to cool yourself off during the heat of the summer, strap on your ice skates and head down to the Sky Rink at Chelsea Piers on Sunday afternoon from noon to 4:00 p.m., late May to late August. They offer four hours of free general skating, but you will have to choke up about $7 for the skate rentals if you don't have your own pair.

TIME'S UP
(212) 802–8222
www.times-up.org

An environmental activist organization puts together bike and skate rides throughout the year with a point: Get rid of the cars! Critical Mass is an

Ladies, Start Your Skates!

You may have thought Roller Derby was a thing of the past (if you bothered to think about it at all), but the sport is making a sub-culture comeback with a feminist twist and punk-rock attitude. The Gotham Girls Rollar Derby is the home of this all-girl sport/spectacle. The league is made up of four teams, Manhattan Mayhem, Brooklyn Bombshells, Queens of Pain, and Bronx Gridlock, with team members who have aliases like Bitchie Slambora, Surly Temple, Stevie Kicks, and Barbara Ambush. And you can play a part in the slam-bash by volunteering to help lay the skating floor and unloading equipment at one of their raucous bouts. Of course, you will get to stick around and enjoy the games for free as well as the live music and after party. They generally have about fif-teen volunteers help out each match, and they need you to commit to showing up a few hours before the skating begins and hang out for about forty-five minutes after. To volunteer, e-mail info@gothamgirlsrollerderby.com, or for more information check out their Web site, www.gothamgirlsrollerderby.com

Get In-Line:
Central Park Skate Patrol

Not too steady on those in-line skates? Don't let that stop you from getting out there and hitting the road, but make your first stop (or crash!) at the Free Braking and Safety Clinic in Central Park, taught by certified volunteers. Stationed at the East and West Side 72nd Street entrances to the park every Saturday and Sunday from 12:30 to 5:30 P.M. (mid-April to mid-October), these kind and patient volunteers will hold your hand while you master the art of staying in an upright position with blades on your feet. Be sure to pick up a copy of their free **Central Park Pocket Guide for Skaters**, *which offers a great map and lots of useful information for the beginning skater. They also offer advanced group classes and lessons (but they charge for those). For more information call (212) 439–1234 or check out the Web site www.skatepatrol.org.*

"organized coincidence" that aims to exercise the rights of skaters and cyclists as road users. Meet at Union Square (14th Street and University Place) at 7:00 P.M. on the last Friday of every month, year-round. The Moonlight Ride/Roll through Central Park happens on the first Friday of every month at 10:00 P.M. The group meets at the Columbus Circle entrance to Central Park at 59th Street. The Prospect Park Moonlight Ride/Roll is the second Saturday of every month at 9:00 P.M. and starts at Grand Army Plaza (Flatbush Avenue and Eastern Parkway). Both are relaxing and easygoing tours through these parks. They also run many other rides throughout the five boroughs; check their Web site for details.

WEDNESDAY EVENING SKATE CLUB
North end of Union Square (17th Street, between Broadway and Park Avenue)
www.weskateny.org
This very popular skate tours different sections of the city each week and meets between 7:30 and 8:00 P.M. The group rides for about two hours. Open to all levels.

BOATING

THE DOWNTOWN BOATHOUSE

Pier 40 (Hudson River at Houston Street); Saturday and Sunday, 9:00 A.M.–6:00 P.M., and holidays.

Pier 96 (56th Street and the Hudson River); Saturday and Sunday, 9:00 A.M.–6:00 P.M., and holidays; open weekdays (June 15 to September 15) 5:00–7:00 P.M.; Wednesday classes, 6:00–8:00 P.M.

Riverside Park (at 72nd Street); Saturday and Sunday, 10:00 A.M.–5:00 P.M.

(646) 613–0375 (recorded information), (646) 613–0740 (daily status line)
www.downtownboathouse.org
May through October.

These three locations offer free kayaking on a first-come, first-served basis. They provide the boats, safety equipment, and brief instructions, and you provide the muscle. You can take a leisurely ride in the local embayment, and once you have some experience, you can join them on their free three-hour rides to the Statue of Liberty or the *Intrepid* Museum. The long rides leave from Pier 40 at 9:00 A.M. every Saturday and Sunday; get there earlier to put your name in the lottery for a slot. They also hold introductory kayaking classes every Wednesday evening from 6:00 to 8:00 P.M. at Pier 96. The boathouse is entirely volunteer-run. Volunteer and get yourself some advanced lessons and extra access to the boats.

FLOATING THE APPLE

Pier 40 (Hudson River at Houston Street); Tuesday and Thursday, 6:00 P.M. to dusk.

Pier 84 (Hudson River at 44th Street); call for schedule.
(917) 929–3670 or (212) 564–5412
www.floatingtheapple.org

Join the crew and hit the high seas . . . well, the choppy Hudson . . . for an exhilarating afternoon of rowing. This volunteer organization builds their own vintage-style Whitehall gigs and puts land-loving New Yorkers on the water. No experience necessary. These friendly folks will deftly guide you through the whole experience, and you will soon feel like you were born with an oar in your hand.

THE GOWANUS DREDGERS CANOE CLUB
2nd Street near Bond Street
Red Hook, Brooklyn
(718) 243–0849
www.waterfrontmuseum.org/dredgers
Weekday evenings and weekends by appointment, spring through fall.
Question: What do Venice and Brooklyn have in common? Answer: Great Italian food, pigeons, and canals. Yes, canals—but you can take a ride through Brooklyn's canals for free! (though the "O Solo Mio" may not be quite as good). E-mail a member of the club through the Web site, and they will be happy to take you on a canoe trip down this undiscovered trail. They also offer introductory canoe classes many Wednesday evenings and Sunday afternoons and the occasional walking or bicycle tour. Check their Web site for schedule and details.

For more free kayaking and conaoeing in Brooklyn, check out the Red Hook Boaters (917–676–6458; www.redhookboaters.org), and in Queens try the Long Island City Community Boathouse (718–228–9214; www.licboathouse.org).

EVERYBODY IN! PUBLIC POOLS

In addition to the pools at the recreation centers (see Appendix D), there are a number of city-run outdoor pools to cool yourself off in during those steamy summer months. These pools are all free and are open from July 4th through Labor Day. Daily hours are generally 11:00 A.M. to 7:00 P.M. You can get more information by clicking on "Things to Do" at the Web site www.nycgovparks.org or by calling the pools directly.

MANHATTAN

ASSER LEVY (MIDTOWN EAST), Asser Levy Place and East 23rd Street; (212) 447–2020.

DRY DOCK (EAST VILLAGE), East 10th Street between Avenues C and D; (212) 677–4481.

HAMILTON FISH (LOWER EAST SIDE), Pitt and Houston Streets; (212) 387–7687.

HIGHBRIDGE (WASHINGTON HEIGHTS), Amsterdam Avenue and West 173rd Street; (212) 927–2400.

JACKIE ROBINSON (HARLEM), Bradhurst Avenue and West 146th Street; (212) 234–9606.

JOHN JAY (UPPER EAST SIDE), East 77th Street east of York Avenue; (212) 794–6566.

LASKER (CENTRAL PARK), 110th Street and Lenox Avenue; (212) 534–7639 (Olympic-size pool).

MARCUS GARVEY (CENTRAL HARLEM), 124th Street and Fifth Avenue; (212) 410–2818.

SHELTERING ARMS, West 129th Street and Amsterdam Avenue; (212) 662–6191.

THOMAS JEFFERSON, East 112th Street and Amsterdam Avenue; (212) 860–1372 (Olympic-size pool).

TONY DAPOLITO (WEST VILLAGE), Clarkson Street and Seventh Avenue South; (212) 242–5228.

WAGNER (EAST HARLEM), East 124th Street between First and Second Avenues; (212) 534–4238.

THE BRONX

CLAREMONT, 170th Street and Clay Avenue; (718) 901–4792.

CROTONA, 173rd Street and Fulton Avenue; (718) 822–4440.

HAFFEN, Ely and Burke Avenues; (718) 379–2908.

MAPES, East 180th Street (between Mapes and Prospect Avenues); (718) 364–8876.

MULLALY, East 164th Street between Jerome and River Avenues; (718) 538–7083.

VAN CORTLANDT, West 242nd Street and Broadway; (718) 548–2415.

BROOKLYN

BETSY HEAD, Boyland, Livonia, and Dumont Avenues; (718) 965–6581.

Everything and Anything

Be sure to get yourself one of the invaluable New York City Department of Parks and Recreation special-events calendars for the year. It lists the vast numbers of activities going on in parks throughout the five boroughs from April through October. Many of these are one-day events that you don't want to miss—the Urban Park Rangers' Falcon Olympics, Haunted Halloween Walks, ethnic celebrations from every corner of the world in every corner of the city, opera, symphony, and philharmonic performances, sports tournaments, and much more. Call 311 or (212) NEW–YORK to get a copy, or check their Web site, www.nycgovparks.org, for an up-to-date schedule. And fear not: The schedule is free, and all the activities are gratis as well.

BUSHWICK HOUSES, Flushing Avenue and Humboldt Street; (718) 452–2116.

COMMODORE BARRY, Flushing and Park Avenues (between Navy and North Elliot Streets); (718) 243–2593.

DOUGLAS AND DEGRAW, Third Avenue and Nevins Street; (718) 625–3268.

THE FLOATING POOL LADY & BROOKLYN BRIDGE PARK BEACH, (718) 222–9742; www.brooklynbridgepark.org.

HOWARD, Glenmore and Mother Gaston Boulevard (at East New York Avenue); (718) 385–1023.

KOSCIUSKO (between Marcy and Dekalb Avenues); (718) 622–5271 (Olympic-size pool).

RED HOOK, Bay and Henry Streets; (718) 722–3211.

SUNSET PARK, Seventh Avenue (between 41st and 44th Streets); (718) 965–6578 (Olympic-size pool).

QUEENS

ASTORIA, 19th Street and 23rd Drive; (718) 626–8620 (Olympic-size pool).

FISHER, 99th Street and Thirty-second Avenue; (718) 779–8356.

FORT TOTTEN, 338 Story Avenue (between Murray Avenue and Shore Road); (718) 224–4031.

LIBERTY, 173rd Street and 106th Avenue; (718) 657–4995.

STATEN ISLAND

FABER, Faber Street and Richmond Terrace; (718) 816–5259.

LYONS, Pier 6 and Victory Boulevard; (718) 816–9571.

TOTTENVILLE, Hylan Boulevard and Joline Avenue; (718) 356–8242.

WEST BRIGHTON, Henderson Avenue (between Broadway and Chappel Street); (718) 816–5019.

BEACHES

While no one would confuse New York City with Maui, it does have its fair share of sandy beaches within city limits. The city parks department maintains 14 miles of public beaches, all of which are open from Memorial Day through Labor Day. And you know New York has a much better subway system than Maui. In fact, all city beaches are accessible by public transportation, though some more easily than others. For more information go to www.nycparks.com and click on "Things to Do," then click "Activities/Facilities."

BRIGHTON BEACH AND CONEY ISLAND
Brighton 1st Street to West 37th Street
Brooklyn
(718) 946–1350
www.nycgovparks.org

These two beaches are really one long stretch of shoreline that's a very popular destination because of its legendary reputation and easy accessibility. It's located at the end of the F, B, W, and Q subway lines. The throngs also show up because the area offers so much more than just sand and sun. A trip to Coney Island isn't complete without a walk through Astroland (what remains of the famous amusement park) and a ride on the oh-so-rickety and oh-so-thrilling roller coaster, the Cyclone (a kick worth paying $6 a ride; 718–372–0275; www.astroland.com). Astroland also has a fireworks display every Friday night with free cabaret performances beginning at 8:00 P.M. during the summer. Don't miss the stalls of antiques/junk/whatever being hawked along Surf Avenue. Farther down the boardwalk is Brighton Beach. Known as "Odessa by the Sea," Brighton has become the home of New York's thriving Russian immigrant community, and a walk along Brighton Avenue certainly makes you feel like you've been transported to the heart of Mother Russia. There are also some amazing deals to be found on fresh fruits, vegetables, and rugelach along the avenue.

JACOB RIIS PARK
Fort Tilden, Gateway National Park
Rockaway, Queens
(718) 318–4300
www.nps.gov/gate
Run by the National Park Service, this small strip of sand located just a short hop from Brooklyn is a very popular destination, particularly on the weekends. When the public beach is overrun, venture onto the private beaches of Rockaway, just a short walk along the dunes. From Brooklyn take the Q35 bus, and from Queens take the Q35 or the Q22 bus.

MANHATTAN BEACH
Oriental Boulevard (from Ocean Avenue to Mackenzie Street)
Brooklyn
(718) 946–1373
www.nycgovparks.org

Open the Gate:
Gateway National Recreation Area

Administered by the National Park Service, Gateway is made up of 26,000 acres of parkland that runs through Brooklyn, Queens, Staten Island, and into northern New Jersey. There's a huge array of activities for kids and adults, from nature walks, concerts, and campfire sing-alongs to sailing lessons, gardening classes, and yoga on the beach. All activities run by the NPS are free and open to all. For a guide to their programs, locations, and activities, call (718) 338–3338 or check their Web site, www.nps.gov/gate.

Located just a bit farther down the shore from Brighton Beach, this more secluded beach isn't quite as populated as the big guys next door and also offers areas for you to fire up the barbecue and picnic. The buses B1 and B49 will take you to the beach.

ORCHARD BEACH
Pelham Bay Park
The Bronx
(718) 885–2275
www.nycgovparks.org
Looking out on Long Island Sound, this is the beach of choice for Bronx residents. The waters are generally calm, and the promenade is quite lively, especially on weekends. They offer free Latin music concerts on the beach every Sunday in the summer. Take the number 12 bus from the Pelham Bay subway station (6 train).

ROCKAWAY BEACH
Beach 9th Street in Far Rockaway to Beach 149th Street
Neponsit, Queens
(718) 318–4000
www.nycgovparks.org
Popular with Brooklyn and Queens residents, this long stretch of beach (7 miles) runs almost the entire length of Rockaway. Take the A train toward Far Rockaway; there are many beach stops along the way. If you are looking to hang ten, head to New York's best surfing beaches from Beach 87th to 92nd Streets (take the A train to Beach 90th Street) or Beach 67th to 69th Streets (take the A train to Beach 67th Street).

SOUTH AND MIDLAND BEACHES
Fort Wadsworth to Miller Field
Staten Island
(718) 987–0709
www.nycgovparks.org
Staten Island's own secret beach that's hardly ever crowded.

"No entertainment is so cheap as reading, nor any pleasure so lasting."

—Lady Mary Wortley Montague

LIBRARIES ARE THE ultimate resource for anyone who wants it all but doesn't want to spend anything to get it. After all, the libraries were established by Mr. "A Penny Saved Is a Penny Earned" himself, Benjamin Franklin. New York has three public library systems: the New York Public Library (in Manhattan, the Bronx, and Staten Island), the Brooklyn Public Library, and the Queens Borough Public Library. The three systems have a network of research libraries and local branches with more than 200 locations throughout the five boroughs (see Appendix C for a complete list of branch locations). At each of these branches, you'll find not only bookshelves full of reading material but also a wide selection of videos and CDs of every kind of music conceivable. Some locations, like the Mid-Manhattan and Donnell Libraries, can rival Blockbuster and Tower Records in their video and CD selections.

You also have access to computers and the Internet as well as computer classes. In fact, you can find free classes in everything from origami and quilting to job placement and starting a small business. Many branches also have a regular schedule of music, films, theater, and readings. There are many private libraries in New York, too; some charge a membership fee to borrow materials, but all can be a great source for in-house research.

RESEARCH CENTERS

THE NEW YORK PUBLIC LIBRARY FOR THE PERFORMING ARTS

40 Lincoln Center Plaza (65th Street and Amsterdam Avenue)
(212) 870-1630
www.nypl.org/research/lpa/lpa.html

Returned to its home at Lincoln Center after a three-year renovation, this is home to one of the world's most extensive collections of materials in the performing arts. Not limited to books, the library is particularly well known for its huge collections of historic recordings, videotapes, CDs, records, autograph manuscripts, correspondence, sheet music, stage designs, press clippings, programs, posters, and photographs. You can borrow a great deal of the materials in the library, though the archival collections are only available for reference. Being the performing arts library, you would expect they might have a performance or two every now and then—and they certainly don't disappoint. You'll find a full schedule of presentations by prominent actors, composers, musicians, writers, choreographers, and dancers throughout the week.

THE NEW YORK PUBLIC LIBRARY HUMANITIES AND SOCIAL SCIENCES LIBRARY

Fifth Avenue and 42nd Street
(212) 930-0830
www.nypl.org/research/chss

This landmark Beaux Arts building is home to more than one million books, 135 miles of hidden bookshelves, and two friendly lions named Patience and Fortitude. You cannot take any books out of this library, but you are welcome to spend endless hours in their stunning reading rooms—and you will want to. The building underwent a multimillion-dollar renovation, and the grandeur of these rooms, particularly the Rose Reading Room, guarantees you'll be thinking exceptionally intelligent thoughts. Don't miss the one-hour tours of the historic facility every Monday through Saturday at 11:00 A.M. and 2:00 P.M. Tours of changing exhibitions in Gottesman Hall begin at 12:30 and 2:30 P.M. They also offer an array of classes at the South Court Training Center.

SCHOMBURG CENTER FOR RESEARCH IN BLACK CULTURE
515 Malcolm X Boulevard (at 135th Street)
(212) 491–2200
www.nypl.org/research/sc
This is a national research library devoted to collecting, preserving, and providing access to resources documenting the experiences of peoples of African descent throughout the world. Their collection is entirely noncirculation, but they make many of the historic materials available to the public through an extensive schedule of exhibitions, publications, and educational, scholarly, and cultural programs. They do charge for some performances, but many are free. Be sure to grab a free MP3 audio tour when viewing any of their exhibitions.

SCIENCE, INDUSTRY, AND BUSINESS LIBRARY
188 Madison Avenue (at 34th Street)
(212) 592–7000
www.nypl.org/research/sibl

Reference Desk

You will find mentions throughout this book of various goings-on at public libraries around the city. Here's a rundown of which chapters contain detailed information on these happenings:

For the complete list of **PUBLIC LIBRARY BRANCH LOCATIONS** *in the five boroughs, see Appendix C.*

For *listing of branch libraries that offer* **REGULARLY SCHEDULED FILMS,** *see pages 53–54.*

For **FILMS FOR KIDS** *at libraries, see pages 131–34.*

For **STORYTELLING AND READING** *at libraries, see pages 143–44.*

For **CLASSES** *at libraries, see page 153.*

For **CONCERTS** *at libraries, see page 33.*

"Get Ya Free Money Heeere!"

Okay, it's not as simple as that, but there is plenty of it out there in the form of grants and scholarships from private and public organizations, and the Foundation Center can help you find it (free of charge, of course). The library will help you sift through the more than 47,000 private and corporate giving programs to find the ones that are the best targets for your project. They have free training sessions on funding research, proposal writing, proposal budgeting, and even the occasional networking breakfast (with free pastries and coffee!). The Foundation Center (79 Fifth Avenue, second floor, at 16th Street) is open Monday, Tuesday, Thursday, and Friday, 10:00 A.M. to 5:00 P.M.; and Wednesday until 8:00 P.M. For more information call (212) 620–4230 or check the Web site www.fdncenter.org.

The nation's largest public information center devoted solely to science and business, the research center houses both a circulating library and an extensive noncirculating collection (1.4 million volumes). The library's Electronic Information Center connects users to the hundreds of internal and external electronic information resources, including Internet databases, CD-ROMs, electronic journals, and online services. The Electronic Training Center offers ongoing classes in computer programs, the Internet, research, and business and industry issues. Combined, the two centers have more than a hundred computer workstations ready for public use. Take the free one-hour tour Tuesday or Thursday at 2:00 P.M. to learn more about the facilities. For tour information call (212) 592–7000.

PRIVATE LIBRARIES

FRENCH INSTITUTE/ALLIANCE FRANÇAISE
22 East 60th Street (between Park and Madison Avenues)
(212) 355–6100
www.fiaf.org
Hours: Monday through Thursday, 11:30 A.M.–8:00 P.M.; Saturday, 9:30 A.M.–1:30 P.M.

Nonmembers do not have borrowing privileges. Membership is $90 a year.

This is the largest collection of all-French materials in the United States. You're welcome to spend all day in the spacious library reading any of the 30,000 French books, perusing the hundreds of French magazines, watching any of the 1,000 French videos, or listening to the many French CDs, French books on tape, or French cassettes. In other words, if it's French, it's here.

Got a Question? Get an Answer!

Q: *Need to know the capital of Lithuania or the correct spelling for Engelbert Humperdinck? Then give a call to free library reference lines. They are there to answer any question you have, from the most obscure facts to the most commonly asked question on all subjects. The New York Public Library's telephone reference line is (212) 340–0849 (Monday through Saturday, 9:00 A.M. to 6:00 P.M.) (Or you can chat with a librarian online though their Web site, www.nypl.org, Monday through Friday, 9:00 A.M. to 5:00 P.M. Click on "Ask a Librarian.") The Brooklyn Public Library's reference phone is (718) 230–2100, ext. 3 (Monday and Friday, 9:00 A.M. to 6:00 P.M.; Tuesday through Thursday, 9:00 A.M. to 9:00 P.M.; Saturday, 10:00 A.M. to 6:00 P.M.; and Sunday, 1:00 to 6:00 P.M.), and the folks at the Queens Borough Public Library can help you (718) 990–0728 (Monday through Friday, 10:00 A.M. to 8:45 P.M. and Saturday, 10:00 A.M. to 4:00 P.M.) Or you can click on "Ask a Librarian" on their Web site (www.queenslibrary.org) to chat online with a librarian during the same hours.).*

A: *The capital of Lithuania is Vilnius. Answer courtesy of the Brooklyn Public Library Telephone Reference Line.*

A: *The correct spelling for both the 1960s nightclub singer and the nineteenth-century German composer of* Hansel and Gretel *is Engelbert Humperdinck. Answer courtesy of the New York Public Library Telephone Reference line.*

GOETHE INSTITUTE

1014 Fifth Avenue (between 82nd and 83rd Streets)
(212) 439–8700
www.goethe.de/uk/ney
Hours: Tuesday and Thursday, noon–7:00 P.M.; Wednesday, Friday, and
Saturday, noon–5:00 P.M.

**Nonmembers do not have borrowing privileges.
Membership is $10 a year.**

This is the German version of the French Institute. The big difference here is
that they have half as many books, videos, CDs, newspapers, and magazines.
(And, of course, they're in German, not French.)

INSTITUTO CERVANTES LIBRARY

211–215 East 49th Street (between Second and Third Avenues)
(212) 308–7720, ext. 104
www.cervantes.org
Hours: Tuesday and Wednesday, 11:30 A.M.–7:30 P.M; Thursday and Friday,
noon–7:00 P.M.; Saturday, 10:00 A.M.–1:30 P.M.

**Nonmembers do not have borrowing privileges.
Membership is $50 a year.**

Okay, this time take the French Institute, double the size of the collection,
translate everything into Spanish, and you have the Instituto Cervantes Library.

THE NEW YORK ACADEMY OF MEDICINE LIBRARY

1216 Fifth Avenue (at 103rd Street)
(212) 822–7300
www.nyam.org
Hours: Monday, Tuesday, Thursday, and Friday, 9:00 A.M.–5:00 P.M.;
Wednesday, 9:00 A.M.–7:00 P.M.

This noncirculating research library houses the second-largest medical collection in the United States, following the National Library of Medicine in
Bethesda, Maryland. Its extensive facilities include more than one million
volumes, more than 1,400 current journal subscriptions, and a variety of
electronic resources. They also offer a full curriculum of free classes in various research methods and techniques to make your use of their library (and
all libraries!) much more effective.

PAT PARKER/VITO RUSSO CENTER LIBRARY
The Lesbian, Gay, Bisexual & Transgender Community Center
208 West 13th Street (between Seventh and Eighth Avenues)
(212) 620–7310
www.gaycenter.org
Hours: Monday through Thursday, 6:00–9:00 P.M.; Saturday,
1:00–4:00 P.M.

 **Nonmembers do not have full borrowing privileges.
Membership is $75.**

The collection at this library is geared toward everything to do with gay, lesbian, bisexual, transgender, and AIDS studies. The library has a collection of about 12,000 books and more than 500 videos (documentaries and features). When you borrow videos, they ask you to leave a refundable deposit for the one-week loan.

"Opinions are the cheapest commodities on Earth."

—Frank Bacic

TIMES, SHMIMES. You don't need to throw away $1.00 a day ($3.50 on Sunday!) to get your fill of information in New York City. Whatever your interest or point of view, there's a free newspaper out there for you. Granted, the news you get from some of the free presses in the city might have a bit of a skewed worldview. But if you're looking for community news, local entertainment listings, and happenings around town, there are plenty of papers to pick up that you don't need to drop a quarter, a dime, a nickel, or even a penny to get. You'll find most of these papers in those ubiquitous newspaper boxes on almost any major street corner in Manhattan. Some can be found throughout the boroughs but are easiest to come by in Manhattan.

AM NEW YORK

(212) 239–5555
www.am-newyork.com
Headline: Pint-size Publication Packs a Punch. One of the most welcome additions to the freescape of New York City, this easily digestible daily newspaper gives you all the news that fits in twenty pages. The perfect companion
for your subway ride to work, the tabloid touches on local, national, and
international topics and has sections (okay, pages) devoted to travel, food,
sports, classifieds, and local events. My favorite feature is their *4 for Free* section, which lists four free events going on around New York every day. Pick
up your free copy any weekday at street-corner boxes throughout the five
boroughs.

BIG APPLE PARENT, BROOKLYN PARENT, AND QUEENS PARENT

((718) 638–8600
www.parentsknow.com
This monthly magazine is dedicated entirely to parenting in New York City.
Each month's issue has intelligent and informative articles, an extensive calendar of events, and lots and lots of advertising. Be aware that the magazine
is targeted toward parents with no shortage of cash, so there's no focus on
doing things on the cheap. There is, however, some very useful information

Extra! Extra!

*I have to confess that there are times when even I read one of
the big daily newspapers, either to get better informed or, in the
case of the* Post, *just for laughs. Still, that's no excuse to spend
money. If you have access to the Web, you have free access to the
newspapers. Every one of the major dailies publishes practically
its entire contents, along with even more information, on the
Web every day. For the* New York Times, *check out www.nytimes.com.
The* New York Daily News *is at www.nydailynews.com, and the*
New York Post's *Web site is www.nypost.com. If you feel the need
to get some ink on your hands, you can always find a copy at
any local library.*

for all to be found within their pages. You can find copies in street-corner boxes and stores throughout Manhattan, in Brooklyn Heights, Carroll Gardens, and Park Slope in Brooklyn, and throughout Queens. Check the Web site or call for specific locations.

DOWNTOWN EXPRESS

(212) 242–6162

www.downtownexpress.com

Downtown Express is a biweekly newspaper covering all the goings-on in Tribeca, Battery Park City, the South Street Seaport, and the Wall Street area in lower Manhattan. This slim publication manages to cover the huge amount of local news, arts, sports, and other happenings below Canal Street. The listings section includes local theater, music, and particularly good coverage of art galleries in the area. The paper is widely distributed in street-corner boxes and stores below Canal Street.

GO NYC

(888) 466–9244

www.gomag.com

This glossy monthly mini-magazine is the place to GO for all things lesbian in NYC. You can find copies in bars and stores all around downtown and selected locations in Brooklyn and Queens. Check their Web site to find a copy near you.

HX

(212) 352–3535

www.hx.com

As you can tell from the full name of this weekly, *Homo eXtra* is a gay magazine. *HX* occasionally touches on such subjects as politics and current events but is best relied on for its bar and club listings, reviews, gossip, and nothing-left-to-the-imagination advertising. You can find copies at every gay bar and store in the city as well as some street-corner boxes in Chelsea.

JEWISH SENTINEL

(212) 244–4949

As you might imagine, this is the source for all things Jewish around New York—from articles on Israel and the Jewish perspective on New York to a selected listing of cultural events, gatherings, galleries, and performances that might be of interest to the Jewish community. You can pick up a copy at street-corner boxes placed randomly around Manhattan; call for specific locations.

METRO SPORTS
(212) 563-7329
www.metrosportsny.com

The source for everything on the go in New York. Articles and listings on running, cycling, skiing, skating, marathons, triathlons, sports medicine, and
new equipment. Most of all, the magazine is a vehicle for a lot of advertising, though the calendar of events is particularly thorough and useful. *Metro
Sports* is published once a month and can be found in any sporting goods
store around the city.

NEW YORK BLADE NEWS
(212) 352-3535
www.nyblade.com

New York's weekly gay community newspaper covers local and national issues,
personalities, and events affecting gay men and lesbians in the city. It's also a
good source for arts listings and community events. The paper is distributed
widely on street corners and stores throughout Manhattan and at selected locations throughout the boroughs; call or check the Web site for specific locations.

NEW YORK PRESS
(212) 244-2282
www.nypress.com

New York's *alternative* alternative newspaper, the *Press* is chock-full of opinionated and often very funny articles on the politics, characters, events, and
arts of the city. Its film, music, and events listings are among the best in the
city. You'll find copies on almost any street corner in Manhattan and parts of
Brooklyn (downtown, Park Slope, and Cobble Hill). Like the *Voice,* grab a copy
early in the week; you may have a hard time finding one once the weekend
rolls around.

NEW YORK RESIDENT
(212) 993-9410
www.newyorkresident.com

A weekly magazine with a focus on the culture and politics of the city.
You'll find regular articles on health, fashion, travel, and restaurants, as
well as weekly theater, film, and music picks. The *Resident* is distributed
widely in street-corner boxes in Manhattan.

NEXT MAGAZINE
(212) 627-0165
www.nextmagazine.net

Almost an exact clone of *HX.*

THE ONION
(212) 627–1972
www.theonion.com

This on-target satirical news weekly takes on national issues, news figures, and "local" events all over the country. While their view on the news can be hysterically funny, their arts section, "The A.V. Club," is surprisingly serious and extensive. The section doesn't include timetables or movie locations, but they do include in-depth reviews and features on almost every film in the theaters at any given time, from Hollywood blockbusters to independents and documentaries. You'll also find good articles on videos and local music picks. You can grab a copy from their boxes located all over Manhattan (most plentifully below 23rd Street and in the Columbia University area) and in Park Slope and Williamsburg in Brooklyn.

VILLAGE VOICE
(212) 475–3300
www.villagevoice.com

The original and still the largest alternative news weekly. Since 1955 the *Voice* has been the place to go to get the other view on anything: politics, art, theater, film, literature, sex, and even a unique take on horoscopes. The paper is sure to annoy you with some of its articles and engage you with others, but you will almost always find them provocative. Even if you never agree with what they have to say, the *Voice* is always worth picking up for the extensive music, film, theater, dance, and art listings, and the sprawling classifieds, which include their no-holds-barred personals. Grab a copy out of one of the red boxes on most street corners around the five boroughs or free at newsstands and stores around the city. Get your copy early in the week; by the time the weekend rolls around, the boxes are usually empty. You can always find a pile of papers outside their downtown office on Bowery between 5th and 6th Streets. Check the Web site to find a place to pick up a copy near you.

WEST SIDE SPIRIT AND OUR TOWN
(212) 268–8600
www.ourtownnyc.com

Both put out by the same publisher and editorial staff, these two weekly papers are basically mirror images of each other, with *Our Town* covering the East Side and the *West Side Spirit* covering (you guessed it) the West Side. Both cover the local politics, crime, and events of their areas and share a good citywide listing of arts and community events, with a strong focus on free activities. Both can be found in corner boxes and stores on their respective sides of town between 59th and 110th Streets.

"There are many things that we would throw away, if we were not afraid that others might pick them up."

—Oscar Wilde

ALL AROUND THE city you'll spot them every other day of the week. Some people call them piles of trash, but the trained eye clearly recognizes them as mountains of treasures. Furnishing New York apartments by "recycling" is not only good for the environment, it's great for the bank account. It's a long-held tradition and a way of life for students, artists, collectors, and anyone with an open mind and a creative eye. You will be shocked at the high caliber of items some people consider garbage, but it makes sense. Consider the fact that New Yorkers on average earn a great deal of money but are forced to live in some of the smallest apartments this side of a shoe box. The result is, folks end up throwing away some mighty fine used stuff to make room for some newer, finer stuff.

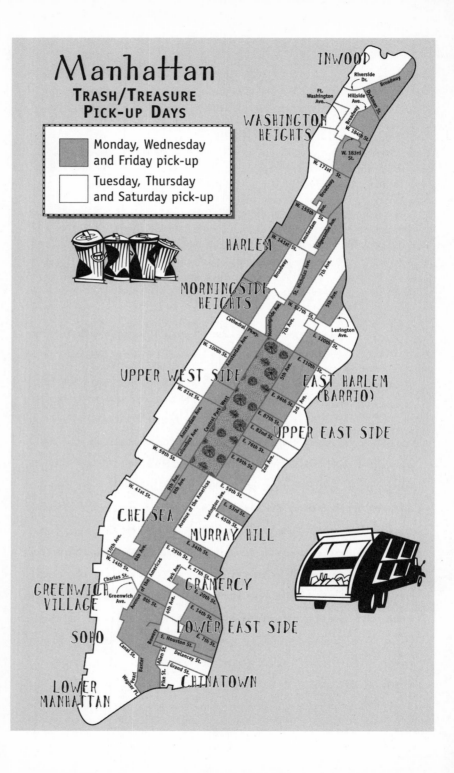

Freecycle:
A Little Give & Take

Here is the scenario: Someone across town has just upgraded to a brand-new couch and wants to get rid of that oh-so-cozy but slightly shoddy pullout that has seen him through the leaner times. You are new to town and just finished shelling out every dime you have to secure that pricey New York studio, but now you have to furnish it. It is a match made in heaven, but how do we make the connection? Freecycle! This Web-based recycling group is in existence to empty out your spare closet and fill your neighbor's, or vice versa. All you have to do is go to their Web site, www.freecycle.org, and connect to the New York branch (this is an international movement verging on two million members worldwide). Once you become a member, for free of course, your inbox will literally be flooded with e-mail offers for stuff (useful and not so useful) every day. A typical day's offerings can run the gamut from the worthwhile (including furniture, books, appliances, clothes) to the kooky (advice, leftovers, broken glass bottles) to the incredibly specific (2 yards of yellow felt, size 9.5 women's sensible brown shoes, 75 small packets of soy sauce). You are even able to post "Wanted" messages for practically anything you might need. The New York list has a membership of more than 25,000 members (and growing), so, anything you want you can get, anything you want to get rid of someone else wants, and many things you did not know you needed are up for grabs.

FAVORITE FINDS

Almost anything you need or want can be found on the street. I can't tell you how many times I have said "I need" this or that, only to come across that exact "this or that" a few days later on the street. You are limited only by your willingness to forage and schlep. Obviously, the smaller the item you're in the market for, the more effort you'll have to put into your search. If you're interested in larger furnishings, however, the sky's the limit. Here are some of my favorite items I've picked up from the street over the years:

Antique trunks	Ironing board
Antique wooden milk crate	Leather easy chair
Artwork	Luggage
Bookcases	Microwave oven
Chest of drawers	Mirrors
Coffee table	Oriental rugs
Couch	Ottoman
Decorative window flower box	Plates, bowls, silverware
Desk	Power Mac computer, monitor,
Desk chairs	and printer
Director's chairs	Spice rack
Doctor's office scale	Storage boxes
End tables	Telephone
Exercise mat	Toaster oven
File cabinets	Vacuum cleaner
Footstool	Wicker basket
Halogen torch lamp	Window screens

Who knows what *you* might find!

CURBSIDE SHOPPING TIPS

Here are some helpful rules to live by when you are on the prowl:

1. **SHOP IN THE BEST NEIGHBORHOODS:** The better off the neighbors, the better the garbage.

2. **KNOW WHEN THE SHOPS ARE OPEN FOR BUSINESS:** Consult the accompanying map to see what days the Department of Sanitation will be around to take away the merchandise. It's best to do your hunting the night before scheduled pick-ups. You'll generally start to notice piles appearing in the late afternoon and early evening.

3. **WHEN IN DOUBT, DON'T LEAVE IT OUT:** If you're considering an item, take it. Undoubtedly it will not be there if you decide to come back for it. But if you take it and it doesn't work or fit your need, you can always redonate it. Nothing ventured, nothing gained.

The Big Salvation (Army)!

Not that I'm endorsing the idea of spending cash, but there are times when you can't wait to stumble across that perfect headboard, desk, or butcher-block countertop, and money must be spent. The best option is always to shop at any of New York's many thrift stores. While whole books have been written on this subject alone, there are some standout shops to head for when you're in the market for furniture, appliances, or knickknacks of any kind. Most local thrift stores offer a smattering of sofas, chairs, and china, but their space is limited, so the selection is as well. Still, in each borough you'll find a main Salvation Army Thrift Store (usually connected to a warehouse) with huge assortments of goods. While these stores may not be around the corner, the prices and selection make them worth the trip. For some other shopping ideas, see the chapter "Shopping: A Tale of Two Streets," and for a good list of thrift stores throughout the city, check out the Web site www.salvationarmy.usa east.org. Here are the super Salvation Army stores in each borough:

MANHATTAN: *536 West 46th Street (between Tenth and Eleventh Avenues); (212) 757–2311.*

BROOKLYN: *436 Atlantic Avenue (between Bond and Nevins Streets); (718) 834–1562.*

22 Quincy Street (between Classon and Downing Streets); (718) 622–5686.

THE BRONX: *4109 Park Avenue (at 175th Street); (718) 583–3500.*

QUEENS: *34–02 Steinway Street (between Thirty-fourth and Thirty-fifth Avenues); (718) 472–2414.*

STATEN ISLAND: *2053 Clove Road (at Mosel Avenue); (718) 442–3080.*

4. DON'T BE A HOG: If you find something that turns out not to fit your need, set it back out on the street right away. The temptation is to hold on to this great find and hope you can find a use for it someday. The problem is, you'll end up cluttering up your small studio apartment with stuff you can't use, and the longer you hold on to it, the harder it will be to part with it. Just like ripping off that Band-Aid, do it quick and it will be less painful. And no doubt, someone else will pick it up and be very grateful to you.

Freegans: Dumpster Dining

The Freegans, truly the masters of the fine art of dumpster diving, are a group that is on a mission to put an end to our society's rampant materialism by recycling and making use of all the handy materials already produced . . . and chucked out. Every week they lead "trash tours" in various neighborhoods throughout the city where they come up with a huge smorgasbord of discards, and they are always happy to share their techniques and bounty. Nothing is off-limits to these folks—furniture, cleaning supplies, household items, office supplies, and food— . . . yes, food! In fact, they specialize in finding gratis goodies. This may sound a bit gross to you, but rest assured we are not talking about half-eaten sandwiches and rotten apples here; this is all packaged and sanitary stuff. Their plan is to "shop" in the trash of some of the finer markets (Food Emporium, Gourmet Garage, Zabars, etc.) and pick out the items that the retailer feels they can't put on their shelves any longer but are perfectly delicious treats for the savvy scavenger. The Freegans also take part in a wealth of other activities every week, including free build-a-bicycle and bicycle-repair workshops and furniture hunts and repair classes. Even if you are not interested in taking part in their tours and hunts, you should definitely sign up for their e-mails. These people are in on the ground floor of every free event and activity in New York, and they send out great listings to all who sign on. Check them out at www.freegan.info or call (347) 724–6954.

5. **A LITTLE WORK GOES A LONG WAY:** Repaint it, refinish it, change the knobs, or reupholster the cushion and presto! It's good as new!

6. **CLEAN IT.** (Hey, you never know.)

7. **ENJOY IT.**

HAPPY HUNTING!

"I always say shopping is
cheaper than a psychiatrist."
—Tammy Faye Messner

IF YOU *MUST* SPEND MONEY—and as a rule I do not endorse the practice—there are a couple of streets you should know about to keep this awful habit in check. Of course, there are thousands of stores throughout the city where you can find "a deal." There are also tons of books that tell you where to find these stores, but I'm just going to include a few of the best. On 17th and 32nd Streets, you'll find clusters of some of my favorite shops in New York City—the places where I shop almost to the exclusion of any other stores in town. What makes them so great? You guessed it: great stuff, really cheap.

On West 32nd Street you will find a couple of stores that can supply you with all the essentials of life (food, dishes, books, clothes, furnishings, office supplies, cosmetics, electronics, toys . . .) and many of the absurdities of life ("As Seen on TV" items, last year's fad items, "has-been" pop star paraphernalia, and more) at ridiculously low prices. West 17th Street is the place to head to check out three of the best thrift stores around. These secondhand shops are not necessarily the cheapest in the five boroughs, but you can snag some amazingly high-quality finds at very respectable prices at these shops.

32ND STREET: BARGAIN PARADISE

JACK'S 99¢ STORES
110 West 32nd Street (between Sixth and Seventh Avenues)
(212) 268–9962

You may have come across other 99-cent stores in your travels, but Jack's is hands-down the best there is. This huge store is overflowing with bargains, from the frozen foods section to every household item or office supply you could ever need. While some of the goods are made by companies you may not recognize, a surprisingly large amount of the merchandise is brand name. The wares change on a daily basis, so you could walk the aisles every day and be almost guaranteed of finding something you can't live without (for 99 cents, that is). Located upstairs is Jack's World, where they have another great selection of bargains on higher-ticket items (appliances, furniture, clothes, housewares, toys and games), but here they don't keep to the 99-cent limit. There is a second Jack's 99¢ location at 16 East 40th Street (between Fifth and Madison Avenues) and another Jack's World at 45th West 45th Street (between Fifth and Sixth Avenues).

WEBERS CLOSEOUTS
116 West 32nd Street (between Sixth and Seventh Avenues)
(212) 564–3606

Just a couple of doors down from Jack's, Webers is another great source for steals, though they no longer rise to the challenge of keeping everything priced less than a buck. Still, there are plenty of good deals to be had if you're willing to do a little work sifting through the schlock. There are many other Webers located in the Bronx and Brooklyn, but none quite as expansive as this one.

17TH STREET: FIRST IN SECONDHAND

HOUSING WORKS THRIFT SHOPS
143 West 17th Street (between Sixth and Seventh Avenues)
(212) 366–0820
www.housingworksauctions.com

Fruit of the Streets

Over the last few years, fruit stands have begun to sprout up on almost every street corner in the city. But one seems to stand above all others as the place to get more bananas for your buck. A guy named Smiley, or "The Fruit Nazi" (depending on whom you talk to), runs a few Midtown stands where you're likely to find the kind of produce you don't usually see other street vendors selling: plump strawberries, mangos, mesclun, kiwis, as well as the usual apples, tomatoes, peppers, and more. The catch is that he sells them for pennies, but only in large quantities—10 large tomatoes for $1.00, four pounds of grapes for $2.00, five pounds of gourmet salad mix for $3.00. Also, he doesn't take too kindly to you picking out the fruit (hence "The Fruit Nazi"). Let him pick your pears and you'll stay on his good side. The main stand is on 48th Street, just east of Sixth Avenue. He runs another stand with much of the same selection at 42nd Street and Third Avenue. These stands are open for business Monday through Friday, after 3:00 P.M.

Think of Housing Works Thrift Shops as the Bergdorf Goodman of secondhand. The designer clothing, furniture, housewares, art, antiques, books, CDs, and records are certainly a cut above what you would find in your neighborhood Salvation Army or Goodwill. The prices are also a bit higher, but not much. They often run daily specials, making the place a steal. There are six other locations around the city (202 East 77th Street, between Second and Third Avenues; 306 Columbus Avenue, between 74th and 75th Streets; 157 East 23rd Street, between Third and Lexington Avenues; 245 West 10th Street, between Hudson and Bleecker Streets; 1730 Second Avenue, on the corner of 90th Street; and in Brooklyn at 122 Montague Street, near the corner of Henry Street). Housing Works is New York's largest provider of housing and supportive services to homeless, formerly homeless, and at-risk men, women, and children living with HIV and AIDS.

ANGEL STREET
118 West 17th Street (between Sixth and Seventh Avenues)
(212) 229–0546
www.angelthriftshop.org
Continue along 17th Street a bit farther, and you'll come across Angel Street. Much like Housing Works, it gets great high-quality donations but with more

of an emphasis on furnishings and accessories than clothes (though the clothes they do sell, they sell very cheaply). You'll also find enticing daily specials at this boutiquelike shop. All proceeds from Angel Street benefit individuals and families affected by substance abuse, HIV, AIDS, and mental illness.

17 @ 17 THRIFT STORE

17 West 17th Street (between Fifth and Sixth Avenues)
(212) 727–7516
www.ujafedny.org/thriftshop

Walk farther down the street. Okay, you do actually have to cross an avenue, but since you're in the neighborhood, it's worth stopping in. This store is almost always so overflowing with furniture, clothes, and tchotchkes that you can count on them having a 50 to 75 percent off sale going on. All proceeds benefit the Women's Campaign of the UJA-Federation of New York, helping Jewish people in need around the world.

"And the turtles, of course . . .
all the turtles are free.

As turtles and, maybe,
all creatures should be."

—Dr. Seuss

PETS: CANINE, FELINE, BOTTOM LINE

WHETHER YOUR PREFERENCE is cats or dogs (or hamsters, rabbits, or even the occasional turtle), there are plenty of little companions to be had for the asking. By opting for an adopted pet, you will not only be saving a cage full of cash and giving a home to a needy (and loving) buddy, but you will also be doing your part to put an end to the animal mills that churn out unhealthy dogs and cats for pet stores. Most of the shelters around the city do require some "donation" to offset their expenses, but here are some ways to increase the size of your household without decreasing the size of your bank account. Also here are some suggestions on where to go to keep your Pekinese in the pink without spending much green.

Surfing for Pets

Here are a few good Web sites to check out for free pet adoptions. There is also no charge to list pets on these sites for adoption.

WWW.ANIMALALLIANCENYC.ORG, *New York City's official animal information site, provides information and links to practically everywhere you can possibly adopt a pet in the five boroughs as well as information on licensing; low-cost spay, neuter, and pet-care options; events; and discounts for services.*

WWW.NEWYORK.CRAIGSLIST.ORG, *the classified section of the Internet, has a listing for every pet need from pet portraits to adopting or buying every kind of pet you can think of. New listings are added every day and throughout the day. Craigslist includes my favorite section, "Free," where you will find listings for furniture, tickets, appliances, books, antiques, classes, and so much more.*

WWW.PETFINDER.ORG, *national and local clearinghouse for shelters and rescue organizations that list thousands of animals by breed and location. Many of these shelters do suggest donations ranging from $30 to $100.*

LOW-COST PET CARE AND ADOPTIONS

ANIMAL CARE & CONTROL OF NEW YORK CITY
Bronx: 464 East Fordham Road (between Washington and Third Avenues)
Brooklyn: 2336 Linden Boulevard (between Essex Street and Shepherd Avenue)
Manhattan: 326 East 110th Street (between First and Second Avenues)
Queens: 92-29 Queens Boulevard (between Eliot and 62nd Avenue)
Staten Island: 3139 Veterans Road West (near Arthur Kill Road)
(212) 788–4000
www.nycacc.org

Charges between $25 and $150 for adoptions.

These shelters in each borough are overflowing with dogs, cats, rabbits, and occasionally some other surprises for you to take home and make a part of your family. Start your search for Fluffy on their Web site, where they post pictures and information on all the pets they have up for adoption. They do charge a fee for adoptions that includes all immunizations, spay or neutering, and microchips. All cats are $25 and most dogs are $100 or less, but they charge $150 for purebred dogs.

ASPCA
Bergh Memorial Animal Hospital & Clinic
424 East 92nd Street (between York and First Avenues)
(212) 876–7700
www.aspca.org

 Charges $75 for an appointment with a doctor and $110 for an emergency visit.

The granddaddy of all humane organizations, the ASPCA's clinic and hospital provide low-cost health care for your little loved ones. They provide the full range of medical care for pets, including spaying and neutering ($40 to $65), vaccines, and an on-site pharmacy. They also offer adoptions of all sorts of pets starting at a $75 donation. The adoption package includes microchip ID, spaying or neutering, follow-up exams, medical support, vaccines, literature, private behavior counseling, and starter equipment.

BIDE-A-WEE
410 East 38th Street, second floor (between First Avenue and FDR Drive)
(212) 532–5884 (clinic)
(212) 532–4455 (adoptions)
www.bideawee.org

 Charges $52.50 for exams, $90.00 for emergency visits, and $70.00 to $80.00 for adoptions.

This full-service veterinary clinic provides everything to keep your feline feeling fine. Appointments are available about a week in advance. They also have a large shelter and offer adoptions for a $70 to $80 fee, which includes spay or neutering, all vaccinations, and two weeks of free clinic services.

PET POSTINGS

Another way to find a free companion is to check out the bulletin boards and windows of local pet stores and veterinarians for notices from your neighbors who need to give up their pets. Whether it's because they're moving and can't take the Tonkinese to Tupelo, or their Labrador just had a litter, or the new hubby is allergic to the husky, often owners and their pets must be parted. Here are some places where you're sure to find postings:

EAST SIDE

CALLING ALL PETS, 1590 York Avenue (at 84th Street); (212) 249–7387.

CALLING ALL PETS, 301 East 76th Street (at Second Avenue); (212) 734–7051.

THE COUNTRY VET, 430 East 75th Street (between First and York Avenues); (212) 535–3250.

LITTER AND LEASHES, 343 East 66th Street (at First Avenue); (212) 734–8400.

THE NATURAL PET, 238 Third Avenue (between 19th and 20th Streets); (212) 228–4848.

PETCO, 560 Second Avenue (at 31st Street); (212) 779–4550.

PETCO, 860 Broadway (at East 17th Street); (212) 358–0692.

WEST SIDE

ANIMAL GENERAL, 558 Columbus Avenue (at 87th Street); (212) 501–9600.

BARKING ZOO, 172 Ninth Avenue (between 20th and 21st Streets); (212) 255–0658.

CLINTON VETERINARY CENTER, 357 West 52nd Street (between Eighth and Ninth Avenues); (212) 333–5548.

THE PET HEALTH STORE, 440 Amsterdam Avenue (at 81st Street); (212) 595–4200.

PET STOP, 564 Columbus Avenue (between 87th and 88th Streets); (212) 580–2400.

SPOILED BRATS, 340 West 49th Street (between Eighth and Ninth Avenues); (212) 459–1615.

WESTSIDE ANIMAL HOSPITAL, 733 Ninth Avenue (between 49th and 50th Streets); (212) 247–8600.

DOWNTOWN WEST

PARROTS AND PUPS, 45 Christopher Street (east at Seventh Avenue); (212) 352–8777.

PET BAR, 132 Thompson Street (between Prince and Houston Streets); (212) 253–9250.

DOWNTOWN EAST

ANIMAL CRACKER, 103 East 2nd Street (between Avenue A and First Avenue); (212) 614–6786.

WHISKERS, 235 East 9th Street (between Second and Third Avenues); (212) 979–2532.

Section 3:

EXPLORING NEW YORK

"Afoot and lighthearted I take to the open road,

Healthy, free, the world before me,

The long brown path before me, leading wherever I choose."

—Walt Whitman

WHETHER YOU'RE A visitor to New York or a native, there is always so much to discover about every corner of the city. The best way to get to know New York is to walk the streets with someone who knows it well. There are free guided tours of every fashion: leisurely strolls; historical, architectural, and nature tours; one-on-one explorations and groups. Most of the tours happen at regularly scheduled times every week, and some can be scheduled at your convenience.

WALKING TOURS BY THE WEEK

TIME	MONDAY	TUESDAY	WEDNESDAY	THURSDAY	FRIDAY	SATURDAY	SUNDAY
8:30 A.M.							
9:00 A.M.							
9:30 A.M.	Federal Reserve Bank (9:30 A.M.–2:30 P.M.) Steinway Factory Tour SEPTEMBER–JUNE	Federal Reserve Bank (9:30 A.M.–2:30 P.M.) Steinway Factory Tour SEPTEMBER–JUNE	Federal Reserve Bank (9:30 A.M.–2:30 P.M.)	Federal Reserve Bank (9:30 A.M.–2:30 P.M.)	Federal Reserve Bank (9:30 A.M.–2:30 P.M.)		
10:00 A.M.		City Hall					
10:30 A.M.	Youth Hostel's Central Park (every other week)						
11:00 A.M.	Columbia University NYPL	Columbia University NYPL WNET	Columbia University NYPL	Columbia University NYPL	Columbia University NYPL	NYPL Lincoln Square JUNE–NOVEMBER	Orchard Street APRIL–DECEMBER
11:30 A.M.						8th Street LATE MAY–SEPTEMBER (selected dates)	
12:00 NOON	Austrian Cultural Forum	Austrian Cultural Forum	Austrian Cultural Forum City Hall	Wall Street Austrian Cultural Forum	Times Square Austrian Cultural Forum	Brooklyn Brewery (noon–6:00 P.M.) Prospect Park Audubon Center Wall Street	
12:30 P.M.	Pennsylvania Station 4th Monday of month		Grand Central Terminal		The Grand Tour		
1:00 P.M.							
1:30 P.M.							
2:00 P.M.	Columbia University NYPL Trinity Church	Columbia University NYPL Trinity Church	Columbia University NYPL Trinity Church	Columbia University NYPL Trinity Church	City Hall Columbia University NYPL Trinity Church	Union Square NYPL Trinity Church	Trinity Church NYPL
2:30 P.M.							
3:00 P.M.	Austrian Cultural Forum	Austrian Cultural Forum	Austrian Cultural Forum	Austrian Cultural Forum	Austrian Cultural Forum	Prospect Park Audubon Center APRIL–NOVEMBER	Prospect Park Audubon Center
3:30 P.M.							
Sunset	Youth Hostel's Twilight in Brooklyn (every other week)						

AUSTRIAN CULTURAL FORUM
11 East 52nd Street (between Fifth and Madison Avenues)
(212) 319-5300
www.acfny.org
Monday through Friday at noon and 3:00 P.M.
A unique addition to the New York skyline, this building is a pure example of making the most out of a little. Stop in for a free tour of this narrow twenty-four-story glass-and-concrete skyscraper that looks like a huge totem pole designed for a science fiction movie. They also host a full schedule of other free events, including readings, concerts, art exhibitions, film screenings, and panel discussions.

BATTERY PARK CITY WALKING TOURS
Battery Park City Parks Conservancy
2 South End Avenue (at West Thames Street)
(212) 267-9700
www.bpcparks.org
Various dates May through October.
They offer a variety of walking tours, including nature walks, garden tours, river walks, art tours, and historic tours. Some tours are offered weekly, others on occasion. Check the Web site or call for schedules.

BIG APPLE GREETERS
1 Centre Street, Room 2035 (at Chambers Street)
(212) 669-8159
www.bigapplegreeter.org
Any day, any place, year-round.
This is your dream-come-true tour of New York. You choose the time and day, you choose the place, and you don't pay anything—in fact, they'll even give you a one-day unlimited-use MetroCard for the subway. You think I'm kidding, don't you? Well, I'm not. Friendly and knowledgeable New Yorkers volunteer their time for this amazing organization to show you around any neighborhood in the city. They usually live in the area they show, so they can give you firsthand accounts of the area's history, off-the-beaten-trail spots, and great tips for finding some tasty (and cheap!) food and drink. Walks can run from two hours to all day. They don't accept tips, but if you offer to buy them lunch, they probably won't argue with you. Call at least two weeks in advance.

BROOKLYN BREWERY

79 North 11th Street (between Wythe Avenue and Berry Street)
Williamsburg, Brooklyn
(718) 486–7422
www.brooklynbrewery.com
Saturday, noon–6:00 P.M. (last tour at 4:00).
Brooklyn's mom-and-pop brewery walks you through the process of mixing up a batch of beer in intricate detail, right down to the molecular physics. And somehow it seems so very interesting once you've been plied full of generous samples of their fine (and fresh!) brew. Also, on Friday night they have free music and cheap beer.

CENTRAL PARK

Central Park Conservancy
(212) 310–6600
www.centralparknyc.org
Various days and times throughout the week, year-round.
Explore the wilds of New York City with the many tours led by volunteers for the Central Park Conservancy. With a wealth of knowledge about the flora, fauna, history, trivia, secret passageways, and hidden trails of Central Park, these tours are always worthwhile for natives and visitors alike. Call for schedule information.

COLUMBIA UNIVERSITY

213 Low Library (116th Street and Broadway)
(212) 854–4900
www.columbia.edu
Monday through Friday, 11:00 A.M. and 2:00 P.M., year-round.
This one-hour tour of New York's very own Ivy League school uncovers the history, architecture, and personalities behind these prestigious walls.

8TH STREET WALKING TOUR

The Village Alliance
(212) 777–2173
www.villagealliance.org
Every other Saturday at 11:30 A.M., late May through September.
The ninety-minute tour called "Discover Places, Tidbits & Gossip That Even New York's Cognoscenti Don't Know" delivers just what it promises as it traipses through the East and West Villages. The tour meets at the northwest

corner of Second Avenue and St. Marks Place (8th Street). Call or check the Web site for the schedule.

THE FEDERAL RESERVE BANK

33 Liberty Street (between Nassau and William Streets)
(212) 720–6130
www.newyorkfed.org
Monday through Friday at 9:30 A.M., 10:30 A.M., 11:30 A.M., 1:30 P.M., 2:30 P.M.; make a reservation one month ahead.

You've heard the sayings "Follow the money" and "Show me the money," right? Well, here's your chance to do both. This sixty-minute tour of the richest bank in the world takes you through their gold vaults, tells you all about the Fed's cash-processing procedures, and even gives you some free money at the end of the tour! Okay, so it happens to be shredded. You can't have everything.

GRAND CENTRAL TERMINAL

42nd Street and Vanderbilt Avenue
(212) 439–1049
www.mas.org
Wednesday at 12:30 P.M., year-round.

 While there's no charge for the tour, they do ask for a donation of any amount, though you aren't obligated to give one.

For more than twenty-five years, the Municipal Art Society has been showing folks around this Beaux Arts landmark. The tour includes the history of the terminal as well as a look at the major restorations completed in 1998. The tour runs a little more than an hour and meets at the main information booth on the main level of Grand Central.

THE GRAND TOUR: GRAND CENTRAL STATION AREA

42nd Street and Vanderbilt Avenue
(212) 883–2420
www.grandcentralpartnership.org
Every Friday at 12:30 P.M., year-round.

This free ninety-minute walking tour organized by the Grand Central Partnership leaves from the Philip Morris Building across the street from Grand Central. This walk points out some of the architectural splendors of

East 42nd Street, including Grand Central Station, the Chrysler Building, the Chanin Building, and many others, as well as passing along some of the area's rich history and curious events.

JOHN J. HARVEY FIREBOAT
  Pier 63 (Hudson River and 23rd Street)
  www.fireboat.org
Various days and times, year-round.
Since she was put into service in 1931, the *John J. Harvey* fireboat has greeted every passenger cruise ship that has made its way into New York Harbor with a spectacular water display. But this boat wasn't made just for show. To this day, although she was officially retired from service by the New York City Fire Department in 1994, she remains one of the most powerful and fastest fireboats ever to take to the water. The ship is now under private ownership and does not rest on her impressive laurels. She's now pressed into action for tours up and down the Hudson and around New York Harbor. The schedule of events is erratic, but they go on throughout the year (more from spring through fall and less in the winter). Some tours have themes and knowledgeable guides, like their "History of Garbage" tour and a tour of historic fires the *Harvey* worked on. Other tours are just pleasant days on the water. All are free, because the boat doesn't meet the strict standards set by the U.S. Coast Guard for the carriage of passengers for hire. If you come onboard, it's as private guests of the boat, and you may be asked to sign a release to this effect. Trips are limited to the first fifty passengers. And yes, they do "fire up" the powerful hoses at some point on every trip, and yes, you will get wet. For schedule information check out the Web site or sign up for their mailing list though the Web site.

LINCOLN SQUARE
  Columbus Circle fountain (59th Street and Broadway)
  (212) 581–3774
  www.lincolnbid.org
Saturday at 11:00 A.M., June through November.
This ninety-minute tour (that can actually run as long as three hours) explores the historic Lincoln Square district, which has become a world center for arts and entertainment—and is also full of historic treasures, architectural jewels, peaceful green areas, and surprising enclaves of public art. The tour meets at the Columbus Circle fountain.

NEW YORK CITY HALL
(212) 788–2170 or 311
www.nyc.gov/artcommission
Tuesday at 10:00 A.M. and Friday at 2:00 P.M. (reservations required);
Wednesday at noon (no reservations required).
Stroll through this early-nineteenth-century Federal-style building that's home to the mayor's office and city council chambers and is chock-full of historic American portraits and artifacts. You can make reservations for tours on Tuesday at 10:00 A.M. and Friday at 2:00 P.M. by calling or through their Web site. The tours are limited to twenty people, so it is a good idea to make a reservation a least a week in advance, but you can try up to two days before. Or you can just show up for the Wednesday tour at noon, which is open to the first twenty people who sign up that morning at the Heritage Tourism Center, located at the southern end of City Hall Park. All tours are free, of course.

NEW YORK INTERNATIONAL YOUTH HOSTEL
891 Amsterdam Avenue (between 103rd and 104th Streets)
(212) 932–2300
www.hinewyork.org
Monday at 10:30 A.M., Central Park (every other week);
Monday afternoons, Twilight In Brooklyn (every other week).
Meet up at the International Youth Hostel every Monday for a morning jaunt to Central Park or at twilight for a tour of Brooklyn Heights. Even if you are not staying at the hostel you can tag along for these fun explorations of top New York destinations. Stroll through Central Park and take in the highlights of the city's green oasis or explore downtown Brooklyn and its spectacular views of Manhattan, as well as a walk over the historic Brooklyn Bridge. These tours take place on alternating Mondays. You are sure to hook up with an interesting mix of international visitors and get the scoop on some of the city's best cheap eats. The hostel also hosts a full schedule of other tours throughout the week, but they do charge a small fee for most of the others. The one tour that might actually be worth shelling out the bucks for is Jerry's Grand Tour ($10). This is a sixteen-hour marathon that covers up to 22 miles and every New York sight you might ever want to see. The Grand Tour takes place every Saturday at 8:30 A.M. You do need to call or stop by the hostel to sign up for all tours at the information desk. Check out their Web site for more details and a schedule of other tours and events, including the free stand-up comedy every Wednesday night at 8:30. And if you are looking for a bed in New York, the hostel is the way to go. It is clean, friendly, fun, and, most importantly, cheap. With beds running only $30 to $38 a night, this is just about the best deal you're going to find in the city.

NEW YORK PUBLIC LIBRARY (NYPL)
Humanities and Social Science Library, 476 Fifth Avenue
(entrance at 42nd Street)
(212) 930–0501
www.nypl.org
Monday through Saturday at 11:00 A.M. and 2:00 P.M., Sunday at 2:00 P.M.,
year-round.
The lions welcome you to a one-hour walk through the stunningly renovated
main branch of the public library. They also offer guided tours through their
major art exhibits daily at 12:30 and 2:30 P.M.

ORCHARD STREET WALKING TOUR
Katz's Deli
205 East Houston Street (at Ludlow Street)
(212) 226–9010
www.lowereastsideny.com
Sunday at 11:00 A.M., April through December.
From pushcarts to pulsing beats, this tour explores a neighborhood that
started out as a hub for immigrants from Russia and Eastern Europe and is
now turning into the newest chic area on the isle of Manhattan. Tours run
about ninety minutes.

PENNSYLVANIA STATION TOURS
34th Street Partnership tourist information kiosk
32nd Street and Seventh Avenue
(212) 719–3434 or (212) 868–0521
www.34thstreet.org
The fourth Monday of every month at 12:30 P.M., year-round.
Tour the grandeur that once was New York's Penn Station. The tour resurrects
this behemoth by using vintage photographs and surviving remnants to tell
the story of New York's lost railroad station. This ninety-minute walk tells the
tale from Penn Station's turn-of-the-twentieth-century beginnings to the
forces that brought about its destruction in the 1960s.

PROSPECT PARK AUDUBON CENTER
Lincoln Road and Ocean Avenue
Brooklyn
(718) 287–3400
www.prospectparkaudubon.org
Saturday at noon: Bird-Watching Tour.
Saturday and Sunday at 3:00 P.M.: Discovery Tour.

The restored boathouse is home to this state-of-the-art wildlife preserve and education center. Their busy schedule abounds with free events, activities, and tours through the wilds of Brooklyn's only forest with a gorge and waterfall (okay, even without the gorge and waterfall, it would still be Brooklyn's only forest). Take the Discovery Tour offered every Saturday and Sunday at 3:00 P.M., the Bird-Watching Tour every Saturday at noon, or stop in for any other of the tons of ongoing activities for kids and adults throughout the week.

STEINWAY & SONS
1 Steinway Place (Nineteenth Avenue and 38th Street)
Long Island City, Queens
(718) 721–2600
www.steinway.com
Monday and Tuesday at 9:30 A.M., September through June.

Take a walk back in time through the Steinway factory, where they still craft each of their world-famous pianos by hand using the same techniques created and patented by Henry Engelhard Steinway (and his sons) starting in 1853. From bending and shaping one long piece of wood into the entire outer rim of the piano to hand-sanding, sawing, rubbing, regulating, voicing, and stringing the instruments, the tour is an in-depth two-and-a-half-hour master class in the art of piano making from those who do it best. Tours are held on Monday and Tuesday mornings September through June, and reservations are required.

TAKE A WALK, NEW YORK!
(212) 228–3126
www.walkny.org
Various locations throughout the five boroughs, year-round.

Your government thinks you're getting too fat. So they want you to hit the streets and start exercising. This federally funded local group organizes guided walks all around the city that aim to stimulate you intellectually and visually so they can sucker you into walking, walking, walking. This is a great chance to explore sections of the city you've never visited before (or may not have even known existed). The walks are always easily accessible by public transportation, led by knowledgeable guides, and free.

THIRTEEN/WNET
450 West 33rd Street (between Ninth and Tenth Avenues)
(212) 560–2711
www.thirteen.org
Tuesday at 11:00 A.M.; reservations required.

A fascinating one-hour peek inside the country's largest public television station.

TIMES SQUARE WALKING TOUR
  Times Square Visitors Center
  1560 Broadway (between 46th and 47th Streets)
  (212) 869–1890
  www.timessquarebid.org
Friday at noon.
What was once a center for horse trading has now become the center of the commercial theater world. This two- to three-hour tour fills you in on all the history, intrigue, and ever-changing architecture of Broadway and its surrounding areas. The visitor center also offers free Internet access, loads of information, and clean bathrooms!

TRINITY CHURCH
  Broadway and Wall Street
  (212) 602–0800
  www.trinitywallstreet.org
Daily at 2:00 P.M., year-round.
A short fifteen- to twenty-minute tour that covers the long history of one of New York's oldest churches (established 1697). Concerts are also offered every Thursday at 1:00 P.M.

UNION SQUARE WALKING TOUR
  16th Street between Union Square East and West (Park Avenue and Broadway)
  (212) 460–1200
  www.unionsquarenyc.org
Saturday at 2:00 P.M., year-round.
Take a ninety-minute, opinionated, totally interactive tour of Union Square's past, present, and future. Meet at the Lincoln statue midpark at 16th Street.

URBAN PARK RANGERS
  Parks throughout the five boroughs
  (866) NYC–HAWK (692–4295)
  www.nyc.gov/parks
Various times, days, and locations, year-round.
Yogi Bear has nothing on New York. Yes, we have our own pack of park rangers, and they're a useful bunch of folks to know. They run an extensive

and ever-changing array of walks, hikes, nature explorations, canoe trips, and even camping trips. Call to get a schedule or check out the Web site.

WALL STREET WALKING TOUR

Museum of the American Indian
1 Bowling Green (at the end of Broadway, across from Battery Park)
(212) 606–4064
www.downtownny.com
Thursday and Saturday at noon, year-round.

Explore this area that takes in everything from founding fathers of the United States to the financial capital of the world. This free ninety-minute tour weaves together the history, events, architecture, and people of downtown with stops at the U.S. Custom House, Trinity Church, New York Stock Exchange, and many other sites along the way. No two walks are ever the same, so join in often.

"We're gonna see America. We take no map. We'll follow the sun. Stay in cheap motels and steal what we need along the way."

—Al Bundy

JUST BECAUSE YOU'RE low on cash is no reason to sit at home. Whether it's getting around the city or getting out of town, there are some great options. Of course, the best way to get to see New York is the cheapest—by foot (biking and in-line skating are great choices as well). More than any other place in America, New York is a walking city—logically laid out, compact, lots to see, and plenty of people to bump into along the way (figuratively and literally). While New York is undoubtedly a big city, as you walk the streets, you realize that it's also very much a small town. There may be eight million people, but you'll be amazed at how many friends and acquaintances you'll run into on the streets and how many familiar faces in the crowds you'll see over and over again. When walking is out of the question, though, the subway is the answer. The unlimited-use MetroCard ($7 for one day, $24 for one week, $76 for one month) makes getting from here to there a bargain. The MetroCard is good for all subways and buses (see below). Here are some other suggestions for getting around and out of New York.

GETTING AROUND NEW YORK

MTA NEW YORK CITY TRANSIT
(718) 330–1234
www.mta.nyc.ny.us/nyct
Okay, I know I'm not offering you any special deals here. Yes, you do have to pay to get on the trains. This isn't Germany; there ain't no such thing as an honor system on these trains. You pay your fare and you ride your train. You will be ticketed if you hop the turnstiles. Don't try it. But the unlimited-use MetroCards make it easy and cheap to get to anywhere in the five boroughs by subway and/or bus.

STATEN ISLAND FERRY
Whitehall Terminal (at Whitehall and South Streets)
311 or (718) 727–2505
www.nyc.gov/dot
This not-to-be-missed trip runs about every twenty minutes most times, but once an hour late at night. It's absolutely free, and with the spectacular views of lower Manhattan and the Statue of Liberty, how can you pass it up? Particularly dramatic views at sunset, but any time of day it's an awe-inspiring voyage.

Get the 411

1–800–FREE–411 is just that, free directory assistance. Forget about paying your phone or cell phone company a buck or two every time you need a number. Simply call this number from your home or cell phone and get any number in the country for free. What's the catch? Well, you will have to sit through a short ad, which is how they make their money, but the call and the info are totally free. Visit their Web site at www.free411.com.

Hacking It in New York

You won't be surprised by this recommendation: Don't ever take a cab. Besides the fact that it's expensive (just hopping in a cab seems to always cost you at least $5), the wild ride will invariably take you longer than grabbing the nearest subway. Fahgeddaboutit!

GETTING OUT OF NEW YORK

AUTO DRIVEAWAY COMPANY (ADC)
2786 Route 23N, Suite B
Stockolm, New Jersey
(973) 208–8700
www.autodriveaway.com

There's a $15 registration fee and a $350 refundable deposit. The registration fee is good for one year and at all locations.

Forget about flying, Greyhound, or Amtrak; here's your chance to see America the way it was meant to be seen, behind the wheel of your very own gas-guzzling, pedal-to-the-metal, "where the hell is the next rest stop" automobile. With sixty-four locations throughout the United States and Canada, these folks can provide you with the free use of a late-model car to practically any major city you want to visit. If your plans are somewhat flexible, this is a great way to drive yourself around the states. The deal is: ADC acts as a kind of matchmaker between people or companies that need vehicles moved from place to place and drivers who want to get from here to there. Call them up to see what's available, pay your registration and deposit, and hit the road. Cars go on a first-come, first-served basis to drivers twenty-three years or older with two photo IDs. They give you time to do plenty of sightseeing along the way by allotting you extra time to get to where you're going (four days to Florida, for instance, and ten days to the West Coast). When you deliver your car, you get back your deposit and call the nearest ADC office to see when you can get a car back or off to your next destination. The looser your travel plans, the better this system will work for you. The cars come with a free first tank of gas; otherwise, all gas and lodging costs along the way are your responsibility.

CLUB GETAWAY
Kent, Connecticut
(800) 643–8292
www.clubgetaway.com

 You must have the ability to teach something fun or provide some useful service to campers in exchange for free weekends.

This summer camp for adults is a "Club Med in Connecticut" and is always on the lookout for volunteers to commit to spending some weekends with their swinging singles. If you can offer some useful service to the paying campers—teaching yoga, arts and crafts, or in-line skating, say, or even cooking up a killer pie—they will give you room, board, and free run of the extensive grounds and facilities in exchange for the time you spend working with the campers. Even if you don't necessarily think you have some great expertise, they're pretty open to any idea; it's definitely worth a shot. The camp has been rated "one of the top ten hottest destinations for singles" by the Travel Channel and has everything you need to do almost any sport under the sun.

ROWE CAMP & CONFERENCE CENTER
Rowe, Massachusetts
(413) 339–4954
www.rowecenter.org

 Chop wood and carry water in exchange for a peaceful week in the mountains.

For one week every spring and fall, the Rowe Center holds "Work Weeks" where folks from far and wide, both young and old, come to help spiff up the grounds and have a great time. This community-oriented camp offers lots of fun activities and free room and board for all those helping out these weeks. Throughout the year they also offer various conferences on a wide variety of artistic and spiritual subjects, and you can work off the cost of these programs through other work-study programs. Check the Web site for more details and schedule.

The Virtual Thumb

There are a number of Web sites where you can find yourself a free ride out of town or a companion to ride with you wherever you're going. These ride share listings are a great way to travel to or from New York, save a load of cash, and maybe even make a good friend along the way. You are usually expected to split the cost of gas, but not always. Check out these sites for details:

www.erideshare.com

www.newyork.craigslist.org

www.hitchhikers.org

www.shareyourride.net

VIPASSANA MEDITATION CENTER

386 Colrain-Shelburn Road
Shelburn Falls, Massachusetts
(413) 625–2160
www.dhamma.org

Donations of any amount are accepted, but not required, at the end of the ten-day retreat.

Vipassana offers its ten-day meditation "Boot Camp" free of charge (including all accommodations, meals, and instructions)—the only hitch is you can't say a word about the service. In fact, you can't say a word about anything; this is a completely silent retreat. No meditation experience is required to take part, and their focus in not religion-based at all. They are all about the technique and practice of meditation as a "universal remedy for universal ills." Fill out an application at their Web site and make a reservation one to two months in advance.

THE TRAIN TO THE PLANE

Getting to New York's three major airports can be an expensive affair. It can cost you $60 by cab, $20 by shuttle van, or $13 by bus service, but it can be done for next to nothing if you have some time and patience.

KENNEDY AIRPORT

This is the easiest and most user-friendly airport to get to by public transportation, with four cheap options for getting there (two dirt cheap and two not-quite-as cheap). The pricier and slightly more convenient plan is to pick up the AirTrain at either the Howard Beach Station (A train) or at the Sutphin Boulevard Station (E, J, or Z trains). The AirTrain is officially part of the MTA system, but your MetroCard will not get you on board. To take the ten-minute monorail ride to the terminals, you will have to cough up an additional $5. But if you are a purist like me, you will hop on one of the two city buses that will get you to the terminals for just the swipe of your unlimited MetroCard or a $2 subway fare (free transfer from the subway!). Grab the Q10 bus from the Kew Gardens/Union Turnpike subway station (E or F trains) or Q3 at Jamaica Center/Parsons/Archer subway station (E, J, or Z trains). The travel time from Manhattan for any of these routes is about sixty to ninety minutes. The big difference is the AirTrain is a bit plusher and luggage friendly, while the buses are, well, buses.

LA GUARDIA AIRPORT

Getting here can be an adventure, but it can be done for the cost of a subway token as well. From 106th Street and Broadway or 125th Street and Lenox Avenue, hop on the M60 bus. The bus winds its way around Upper Manhattan and Queens and takes you directly to the airport. Travel time is forty-five to ninety minutes (depending on traffic). Another option is to take the E or the F train to the 74th Street and Roosevelt Avenue stop, then catch the Q33 bus. Neither of these are specifically meant to be airport shuttles. That means they make many stops along the way before getting to the terminals, and they do not have any special luggage racks. You won't be making friends with your fellow passengers if you block the aisle with your steamer trunk. For information on all MTA buses and subways, call (718) 330–1234 or check the Web site www.mta.nyc.ny.us/nyct.

NEWARK LIBERTY AIRPORT

Making it to Newark Liberty Airport from Manhattan can be pretty cheap and easy, as long as you know the schedules ahead of time. If you head off without a plan, it could take you a while or wind up costing you a few more bucks than you planned on. The easiest option is to hop on the New Jersey Transit bus #107 ($5.75) at Port Authority in midtown (41st Street and Eighth Avenue) and take it straight to the airport. The good news is this bus will get you to the airport in about thirty minutes and for only $5.75; the bad news is it has a very limited schedule. If that doesn't work for you, take

Next Year in Jerusalem

How about an all-expenses-paid ten-day trip to Israel? Well, if you're between eighteen and twenty-six years old, Jewish, and have never been to the Holy Land before, Birthright Israel wants to take you for free.

Sound inviting? To date they have sent more than 90,000 people from all around the country (including many groups from New York City), and they're looking for more every year. The aim is to build a strong link between young American Jews and Israel. While they try to keep the proselytizing to a minimum, there are many discussions of all things Jewish while you visit historic sites like Masada, the Wailing Wall, and the Dead Sea. Of course, they wouldn't mind you spending your own cash to come back to Israel in the future, or even deciding to settle in Israel, but there's no pressure to do either.

Birthright Israel puts together more than thirty groups to make the trip each winter and spring. These trips take into account the full spectrum of ideological, religious, educational, and cultural backgrounds of the Jewish community. There are groups for those who are nonobservant, Reform, Conservative, and Orthodox. Some trips have a traditional hotel and sightseeing agenda, while others are for those with special interests like biking, sports, or history. In recent years they have also begun to coordinate their activities with the Israeli government to ensure the safety and security of those on the trips. For more information stop by the Birthright Israel offices at 521 Fifth Avenue, twenty-seventh floor (at 43rd Street); call (888) 99–ISRAEL (994–7723); or check the Web site www.birthrightisrael.com.

the Path Train to Newark Penn Station ($1.50) and get the New Jersey Transit bus #62 ($1.35) to the airport. The bus runs about every ten to twenty minutes and is about a twenty-minute ride. The more convenient but much pricier option is to take the AirTrain from Penn Station in Manhattan directly to the airport ($14.00), or you can save a few bucks by taking the Path Train to Newark Penn Station and grabbing the AirTrain there ($7.75). For detailed schedules and more information, call (800) 772–2222 or check the Web site www.panynj.gov.

"Your first job is to prepare the soil. The best tool for this is your neighbor's motorized garden tiller. If your neighbor does not own a garden tiller, suggest that he buy one."

—Dave Barry

GARDENS AND GARDENING: DIRT CHEAP

GARDENS MAY NOT be the first thing you think of when you think of New York, but there's a surprising amount of greenery to be found within this urban jungle—and I'm not just talking about fire-escape gardens. From quaint community gardens to grand botanical gardens, some of the most stunning horticulture anywhere in the world is within the city limits. Not only can you partake in the sights and smells of the gardens, but you can also produce some lovely flowers and vegetables yourself. Cultivate your own free plot of land in one of New York's many community gardens, get free bulbs and cuttings, or develop your own green thumb through free gardening classes around town.

PUBLIC GARDENS

THE BROOKLYN BOTANIC GARDEN (BBG)
1000 Washington Avenue (at Flatbush Avenue)
(718) 623–7200 (info) or (718) 623–7333 (events hotline)
www.bbg.org

 Free Hours: Tuesday and Saturday from 10:00 a.m. to noon; seniors are also free all day Friday.

Hailed by the *New York Times* as "the premier horticultural attraction in the region," the BBG's endless gardens and greenhouses will bring your senses to life. They also provide free gardening and composting classes and workshops throughout the year (see below for details).

THE CENTRAL PARK CONSERVATORY GARDENS
105th Street and Fifth Avenue
(212) 360–2766 or (212) 310–6600
www.centralparknyc.org

Always free, this is the only formal garden in Manhattan open to the public. It covers a relatively small area (when compared to the other botanical gardens in New York) but provides a welcome escape from the clamor of city life. They offer free tours of the gardens from spring through fall on Saturday at 11:00 A.M. Also be on the lookout for their annual plant giveaways—tulips in May and mums in November.

THE NEW YORK BOTANICAL GARDEN
200th Street and Kazimirov Boulevard
The Bronx
(718) 817–8700
www.nybg.org

 Free Hours: Wednesday and Saturday from 10:00 A.M. to noon. Additional fees apply to certain exhibits within the garden.

Who could want anything more than 250 acres of flora from every corner of the world, including forty-eight gardens and plant collections and fifty acres of forestland? This is one of the oldest and largest gardens in the world and should not be missed. They offer free admission to the grounds on Wednesday and Saturday mornings, but you will still have to pay additional fees to gain entry into some venues within the gardens. They also run an extensive adult education curriculum, which you can get free or at reduced tuition by taking part in their work-study program.

THE QUEENS BOTANICAL GARDEN (QBG)
Flushing Meadows Park, 43–50 Main Street (at Dahlia Avenue)
(718) 886–3800
www.queensbotanical.org

Always free admission to this twenty-acre garden (closed Monday). QBG also presents a free concert series during the summer and many free classes throughout the year.

THE STATEN ISLAND BOTANICAL GARDEN
1000 Richmond Terrace
(718) 273–8200
www.sibg.org

 Free admission to the garden grounds, but they do charge admission to the Chinese and Secret Gardens.

This is a small garden when compared to the big guys in the Bronx and Brooklyn, but it makes a lovely place to take a respite. Admission to the garden grounds is free every day, but you will need to pay your way into the enticing and well-regarded Chinese Scholar's Garden.

WAVE HILL PUBLIC GARDEN AND CULTURAL CENTER
675 West 252nd Street (enter at 249th Street and
Independence Avenue)
The Bronx
(718) 549–3200
www.wavehill.org

 Free Hours: Tuesday and Saturday from 9:00 A.M. to noon; no admission charges during December, January, and February.

This former private estate, now a city-owned garden, offers some outstanding views of the Hudson River and New Jersey (yes, it is possible), and some gorgeously maintained gardens.

GARDENING EDUCATION

BROOKLYN GREENBRIDGE & URBAN COMPOSTING PROJECT

Brooklyn Botanic Garden
1000 Washington Avenue (at Flatbush Avenue)
(718) 623–7250 or (718) 623–7209
Compost Help Line (718) 623–7290
www.bbg.org/edu/greenbridge

Classes and workshops are free, but you must register at least one week in advance.

Classes and workshops offered throughout the year on such topics as "Composting in the City," "Perennial Flowers Basics," "Introduction to Horticulture Therapy," "Gardening with Native Plants," and "Battle the Asian Long Horn Beetle!" The classes are targeted toward community gardeners, but all are welcome.

Get the Dirt

Visitors occasionally comment on how dirty New York is. Well, this just might be the reason why. Through a program of the Department of Sanitation and the various botanical gardens of New York, every New Yorker is entitled to an unlimited amount of compost free of charge. Compost is considered to be the "black gold" of gardening and is an essential ingredient for any lush fire-escape garden, window box, or houseplant. The compost give-back days are scheduled each spring and fall. Call or check the Web site for the dates and locations you can show up to shovel yourself a load of this messy but useful, nutrient-rich, organic plant food. They also sell discounted compost bins for $20 ($70 retail price); visit www.nyccompost.org or call (718) 817–8543 (the Bronx and Manhattan), (718) 623–7290 (Brooklyn), (718) 539–5296 (Queens), or (718) 362–1007 (Staten Island).

And if you can't wait for those official give-back days, you can grab some free compost to go anytime at any local Starbucks Coffee. Yes, the ubiquitous coffee pusher gives away its used grounds to anyone who wants them. The nitrogen-rich grinds and any soil make the perfect blend to wake up any houseplant. To find a location near you, walk down any street or check the Web site www.starbucks.com.

NEW YORK BOTANICAL GARDEN SCHOOL OF CONTINUING EDUCATION

200th Street and Kazimirov Boulevard
The Bronx
(718) 817–8610
www.nybg.org/edu/conted

> **Work-study is available: Perform administrative duties in exchange for free or discounted classes. The math: 2 hours of work=1 free classroom hour.**

Choose from more than 700 courses in botanical art and illustration, botany, crafts, floral design, gardening, commercial horticulture, landscape design, and horticultural therapy. Take a short how-to class, explore a topic in depth, or pursue a new career in one of their seven certificate programs.

COMMUNITY GARDENS

Community gardens are generally free to join. They provide you with a plot of land to plant in and all the supplies and materials you need, from seeds and soil to how-tos and hothouses. Some long-established, centrally located gardens have long waiting lists, while newer, off-the-beaten-trail gardens have many spots available. These gardens are not only a good place to grow rutabagas but also great gathering spots for the communities they are in. Many of the gardens have full schedules of free classes, performances, and activities for all.

GREEN GUERILLAS

151 West 30th Street, tenth floor (between Sixth and Seventh Avenues)
(212) 402–1121
www.greenguerillas.org

A good starting point to find a community garden in your neighborhood to participate in.

GREENTHUMB
49 Chambers Street, Room 1020 (between Broadway and
Center Street)
(212) 788–8070
www.greenthumbnyc.org

This organization has more than 600 member community gardens in practically every neighborhood in the five boroughs. The Web site also has a great events calendar where you will find all kinds of free goings-on in the gardens: classes (tai chi, writing, yoga, drawing), concerts, barbecues, community gatherings, film screenings, and more. Check the Web site or call for the community garden near you.

"I hate flowers. I paint them because they're cheaper than models and they don't move."

—Georgia O'Keeffe

ART GALLERIES: SHOW ME THE MONET

NEW YORK IS HOME to hundreds, perhaps thousands, of art galleries, and every one of them is free for you to wander through. In this city where space is at a premium, many of these are small single-room galleries with limited exhibition space, yet there are others that rival some of the major museums around town in the caliber of artists they show and their vast spaces. In some cases, in fact, the line between commercial gallery and museum is hard to define. Ultimately, though, the prime difference between the two remains simple and clear: money. You will never pay an admission charge at a commercial gallery, because everything you see hanging on the walls, lying on the floor, and dangling from the ceiling is for sale. Does the Gap charge you to browse? New York being the center of the art world, the artists you'll find at these galleries are the same ones you'd see at any major contemporary or modern art museum around the world. The styles of works you will find in these galleries run the full spectrum from fine art to the kind of contemporary installations that keep right-wing Republicans in business.

While there are galleries scattered all over the city, you'll find a large concentration of them clustered in just a few neighborhoods: Chelsea, Soho, and Williamsburg, Brooklyn. Each of these areas caters to a different clientele and mind-set, but all have a huge variety of styles, techniques, and talents within their own worlds. The galleries I'm including in this listing are those where you're sure to find some of the most intriguing, world-class, cutting-edge, or otherwise eye-opening works in these neighborhoods and around the city. Don't take this list as the comprehensive survey of galleries in the five boroughs but as a jumping-off point. Galleries generally change shows every four to six weeks. The best way to take them in is to wander these neighborhoods with an open mind (but you can keep the purse closed).

CHELSEA

Chelsea has become the most popular area in Manhattan for galleries. Most of those located here are considered blue-chip galleries that work with lists of established, well-known, high-profile artists. In other words, the galleries can charge thousands of dollars for any given work. There are about 150 galleries crammed into a 10-block area, and most are open Tuesday through Saturday, 10:00 A.M. to 6:00 P.M. Below are some of the big-shot galleries you don't want to miss, but the best way to discover a favorite spot is to walk the streets and check out everything that looks inviting. Most of the galleries are located between 21st and 26th Streets, and between Tenth and Eleventh Avenues.

BARBARA GLADSTONE GALLERY
515 West 24th Street (between Tenth and Eleventh Avenues)
(212) 206–9300
www.gladstonegallery.com
Known for presenting high-minded shows with a focus on conceptual sculpture.

CHEIM & READ
547 West 25th Street (between Tenth and Eleventh Avenues)
(212) 242–7727
www.cheimread.com

This large gallery presents the works of such artists as Diane Arbus, Louise Bourgeois, Robert Mapplethorpe, and Andy Warhol.

FEATURE INC.
530 West 25th Street (between Tenth and Eleventh Avenues)
(212) 675–7772
www.featureinc.com

Specializes in contemporary artists that they consider to be on the cutting edge.

GAGOSIAN GALLERY
555 West 24th Street (between Tenth and Eleventh Avenues)
(212) 741–1111
522 West 21st Street (between Tenth and Eleventh Avenues)
(212) 741–1717
www.gagosian.com

Shows are always headline grabbing, and the huge space allows them to present works on a grand scale.

GALERIE LELONG
528 West 26th Street (between Tenth and Eleventh Avenues)
(212) 315–0470
www.galerie-lelong.com

The gallery's long history includes a dedication to abstract and minimalist paintings, contemporary sculpture, and contemporary Latin American artists.

Where Else to (van) Gogh

Stop into any gallery along the way and pick up a copy of ChelseArt *and Art Now's* Gallery Guide. ChelseArt *is a concise map and up-to-date listing of all the goings-on in the Chelsea area. The* Gallery Guide *is a monthly publication of happenings at every major gallery in Manhattan and selected listings in the other boroughs and beyond. You can get both of these free at any gallery. You may notice the $3 price tag on the* Gallery Guide, *but don't pay any attention; everyone gives it away for free. You can also view the guide online at www.art info.com. Click on "Gallery Guide" to get to the New York listings.*

A Feast for the Eyes (with an Open Bar!)

You are cordially invited to rub shoulders with the trendsetters of the New York art scene, be the first to see what's happening at the happening galleries, and grab yourself a glass (or three) of fine wine or a few bottles of beer. Whenever you stop in to view a gallery, be sure to put your name on their mailing list, and you will start receiving invitations to their upcoming shows, including information about the opening reception. Every gallery holds an opening reception a couple of days before the show opens to the public, where anyone has a chance to meet the artist(s), mix and mingle, drink, and sometimes even eat. These events are almost always open to anyone in the know, and now that means you. Other ways to find out about openings is to check out the Web site http://dks.thing.net pick up a free copy of the Gallery Guide at any gallery.

LUHRING AUGUSTINE GALLERY

531 West 24th Street (between Tenth and Eleventh Avenues)
(212) 206–9100
www.luhringaugustine.com
Cutting-edge, big-budget shows.

MATTHEW MARKS GALLERY

523 West 24th Street (between Tenth and Eleventh Avenues)
(212) 243–0200
www.mmarks.com
One of the first galleries to settle in Chelsea, its space is always home to an unpredictable but intriguing array of works.

METRO PICTURES

519 West 24th Street (between Tenth and Eleventh Avenues)
(212) 206–7100
www.metropicturesgallery.com
Primarily presents photography shows by such artists as Cindy Sherman and Robert Longo.

PACEWILDENSTEIN
545 West 22nd Street (between Tenth and Eleventh Avenues)
(212) 929–7000
www.pacewildenstein.com
The list includes such artists as Chuck Close, Isamu Noguchi, Pablo Picasso, Robert Rauschenberg, Mark Rothko, and Julian Schnabel.

303 GALLERY
525 West 22nd Street (between Tenth and Eleventh Avenues)
(212) 255–1121
www.303gallery.com
Represents a battery of young artists working in a variety of forms, including photography, film, painting, sculpture, and whatever else moves them.

SOHO

Soho is the original art gallery neighborhood of New York, and while gentrification and skyrocketing real estate prices have forced many galleries to relocate, it still remains well populated by galleries presenting vital work. The galleries are often smaller than those in Chelsea, but they display works that are generally more cutting edge and riskier. The spaces are sometime storefronts and clearly marked, but they're often up a few flights and out of the way. Most galleries are open Tuesday through Saturday, 11:00 A.M. to 6:00 P.M. You will find most of the galleries located between West Broadway and Mercer, from Grand to Houston. There's a good map and extensive area listings in the *Gallery Guide,* available free at any gallery. Here are some of the highlights.

ARTISTS SPACE
38 Green Street (between Grand and Broome Streets)
(212) 226–3970
www.artistsspace.org
This nonprofit gallery is often the first stop in a professional career for artists. Since 1972 this large gallery has played host to the first works of many artists who've gone on to international recognition working in almost any style and medium.

DEITCH PROJECTS

18 Wooster Street (between Canal and Grand Streets)

76 Grand Street (between Wooster and Greene Streets)

(212) 343–7300
www.deitch.com

These two galleries play host to wildly diverse solo and group shows of contemporary artists.

DIA CENTER FOR THE ARTS

393 West Broadway (between Spring and Broome Streets)

141 Wooster Street (between Prince and Houston Streets)
www.diacenter.org

Without giving too much away about these two long-term installations, they are worth viewing if only to ponder the question, *What would Starbucks give to get this real estate?* These two works, the *Earth Room* and the *Broken Kilometer,* have been on display in these spaces since 1977 and 1979, respectively. Open Wednesday through Saturday noon to 6:00 P.M., but closed from 3:00 to 3:30 P.M.

THE DRAWING CENTER

35 Wooster Street (between Grand and Broome Streets)
(212) 219–2166
www.drawingcenter.org

A cross between a museum and a gallery, this is the only institution in the United States dedicated exclusively to the exhibition, study, and promotion of the medium of drawing.

RONALD FELDMAN FINE ARTS

31 Mercer Street (at Grand Street)
(212) 226–3232
www.feldmangallery.com

One of the oldest and best-respected galleries in Soho, they have a strong focus on performance, installation, political, and conceptual works from both emerging and long-established artists. Among the collection is the largest selection of Andy Warhol prints of any gallery.

ROSENBERG + KAUFMAN FINE ART

115 Wooster Street (between Prince and Spring Streets)
(212) 431–4838
www.artnet.com (search for "Rosenberg + Kaufman")

Up four flights you'll find this small gallery that's well worth the haul. Working with emerging and midcareer artists, the studio specializes in what it calls contemporary contemplative art. They seek out art that reveals itself slowly to the viewer, operating under the motto, "The more you look, the more you see."

WILLIAMSBURG, BROOKLYN

The Williamsburg art galleries are the newest and freshest additions to the New York art world. Since the late 1990s a set of young, brash, daring, less serious, more innovative galleries has begun to sprout up in some unusual settings in this formerly industrial/working-class, now artsy-hip neighborhood. Spread throughout the area, there are about forty spaces located in lofts, storefronts, and even a backyard toolshed. The spaces are a mix of larger studios and some closet-size galleries that are not always clearly marked, and can be off the beaten trail, but a hearty stroll around the neighborhood should give you a chance to see most of the sights. There is a good continually updated map of all the area galleries at the Web site www.williamsburggalleryassociation.com. Most galleries are open Friday through Monday or just on weekends. Here are some of the area galleries where you can always count on seeing something interesting.

CAPLA KESTING FINE ART
   121 Roebling Street (at North 5th Street)
   (917) 650–3760
   www.caplakesting.com
Capla Kesting presents the works of neighborhood and international artists working in all forms. The shows are always full of humor, and they are daring and thought-provoking. During the summer don't miss their free film festival every Tuesday evening and the free-flowing Kelso beer at their openings thoughtout the year.

HOLLAND TUNNEL
   61 South 3rd Street (between Berry and Wythe Avenues)
   (718) 384–5738
   http://hollandtunnel.nfshost.com
   Hours: Saturday and Sunday, 1:00–5:00 P.M.

You might call it intimate, petite, confined, even claustrophobic, but whatever you call it, there's no getting around the fact that this gallery started out in life as a toolshed from Home Depot. This space has gained quite a reputation partly because of the space itself, but also because of its daring programming. At times, this two-by-four of a gallery has hosted as many as one hundred artists in a single show.

MOMENTA ART

359 Bedford Avenue (between South 4th and South 5th Streets)
(718) 218–8058
www.momentaart.org
Hours: Thursday through Monday, noon–6:00 P.M.
Momenta is a not-for-profit gallery dedicated to giving opportunities to emerging artists. Many exhibitions are the first solo shows by these artists.

PIEROGI 2000

177 North 9th Street (between Bedford and Driggs Avenues)
(718) 599–2144
www.pierogi2000.com
Hours: Friday through Monday, noon–6:00 P.M.
One of the oldest, best-respected, and most spacious of the area galleries, Pierogi 2000 highlights the works of Brooklyn artists in a series of mostly solo shows.

Beer Here!

If your style is more Budweiser than Beaujolais, Williamsburg art may be right up your alley. At these decidedly less pretentious Brooklyn galleries, beer is the official drink of choice for the opening receptions. So chugalug your way down to these opening nights for some free beer and intriguing art. For information on openings, check out the calendar at www.williamsburggallery association.com or put your name on each gallery's mailing list to receive invitations.

OTHER GALLERIES AND SHOWS AROUND NEW YORK

BROADWAY WINDOWS
Broadway at East 10th Street
(212) 998–5751
www.nyu.edu/pages/galleries
Hours: 24/7.
Five innocent-looking shop windows that serve as a gallery. They display a wide range of styles including paintings, sculpture, and site-specific work. Be careful when walking in this neighborhood: People are forever crashing into each other, because they can't take their eyes off these often surprising windows.

BWAC PIER SHOWS
141 Beard Street
Red Hook, Brooklyn
(718) 596–2507
www.bwac.org
Hours: Saturday and Sunday, noon–6:00 P.M., May through September only.
The Brooklyn art scene is brought to the public's eye at this series of annual events showcasing more than 200 emerging and established artists. Painting, sculpture, installation art, photography, and experimental forms are on display. It's a bit of a haul to get there, but the Civil War–era warehouse location, amazing view of the Statue of Liberty, passing barge traffic, and enough art to fill the Louvre all make it worth the effort. Call or check their Web site for a schedule of shows.

80 WASHINGTON SQUARE EAST GALLERIES
New York University
80 Washington Square East
(212) 998–5747
www.nyu.edu/pages/galleries
Hours: Tuesday, 10:00 A.M.–7:00 P.M.; Wednesday and Thursday, 10:00 A.M.–6:00 P.M.; Friday and Saturday, 10:00 A.M.–5:00 P.M.
Eight galleries consisting of different solo shows or one group show. Don't miss the "Small Works" international competition every February.

KENKELEBA GALLERY
214 East 2nd Street (between Avenues B and C)
(212) 674–3939
Hours: Wednesday through Saturday, 11:00 A.M.–6:00 P.M.
This gallery specializes in works by African-American and third-world artists, emerging artists, and experimental works.

PERFORMANCE SPACE 122 GALLERY
150 First Avenue (entrance on 9th Street)
(212) 228–4249
www.ps122.org
Hours: Thursday and Friday, noon–6:00 p.m.; Saturday and Sunday, noon–4:00 p.m.
The gallery wing of the birthplace of downtown performance art, where you'll find shows of paintings, photography, drawings, sculptures, videos, installations, multimedia, and many other things sure to upset Bill O'Reilly and his conservative friends. You can also volunteer-usher to see performances here for free. (See the chapter, "Theater: Free Speech" for details.)

THE ROTUNDA GALLERY
33 Clinton Street (at Pierrepont Street)
Brooklyn
(718) 875–4047
www.brooklynx.org/rotunda
Hours: Tuesday through Friday, noon–5:00 P.M.; Saturday, 11:00 A.M.–4:00 P.M.
Exhibits all Brooklyn-based artists working in all forms, from painting and sculpture to installations and performance art.

SOCRATES SCULPTURE PARK
Broadway at Vernon Boulevard
Long Island City, Queens
(718) 956–1819
www.socratessculpturepark.org
Hours: Daily, 10:00 A.M.–sunset.
This four-and-a-half-acre stretch of land along the Queens side of the East River has been transformed into a delightful green space that highlights the works of up-and-coming artists. They also offer free tours and occasionally free films and music as well. Call or check the Web site for details and schedule.

WEST SIDE ARTS COALITION
On the mall at Broadway and 96th Street
(212) 316–6024
www.wsacny.org
Hours: Saturday and Sunday, noon–6:00 P.M.; Wednesday, 6:00–8:00 P.M.
From cheesy kitsch to winsome watercolors, you never know what you'll find at this little gallery showcasing the works of community artists in the middle of the road, literally (it's located on the median between the traffic running up and down Broadway). Stop by and take a look; it'll just take you a minute, again, literally.

WHITE COLUMNS
320 West 13th Street (enter on Horatio Street, between Eighth
Avenue and Hudson Street)
(212) 924–4212
www.whitecolumns.org
Hours: Tuesday through Saturday, noon–6:00 P.M.
Specializing in large-scale installations by emerging and underrepresented artists, White Columns was the first to commission works by many artists who have gone on to international fame (and infamy), including William Wegman and Andres Serrano.

> "I went to the museum
> where they had all the
> heads and arms from
> the statues that are in
> all the other museums."
>
> —Stephen Wright

MUSEUMS: FREE TO SEE

THE MUSEUMS OF New York City are world-class, abundant—and most of these collections can be seen free of charge. Whatever your taste or interest, whatever your age, background, or curiosities, there are museums to satisfy you. Many are completely free of charge at all times, while others have specific days and hours when they allow the public in for free or "pay what you want" (and you know what I want to pay!). Chances are, if the institution you would like to visit does not fit into one of those two categories, the admission charge is a "suggested donation." (Can you guess what I suggest you donate?)

AMERICAN FOLK ART MUSEUM

Eva and Morris Feld Gallery
2 Lincoln Square (Columbus Avenue, between 65th and 66th Streets)
(212) 595–9533
www.folkartmuseum.org

Hours: Tuesday through Saturday, noon–7:30 P.M.; Sunday, noon–6:30 P.M.

While much of the Folk Art Museum has moved down to fancier digs on 53rd Street where they charge you to get in (except Friday evening), they still maintain these galleries at the original location of the museum, filled with enticing selections from their extensive permanent collection as well as temporary exhibitions. It's always a joy to take a walk through these halls and see what new treasures they have discovered. A sign at the front desk suggests a $3 donation, but no one seems to take any notice of that, and the staff doesn't stop you and ask for any cash. (See pages 256–57 for more information on the 53rd Street location.)

AUDUBON TERRACE

Hispanic Society of America, (212) 926–2234;
www.hispanicsociety.org

Hours: Tuesday through Saturday, 10:00 A.M.–4:30 P.M.; Sunday, 1:00–4:00 P.M.

American Academy of Arts and Letters, (212) 368–5900;
Broadway, between 155th and 156th Streets
www.artsandletters.org

These regal buildings in Upper Manhattan are home to two small but impressive collections. The Hispanic Society is a collection of paintings, sculpture, archaeological finds, textiles, rare books, and manuscripts from Spain, Portugal, and Latin America dating as far back as the seventh century B.C. and is always free and open to the public. The Academy of Arts and Letters is a private organization of 250 preeminent American writers, composers, painters, sculptors, and architects. The building is home to many of the works of these artists and is free, but it's open to the public only for exhibitions during the spring and fall. Call for a schedule and details.

CARNEGIE HALL

The Rose Museum
154 West 57th Street, second floor (between Sixth and Seventh Avenues)
(212) 903–9629
www.carnegiehall.org

Hours: Daily, 11:00 A.M.–4:30 P.M., and during concert intermissions.
Explore the history of the architectural splendor and acoustical wonder that is Carnegie Hall. From Toscanini's baton to Benny Goodman's clarinet, this museum has hundreds of artifacts, photographs, and memorabilia from its legendary past.

CASTLE CLINTON
Battery Park
(212) 344–7220
www.nps.gov/cacl
Hours: Daily, 8:30 A.M.–5:00 P.M.
Originally built in 1811 as the vanguard in the defense of New York Harbor off the shores of the southwest tip of Manhattan, Castle Clinton has over its long history served as a fort, an opera house, and the New York Aquarium; it was finally saved from destruction and returned to its original fort design to serve as a national monument. A small museum and video display tell you about the long and varied history of the building, as does a well-marked self-guided tour. Be sure to check out the tours and programs led by the park rangers throughout the day.

FASHION INSTITUTE OF TECHNOLOGY MUSEUM
Shirley Goodman Resource Center
Seventh Avenue between 27th and 28th Streets
(212) 217–5800
www.fitnyc.edu/museum
Hours: Tuesday through Friday, noon–8:00 P.M.; Saturday, 10:00 A.M.–5:00 P.M.
Located in the fashion district, this school museum is home to the largest collection of costumes, textiles, and apparel dating from the eighteenth century in the world. You won't find all their finery on display at all times, though; exhibitions change throughout the year. Still, whatever they have on display is sure to thrill any fashion bug.

FEDERAL HALL NATIONAL MEMORIAL
26 Wall Street (at Broad Street)
(212) 826–6888
www.nps.gov/feha
Hours: Monday through Friday, 9:00 A.M.–5:00 P.M.
The site of George Washington's first inauguration as president and the first home of the U.S. Congress, this building now houses a museum about its role in the early history of the city and country. Free guided tours at 10:00 A.M., noon, and 2:00 P.M.

THE FISHER LANDAU CENTER FOR ART
38–27 30th Street (between Thirty-eighth and Thirty-ninth Avenues)
Long Island City, Queens
(718) 937–0727
www.flcart.org
Hours: Thursday through Monday, noon to 5:00 P.M.
A spacious museum dedicated to contemporary art from the 1960s until today. The collection of over 1,100 pieces contains the works of such artists as Jasper Johns, Donald Judd, Robert Rauschenberg, Kiki Smith, and Andy Warhol. They also occasionally offer free walking tours in conjunction with other nearby arts organizations. Check their Web site for schedules and exhibitions.

FORBES MAGAZINE GALLERIES
62 Fifth Avenue (at 12th Street)
(212) 206–5548
www.forbesgalleries.com
Hours: Tuesday, Wednesday, Friday, and Saturday, 10:00 a.m.–4:00 P.M.
The business magazine shows its lighter side in their galleries with a permanent collection that includes thousands of toy soldiers, hundreds of toy boats, the untold history of the game Monopoly, and hundreds of unusual trophies. Their other galleries house changing exhibits of jewelry and historical letters and documents, as well as classical and contemporary art.

GENERAL GRANT'S NATIONAL MONUMENT
Riverside Drive and 122nd Street
(212) 666–1640
www.nps.gov/gegr
Hours: Daily, 9:00 A.M.–5:00 P.M.
Here you'll finally get an answer to that age-old question: Who's buried in Grant's Tomb? You can also see some exhibits about U. S. Grant's life (childhood, the Civil War years, and the presidency) as well as some pretty stunning views of the Hudson River.

HALL OF FAME FOR GREAT AMERICANS
Hall of Fame Terrace
181st Street and University Avenue
The Bronx
(718) 289–5161
www.bcc.cuny.edu/halloffame
Hours: Daily, 10:00 A.M.–5:00 P.M.
If there was a hall of fame for halls of fame, this one would certainly be in it, because this is where the whole idea began. On this covered walkway

FREE OR PAY-WHAT-YOU-WISH DAYS AT MUSEUMS

MUSEUM	MONDAY	TUESDAY	WEDNESDAY	THURSDAY	FRIDAY	SATURDAY	SUNDAY
American Folk Art Museum					5:30–7:30 P.M.		
Asia Society					6:00–9:00 P.M.		
Bartow-Pell Mansion Museum					First Friday of Every Month 5:30–9:00 P.M.		
Bronx Museum of the Arts					NOON–8:00 P.M.		
Brooklyn Museum of Art						First Saturday of Every Month 5:00–11:00 P.M.	
Guggenheim Museum					5:45–7:45 P.M.		
International Center of Photography (ICP)					5:00–8:00 P.M.		
Jewish Museum						11:00 A.M.– 5:45 P.M.	
Museum of Arts and Design				6:00–8:00 P.M.			
Museum of Chinese in America (MoCA)					noon–6:00 P.M.		
Museum of Jewish Heritage			4:00–8:00 P.M.				
Museum of Modern Art (MoMA)					4:00–8:00 P.M.		
Museum of the Moving Image					4:00–8:00 P.M.		
New York Hall of Science					2:00–5:00 P.M. (EXCEPT JULY AND AUGUST)		10:00–11:00 A.M. (EXCEPT JULY AND AUGUST)
The Noguchi Museum					First Friday of Every Month 10:00 A.M.– 5:00 P.M.		
The Studio Museum in Harlem						First Saturday of Every Month 10:00 A.M.–6:00 P.M.	
Whitney Museum					6:00–9:00 P.M.		

you'll find bronze busts of great American political leaders, scientists, soldiers, and authors.

LOUIS ARMSTRONG ARCHIVES
Queens College
65–30 Kissena Boulevard (at the Long Island Expressway)
(718) 997–3670
www.satchmo.net
Hours: Monday through Friday, 10:00 A.M.–5:00 P.M.
Home to more than 5,000 photographs, home recordings, scrapbooks, music, and instruments from the home of one of the (if not *the!*) greatest trumpet players in the history of jazz. They also lead tours through the Armstrong house at 34–57 107th Street in Corona, Queens, but they charge for that. The archives are free and open to the public, but by appointment only.

MUSEUM OF AMERICAN ILLUSTRATORS
128 East 63rd Street (between Park and Lexington Avenues)
(212) 838–2560
www.societyillustrators.org
Hours: Tuesday, 10:00 A.M.–8:00 P.M.; Wednesday through Friday,
10:00 A.M.–5:00 P.M.; Saturday, noon–4:00 P.M.
This East Side town house is home to a private club for illustrators, but the public is always invited to explore their two gallery spaces. They put up anywhere from fifteen to twenty-two shows a year from their extensive permanent collection of historical book and magazine covers and illustrations. Some of the true prizes of the collection reside in the upstairs dining room, which is not officially open to the public. If you ask nicely, though, they'll be happy to let you up there to see the Norman Rockwell, Maxfield Parrish, and other treasures.

NATIONAL MUSEUM OF THE AMERICAN INDIAN
1 Bowling Green Place (between State and Whitehall Streets)
(212) 514–3700
www.si.edu/nmai
Hours: Daily, 10:00 A.M.–5:00 P.M.; Thursday until 8:00 P.M.
A branch of the Smithsonian Institution, this museum is overflowing with dazzling artifacts, interactive displays, firsthand oral histories, music, and crafts of Native Americans. The changing exhibits explore the histories, beliefs, customs, and cultures of these once vast civilizations. The museum offers free workshops in such things as traditional basket weaving and bead-

work (small materials fees are required), and free guided tours at 2:00 P.M. every day. If you miss the official guided tour, drop by the information desk on the second floor anytime—there's usually someone available to show you around free of charge. They also have a schedule of free films and live performances. Call or check the Web site for a schedule and details.

NEW YORK UNEARTHED
17 State Street (at Pearl Street)
(212) 748–8628
www.southstseaport.org
By appointment only.
Explore 5,000 years of New York history in fifteen minutes at this free branch of the South Street Seaport Museum. The museum is free, but you must call to make an appointment.

NICHOLAS ROERICH MUSEUM
319 West 107th Street (between Broadway and Riverside Drive)
(212) 864–7752
www.roerich.org
Hours: Tuesday through Sunday, 2:00–5:00 P.M.
Houses more than 200 works by the artist Nicholas Roerich that deal mainly with Himalayan scenery and spiritual subject matter. Sundays they also almost always present a free classical concert or poetry reading. Call or check the Web site for details.

QUEENS COUNTY FARM MUSEUM
73–50 Little Neck Parkway
Floral Park, Queens
(718) 347–FARM (3276)
www.queensfarm.org
Hours: Monday through Friday, 9:00 A.M.–5:00 P.M. (outside only);
Saturday and Sunday, 10:00 A.M.–5:00 P.M.
Where the City Mouse meets the County Mouse. This forty-seven-acre working farm is the last remaining tract of undisturbed farmland in New York City and dates back to the seventeenth century. On the weekend take a free guided tour of the farmhouse and greenhouse, wander the farmyards, and—*hey!*— they even have hayrides (for $2).

TIBET HOUSE NEW YORK

22 West 15th Street (between Fifth and Sixth Avenues)

(212) 807–0563

www.tibethouse.org

Hours: Monday through Friday, noon–6:00 P.M.

The galleries host exhibitions of artworks having to do with the culture, beliefs, history, and mythology of Tibetan Buddhism. They also hold open meditations every Tuesday evening with talks afterward. They ask for a $10 donation or "whatever you like."

URBAN CENTER

Architectural League of New York; (212) 753–1722; www.archleague.org

The Municipal Art Society; (212) 935–3960; www.mas.org

457 Madison Avenue (between 50th and 51st Streets)

Hours: Monday through Wednesday, Friday, and Saturday, 11:00 A.M.– 5:00 P.M.

The galleries on the first two floors of the Urban Center play host to exhibitions from both of these organizations. The Municipal Art Society works usually highlight the city as a work of art, while the Architectural League's shows concentrate on the art of making the city.

WHITNEY MUSEUM AT ALTRIA

120 Park Avenue (at 42nd Street)

(917) 663–2453

www.whitney.org

Hours: Monday through Wednesday and Friday, 11:00 A.M.–6:00 P.M.; Thursday until 7:30 P.M.

A branch of the Whitney Museum, this small gallery and atrium plays host to four or five shows a year with a focus on contemporary emerging artists. There isn't much gallery here, but it's a nice indoor public space for a brown-bag lunch. They also host a series of performances every spring.

SOMETIMES FREE

AMERICAN FOLK ART MUSEUM

45 West 53rd Street (between Fifth and Sixth Avenues)

(212) 265–1040

www.folkartmuseum.org

Hours: Tuesday through Sunday, 10:30 A.M.–5:30 P.M.; Friday until 7:30 P.M.

When free: Friday, 5:30–7:30 P.M.

This glorious building is home to a huge collection of American folk art. The works on display from their permanent collection or from temporary exhibitions are created by artisans and artists from all walks of life throughout American history to the present time. These mostly self-taught artists have created pieces that are often whimsical and surprising, and could be anything from weather vanes or painted furniture to handwoven Shaker rugs or duck decoys. The Lincoln Center gallery is open Tuesday through Sunday and is always free. (See page 250 for details on the museum's other location at 2 Lincoln Square.)

ASIA SOCIETY
725 Park Avenue (between 70th and 71st Streets)
(212) 288–6400
www.asiasociety.org
Hours: Tuesday through Saturday, 11:00 A.M.–6:00 P.M.;
Friday until 9:00 P.M.; Sunday, noon–5:00 P.M.
When free: Friday, 6:00–9:00 P.M.
A terrifically modern museum with exhibits from every corner of Asia that encompass antiquities as old as humankind as well as the most startling new technologies and contemporary art commissions. They offer free guided tours and audio tours on Free Fridays as well.

BARTOW-PELL MANSION MUSEUM
895 Shore Road North
Pelham Bay Park, the Bronx
(718) 885–1461
www.bartowpellmansionmuseum.org
Hours: Wednesday, Saturday, and Sunday, noon–4:00 P.M.
When free: The first Friday of every month, 5:30–9:00 P.M.
Travel back to the early part of the nineteenth century, when living in the Bronx was considered living in the country. The estate predates the signing of the Declaration of Independence, and the mansion was built and furnished in the early 1800s. The museum has returned the home, carriage house, and gardens to their original splendor. You are welcome to make yourself at home on the first Friday of every month from 5:30 to 9:00 P.M., when they open the doors for free and also offer free music, refreshments, and crafts.

BRONX MUSEUM OF THE ARTS
1040 Grand Concourse (at 165th Street)
The Bronx
(718) 681–6000
www.bronxmuseum.org

Hours: Wednesday, Thursday, Saturday, and Sunday noon—to 6:00 P.M.; Friday until 8:00 P.M.
When free: Friday.
Primarily shows twentieth-century contemporary art by African, African-American, Latino, and Asian artists as well as artists who have lived in the Bronx.

BROOKLYN MUSEUM OF ART

200 Eastern Parkway (at Washington Avenue)
(718) 638–5000
www.brooklynmuseum.org
Hours: Wednesday through Friday, 10:00 A.M.–5:00 P.M.; Saturday and Sunday, 11:00 A.M.–6:00 P.M.
When free: The first Saturday of every month, 5:00–11:00 P.M.
Don't miss the First Saturday event every month: free theater, free music, free movies, free dancing, free art, free guided tours. What a night! All other times they have a "suggested" donation of $8 for admission, but you can give as much (or as little!) as you would like.

GUGGENHEIM MUSEUM

1071 Fifth Avenue (at 89th Street)
(212) 423–3500
www.guggenheim.org
Hours: Sunday through Wednesday, 10:00 A.M.–6:00 P.M.; Friday and Saturday until 8:00 P.M.
When free: Friday 5:45–7:45 P.M. is "Pay What You Wish."
The art museum that is a work of art itself. Designed by Frank Lloyd Wright, the building houses modern works that are sometimes controversial, sometimes commercial, but always worth seeing.

INTERNATIONAL CENTER OF PHOTOGRAPHY (ICP)

1133 Avenue of the Americas (at 43rd Street)
(212) 857–0000
www.icp.org
Hours: Tuesday through Thursday, 10:00 A.M.–6:00 P.M.; Friday until 8:00 P.M.; Saturday and Sunday until 6:00 P.M.
When free: Friday 5:00–8:00 P.M. is "Pay What You Wish."
The huge gallery spaces of the ICP mount shows that celebrate the art, craft, and images caught in the blink of an eye by the finest photographers from around the world and throughout the history of this ever-evolving art form.

JEWISH MUSEUM

1109 Fifth Avenue (at 92nd Street)
(212) 423–3200
www.jewishmuseum.org

Hours: Saturday through Wednesday, 11:00 A.M.–5:45 P.M.; Thursday until 8:00 P.M.; closed Friday. The shops have the same hours with the exception of being closed Saturday and open Friday, 11:00 A.M. to 3:00 P.M.

When free: Saturday 11:00 A.M.–5:45 P.M.

Ancient traditions and modern sensibilities clash, collide, and mesh in this museum that follows the development and culture of the Jewish experience from antiquity to the present day. The walls are full of rare artifacts, interactive displays, and intriguing works of art that span the centuries.

MUSEUM OF ARTS AND DESIGN

40 West 53rd Street (between Fifth and Sixth Avenues)
(212) 956–3535
www.madmuseum.org

Hours: Daily, 10:00 A.M.–6:00 P.M.; Thursday until 8:00 P.M.

When free: Thursday 6:00–8:00 P.M. is "Pay What You Want."

This elegant three-story museum essentially serves as an excuse for a very popular gift shop. The museum displays functional objects handcrafted by contemporary American artists working in such areas as glass, baskets, quilts, furniture, instruments, utensils, and even boats, kites, brooms, and paper plates. And yes, many of the artists on display in the museum have pricey items available at the gift shop.

MUSEUM OF CHINESE IN AMERICA (MoCA)

70 Mulberry Street, second floor (at Bayard Street)
(212) 923–3700
www.moca-nyc.org

Hours: Tuesday through Sunday, noon–6:00 P.M.

When free: Friday.

A small museum dedicated to preserving and chronicling the full experience of Chinese immigrants and their descendants.

MUSEUM OF JEWISH HERITAGE

36 Battery Place (in Battery Park City Park)
(646) 437–4200
www.mjhnyc.org

Hours: Sunday through Thursday, 10:00 A.M.–5:45 P.M.; Wednesday until 8:00 P.M.; Friday and the eve of Jewish holidays, 10:00 A.M.–3:00 P.M.

When free: Wednesday, 4:00–8:00 P.M.

The museum exists as a living memorial to the Holocaust and uses the two quotes *"Remember, Never Forget"* and *"There Is Hope for Your Future"* to define its mission. The lives, culture, beliefs, and traditions of those who perished in the Holocaust are celebrated while the museum also looks forward to the present-day Jewish communities around the world that are the legacy of those Holocaust victims.

MUSEUM OF MODERN ART (MoMA)
11 West 53rd Street (between Fifth and Sixth Avenues)
(212) 708-9480
www.moma.org
Hours: Monday, Wednesday, Thursday, Saturday, and Sunday, 10:30 A.M.–5:30 P.M.; Friday, 10:00 A.M.–8:00 P.M.
When free: Friday 4:00–8:00 P.M. is "Pay What You Wish."
From Monet to milk cartons, everything modern can be found here. Films, gallery talks, and jazz in the sculpture garden as well as high-profile temporary exhibitions and the permanent collection are all available during the "Pay What You Wish" Friday hours.

MUSEUM OF THE MOVING IMAGE
Thirty-fifth Avenue at 36th Street
Astoria, Queens
(718) 784-4520
www.ammi.org
Hours: Wednesday and Thursday, 11:00 A.M.–5:00 P.M.; Friday, 11:00 A.M.–8:00 P.M.; Saturday and Sunday, 11:00 A.M.–6:30 P.M.
When free: Friday, 4:00–8:00 P.M.
With the nation's largest collection of film, television, and digital media artifacts, the museum explores, catalogs, entertains, and educates visitors on the complete history of everything having to do with the moving image. Its many exhibits go behind the scenes and delve into every area from penny arcades to the secrets of Yoda's puppetry. There is an additional charge for screenings during the free hours, but there are enough fascinating galleries and interactive exhibits to keep any film buff happy.

NEW YORK HALL OF SCIENCE
47-01 111th Street
Flushing Meadows–Corona Park, Queens
(718) 699-0005
www.nyhallsci.org
Hours: Tuesday through Thursday, 9:30 A.M.–2:00 P.M.; Friday, 9:30 A.M.–5:00 P.M.; Saturday and Sunday, 10:00 A.M.–6:00 P.M.

When free: Friday, 2:00–5:00 P.M.; Sunday, 10:00–11:00 A.M.; except in July and August.
Kids of all ages love this place. A lot of hands-on science experiments, space stuff, and a big glowing brain—who could ask for anything more?

THE NOGUCHI MUSEUM
32–37 Vernon Boulevard (at 33rd Road)
Long Island City, Queens
(718) 204–7088
www.noguchi.org
Hours: Wednesday through Friday, 10:00 A.M.–5:00 P.M.; Saturday and Sunday, 11:00 A.M.–6:00 P.M.
When free: The first Friday of every month.
Housed in a former photo-engraving factory, the museum is devoted entirely to the sculpture and art of Isamu Noguchi. Noguchi sculptures and designs are on display in public and private spaces throughout the world, and the museum houses many of his most striking and noted works in its thirteen galleries and garden space.

THE STUDIO MUSEUM IN HARLEM
144 West 125th Street (between Lenox and Seventh Avenues)
(212) 864–4500
www.studiomuseuminharlem.org
Hours: Wednesday through Friday and Sunday, noon–6:00 P.M.; Saturday, 10:00 A.M.–6:00 P.M.
When free: The first Saturday of each month.
The leading museum dedicated to the works of African-American artists.

WHITNEY MUSEUM OF AMERICAN ART
945 Madison Avenue (at 75th Street)
(212) 570–3600
www.whitney.org
Hours: Wednesday, Thursday, Saturday, and Sunday, 11:00 A.M.–6:00 P.M.; Friday, 1:00–9:00 P.M.
When free: Friday, 6:00–9:00 P.M. is "Pay What You Wish."
One of the most impressive collections of modern art in the world, the permanent collection follows the developments of modern work from Hopper to Pollock and from Rauschenberg to today's cutting-edge artists. A couple of floors of the museum are always reserved for changing shows, from historic solo works to daring group shows. Drop by any Friday for pay-what-you-wish-night and also take in the free live music and guided and audio tours.

MUSEUMS WITH SUGGESTED DONATIONS

A large selection of major and smaller museums in New York operate under a "suggested donation" system. So, while they may "suggest" a $20 "donation," you are under no obligation to make that specific donation. There's no reason to feel bad about giving less than they ask or as little as you can afford. The fact of the matter is, most of these institutions are members of the Cultural Institutions Group (CIG) and receive a tremendous amount of money from the city of New York. One of the obligations that goes along with this cash from the city is that they have to let folks into their museums for whatever they are willing to pay. In essence, you've already paid your admission when you pay your taxes. You can get away with giving as little as a penny. My standard contribution is a quarter (see, I can be generous).

AMERICAN MUSEUM OF NATURAL HISTORY, Central Park West (at 79th Street); (212) 769–5100; www.amnh.org.

BROOKLYN MUSEUM OF ART, 200 Eastern Parkway (at Washington Avenue); (718) 638–5000; www.brooklynmuseum.org.

THE CLOISTERS, Fort Tryon Park, Washington Heights; (212) 923–3700; www.metmuseum.org.

EL MUSEO DEL BARRIO, 1230 Fifth Avenue (at 105th Street); (212) 831–7272; www.elmuseo.org.

METROPOLITAN MUSEUM OF ART, 1000 Fifth Avenue (at 82nd Street); (212) 535–7710; www.metmuseum.org.

MUSEUM OF CHINESE IN AMERICA, 70 Mulberry Street, second floor (at Bayard Street); (212) 619–4785; www.moca-nyc.org.

MUSEUM OF THE CITY OF NEW YORK, 1220 Fifth Avenue (at 103rd Street); (212) 534–1672; www.mcny.org.

NEW YORK CITY POLICE MUSEUM, 100 Old Slip (between Water Street and FDR Drive); (212) 480–3100; www.nycpolicemuseum.org.

NEW YORK FIRE MUSEUM, 278 Spring Street (between Varick and Hudson Streets); (212) 691–1303; www.nycfiremuseum.org.

P.S. 1 CONTEMPORARY ART CENTER, 22–25 Jackson Avenue (at 46th Avenue), Queens; (718) 784–2084; www.ps1.org.

QUEENS MUSEUM OF ART, Flushing Meadows Park; (718) 592–9700; www.queensmuseum.org.

"All good things are wild,
and free."

—Henry David Thoreau

ZOOS: BORN FREE

IT USED TO BE that the best place to see the wildlife for free in New York was to walk around Times Square on any late night. But now that 42nd Street has gotten its face-lift, the closest you will come to seeing anything too wild on those streets are the fake furs and leather worn by visitors to the Disney Shop and Madame Tussaud's. So for some real roars, New York offers some fine collections of everything from African lions, Chilean flamingos, Indian elephants, and Australian lizards to grizzly bears, Goliath beetles, lowland gorillas, and Grevy's zebras. You will find zoos in each of the boroughs, but the only ones that have free hours are the Bronx and Staten Island Zoos. Free days for both zoos are on Wednesday.

THE BRONX ZOO
Fordham Road and the Bronx River Parkway
(718) 367–1010
www.bronxzoo.com

 Free general admission all day on Wednesday, but you will have to pay to get into some exhibits (which can add up!).

The rain forest of the Congo or the African savannah may not be what you expect to see in the Bronx, but at this, the largest metropolitan zoo in the country, you'll find more than 6,000 animals and exhibits set in startlingly realistic natural habitats. As part of the Wildlife Conservation Society, the Bronx Zoo has played an integral part in saving such endangered species as the snow leopard, the American bison, lowland gorillas, Chinese alligators, Mauritius pink pigeons, and more than forty other species. And bring the family by on any Wednesday to save a fistful of cash. Wednesday is Donation Day, and everyone gets in for whatever they want to pay, even if that's nothing. Beware, many of the more enticing and exciting exhibits and rides do charge additional fees (even on Wednesday), so you might want to pony up some cash for their Pay-One-Price ticket upgrade ($15) if you plan on taking in all the wild sights.

STATEN ISLAND ZOO
614 Broadway (off Glenwood Avenue)
(718) 442–3100
www.statenislandzoo.org

 Free on Wednesday after 2:00 P.M.

Particularly well known for its collection of snakes and other reptiles, this small zoo also boasts an aquarium, children's zoo, rain forest, and African savannah habitats and free parking.

"If you want to say it with flowers, a single rose says: 'I'm cheap!'"
—Delta Burke

HEY, EVEN CHEAP BASTARDS need love. And while it's true that introducing yourself as a Cheap Bastard may not be the most successful way to get a date, being a Cheap Bastard shouldn't get in the way of having a great time. In fact, you might even score extra points by coming up with some original ideas for romantic liaisons around New York. Here are some great ways to spend days and evenings with that special someone that won't cost you a thing (except maybe your heart).

THE UNTRADITIONAL TRADITIONAL DATE: Why not put a twist on the usual date by seeing a free movie? In the summer there are any number of starlit nights for you to set out a blanket and cuddle while you watch the stars of Hollywood twinkle on the screen. My personal favorite romantic setting is the Movies With A View, at the foot of the Brooklyn Bridge—not too crowded, the skyline of New York as a backdrop, and fun films on the screen. During the cooler months move indoors with the free screenings at RiFiFi or Casa Italiana at NYU. For more details and other film ideas, see the chapter titled "Film: Cheap Shots."

THE SWEEP-HER-OFF-HER-FEET DATE: Swing down to the MoonDance at Hudson River Park any Sunday during the summer for dancing under the stars to live music. Show up early for a free lesson. During the cooler months, stick a rose in her mouth and heat things up by going down to Chelsea Market to do the Dance of Love any Saturday afternoon, when they offer a traditional Argentinean tango *milonga*. For details and more dance ideas, see the chapter titled "Dance: Free Expression."

THE SURE-WAY-TO-SCORE DATE: Spend a day of fun and games in Central Park by borrowing a free Field Day Kit from the folks at the North Meadow Recreation Center. They throw in all kinds of equipment for almost any sport you can think of. Your big sack of fun includes a basketball, bats, Wiffle balls, football, Nerf ball, horseshoe set, Frisbee, jump rope, and even hula hoops. If that doesn't get the two of you working up a sweat, nothing will. For more information see page 283.

THE THIS-ISN'T-QUITE-VENICE-BUT-HEY-YOU-AREN'T-QUITE-SOPHIA-LOREN DATE: Your gondola awaits you at the Downtown Boathouse on Pier 40 or Pier 96. The bad news is, you have to do all the rowing and serenading yourself; the good news is, it's free. Borrow a kayak for you and your love to paddle up and down the Hudson any weekend from May through October. For details see pages 178.

THE TROUBADOUR DATE: If you don't have the voice to serenade your sweetheart by yourself, here's the next best thing. Catch one of the very intimate performances at the Postcrypt Coffeehouse on the campus of Columbia University any Friday or Saturday night during the school year. Any candlelit evening of acoustic music is the perfect setting for a romantic evening for two. And hey, there's even free popcorn. For details see page 28.

THE MAKE-'EM-LAUGH DATE: A surefire way to win someone's heart is to put a smile on their face, and there are many free funny nights every week around the city. During the week you'll find some top-notch comedy performances at the Upright Citizens Brigade on Wednesday and Sunday nights.

For more details and other comedy destinations, see the chapter titled "Comedy: Cheap Jokes."

THE LOVE-BIRDS DATE: See if a walk among the birds and the bees inspires anything for you. Stop by Belvedere Castle in Central Park and borrow a free Birding Kit for a delightful stroll through the wilds of the park. Your kit comes equipped with your very own set of binoculars, a field guide, a sketch pad, and colored pencils. For more details see page 137.

THE PRETENTIOUS DATE: Show your date you can bandy around words like *cubist, conceptual, minimalistic,* and *postmodernist* with the best of them at any of the many art gallery openings that go on every week. If that doesn't have any effect, maybe all the free wine or beer will. For more details see the chapter titled "Art Galleries: Show Me the Monet."

THE FUN-IN-THE-SUN DATE: Spend a day at any one of the local beaches. An old reliable free day. Sorry, they can't all be gems. See pages 182–84 for beaches.

THE SHOW-'EM-YOU-GOT-CLASS DATE: Take in a museum on one of the many free, suggested donation, or pay-what-you-want nights. The best one is First Saturday Night at the Brooklyn Museum—free live music and dancing, free films, and, oh yeah, there's some art there, too. For more museum details see the chapter titled "Museums: Free to See."

THE NOT-QUITE-THE-GREAT-WHITE-WAY DATE: Take my advice: If you want a second date, don't try this on a first date. If you've been dating for a while, though, and it's clear that you're both Cheap Bastards, then why not pick a Broadway or Off Broadway show for you to volunteer-usher at together? For a list of theaters to usher at, see the chapter titled "Theater: Free Speech." If you don't want to seem chintzy, get free tickets to a production or concert at Juilliard or NYU or any of the other free theaters listed on pages 19–24.

THE YOU-THINK-*WE'VE*-GOT-PROBLEMS? DATE: Hitting one of those rough patches in the relationship? Well, there's nothing like reveling in someone else's misery to make you feel good about your own life. Take your date to see a taping of *The Montel Williams Show, The People's Court,* or *Maury* and by comparison, your troubles will surely seem insignificant. For details and more TV taping ideas, see the chapter titled "Television Tapings: Public Access."

THE GETTING-TO-KNOW-YOU DATE: Why not take the time to get to know each other as you get to know a bit of New York? There are some great walking tours that will give you the time to walk and talk your way around the city. Check out Take a Walk, New York!, Urban Park Rangers tours, or the delightful jaunts through Central Park given by the Central Park Conservancy. For more details see the chapter titled "Walking Tours: The Freedom Trail."

THE HEY-THIS-IS-GOING-PRETTY-SWELL-I-MAY-JUST-WANT-TO-KISS-YOU SPECIAL ADD-ON TO ANY DATE: It may not be as romantic as the *Titanic,* but a ride on the Staten Island Ferry will leave you feeling like you're on top of the world. Particularly if you end that date with a romantic kiss on the boat while you ride by the dramatic New York skyline with the wind in your hair. For more details see page 226.

FINDING A CHEAP DATE . . .

Um, I mean *finding a date, cheap*. It's a big city with lots of single folks out there trying to find each other, but hanging out in bars or going to "singles" parties and events can be costly, not to mention depressing. Here are a couple of alternative ways to make the connection by volunteering and just being your own cheap self.

DATE BAIT
(212) 971–1084
www.datebait.com
DateBaitNY@yahoo.com

Volunteers arrive forty-five minutes early to help with registration and stay a few minutes after to help with cleanup, but they fully participate in the event.

These are structured, results-oriented mixers for single people. The way it works is that when you register, you get a name tag with a number. Once the whole group has gathered—and these events do attract large crowds— everyone gets up to one minute to introduce themselves in front of the assembled. Then there's time to mingle and get to know each other; at the end of the night, you hand in a card with the numbers of those people you're interested in having a date with. If you're on their card as well, it's a match. If not . . . well, at least there was no face-to-face rejection. They have straight, gay, and lesbian events almost every week, and they're always surprisingly unintimidating, fun, and well put together. Call or e-mail at least a few weeks in advance to make a reservation to volunteer.

HURRYDATE
(646) 435–8264
www.hurrydate.com

Door Hosts help set up the event and welcome paying guests. They are not always guaranteed a chance to participate in the "dating" but can mingle and meet potential dates . . . and get paid for it!

Got a minute? Have a date . . . or a dozen. HurryDate puts together energetic evenings where throngs of New York singles meet each other in a rapid-fire succession of mini-dates. They hold events targeted for gay and straight daters of all ages. There are two parts to any HurryDate evening. The evening starts and ends with the usual mix-and-mingle that you'd expect in any singles soiree, but what makes this different is that you're guaranteed twelve to twenty on-the-spot dates. Each date consists of a four-minute conversation where you two can get to know the basics about each other and see if there is enough chemistry there to give the real thing a try. If you both check off "Yes" on your scorecards, HurryDate will hook you up through their Web site and let nature take its course. You can take part in the evening by being a Door Host, which basically means they will pay you about $40 to help organize the event and greet the paying daters. Door Hosts are able to participate in the face-to-face dating only when there is an odd number of participants and you fit into the age or category of the evening. In any case, you are always able to participate in the schmooze-fest part of the evening.

"Every crowd has
a silver lining."

—P. T. Barnum

NEW YORKERS DON'T need much of an excuse to throw a parade, and nobody does a parade bigger or better than us. Either celebrating a national holiday, one of New York's many ethnic groups, or just to whoop it up, if it is the weekend, there is almost always a parade heading down a major avenue near you. Here is a detailed list of most New York City parades throughout the year, including approximate dates and locations. For more information on specific dates and locations, I have included contact information wherever possible. For further information call 311, the New York City information line.

JANUARY

THREE KINGS DAY PARADE, Third Avenue from 106th to 116th Street; (212) 831–7272; www.elmuseo.org/3kings.html; January 6.

MARTIN LUTHER KING JR. DAY PARADE, Fifth Avenue from 61st to 86th Street; third Monday in January.

IDIOT-AROD, a wild and drunken shopping cart race from Fulton Ferry Pier at the foot of the Brooklyn Bridge, over the bridge and through downtown Manhattan to Tomkins Square Park; www.cartsofbrooklyn.com; last weekend in January.

FEBRUARY

CHINESE LUNAR NEW YEAR CELEBRATION AND FESTIVAL, Mott Street; www.explorechinatown.com.

MARCH

ST. PATRICK'S DAY PARADE, Fifth Avenue from 44th to 86th Street; March 17; www.saintpatricksdayparade.com.

BROOKLYN IRISH AMERICAN PARADE, Park Slope, Brooklyn; Seventh Avenue and Prospect Park West from 15th to Union Street; www.brooklyn irishamericanparade.com.

There are many other local St. Patrick's Day Parades throughout the city on the weekends near March 17th; visit www.saintpatricksdayparade.com for all the listings.

RINGLING BROTHERS, BARNUM & BAILEY CIRCUS' ELEPHANT WALK, 34th Street from the Queens Midtown Tunnel to Madison Square Garden; (212) 465–6741; www.ringling.com; the parade of elephants and other circus animals usually takes place on the Tuesday night before the first performance at Madison; mid-March.

GREEK INDEPENDENCE DAY PARADE, Fifth Avenue from 62nd to 79th Street; www.greekparade.org.

PERSIAN-IRANIAN PARADE, Madison Avenue from 41st to 27th Street; www.persianparade.org.

APRIL

EASTER PARADE, Fifth Avenue between 49th and 57th Street; (212) 484–1200; www.nycvisit.com.

NEW YORK TARTAN DAY PARADE, Sixth Avenue from 45th to 58th Street; (212) 980–0844; www.tartanweek.com.

PHAGWAH: HINDU NEW YEAR'S PARADE, Queens, Liberty Avenue from 133rd to 123rd Street to Smokey Oval Park.

SIKH CULTURAL SOCIETY PARADE & FESTIVAL, Madison Avenue from 41st to 23rd Street.

MAY

CUBAN DAY PARADE (LA GRAN PARADA CUBANA), Sixth Avenue from 34th to 59th Street; (212) 348–8270; first Sunday in May.

MARIJUANA MARCH, Broadway from Houston Street to Battery Park; (212) 677–7180; www.cures-not-wars.org; the first Saturday of May.

TURKISH AMERICAN DAY PARADE, Madison Avenue and 56th Street to Second Avenue and 47th Street; www.tadf.org; a Saturday in mid-May.

HAITIAN FLAG DAY PARADE, Brooklyn; Eastern Parkway from Utica Avenue to Grand Army Plaza; third Sunday in May.

NORWEGIAN-AMERICAN 17TH OF MAY PARADE, Brooklyn; Fifth Avenue and 90th Street to Seventh Avenue and 67th Street; www .norway.org/culture/heritage.

SALUTE TO ISRAEL PARADE, Fifth Avenue from 52nd to 79th Street; (646) 472–5388; www.salutetoisrael.com.

JUNE

PHILIPPINE INDEPENDENCE DAY PARADE, Madison Avenue from 40th to 23rd Street; (212) 764–1330; www.pcgny.net.

QUEENS PRIDE PARADE, Queens; Thirty-seventh Avenue from 89th to 75th Street; www.queenspride.com; first Sunday in June.

PUERTO RICAN DAY PARADE, Fifth Avenue from 44th to 86th Street; (718) 401–0404; www.nationalpuertoricandayparade.org; second Sunday in June.

HARE KRISHNA PARADE, Fifth Avenue from 59th Street to Washington Square Park; (718) 855–6714; www.radhagovinda.net; second Saturday in June.

BROOKLYN PRIDE PARADE AND FESTIVAL, Brooklyn; Seventh Avenue from 15th Street to Lincoln Place; (718) 670–3337.

CHILDREN'S EVANGELICAL PARADE, Third Avenue from 96th Street to 122nd Street; third Sunday in June.

BRONX WEEK PARADE, the Bronx; Moshulu Parkway; www.ilovethe bronx.com; last Saturday in June.

INTERNATIONAL CULTURES PARADE, Sixth Avenue from 35th to 56th Street; www.10.org.

MERMAID PARADE, Brooklyn; Coney Island boardwalk from Stillwell Avenue to West 15th Street; (718) 372–5159; www.coneyisland.com; last Saturday in June.

HERITAGE OF PRIDE PARADE, Fifth Avenue from 52nd Street to Christopher Street; (212) 807–7433; www.hopinc.org; last Sunday of June.

JULY

MACY'S FOURTH OF JULY FIREWORKS, FDR Drive from 14th to 42nd Street; (212) 494–4495; www.macys.com; 9:00 P.M. on July 4th.

TRAVIS FOURTH OF JULY PARADE, Staten Island; Victory Boulevard and Cannon Street.

CHINATOWN INDEPENDENCE DAY PARADE AND FESTIVAL, Canal Street to Mott Street and through Chinatown; www.explorechinatown.com; Sunday closest to July 4th.

CAPTIVE NATIONS PARADE, Fifth Avenue from 59th to 72nd Street; third Sunday in June.

GRAN PARADA DOMINICANA DEL BRONX, the Bronx; Grand Concourse from East Tremont Avenue to 161st Street; (718) 993–4463; third Sunday in July.

COLOMBIA DAY PARADE, Queens; Northern Boulevard from 70th to 90th Street; third Sunday in July.

AUGUST

BRONX PUERTO RICAN DAY PARADE, the Bronx; Grand Concourse from East Tremont Avenue to 161st Street; (718) 401–0404; first Sunday in August.

DOMINICAN REPUBLICAN DAY PARADE, Sixth Avenue from 36th to 58th Street; (212) 795–0107; mid-August.

BROOKLYN PUERTO RICAN DAY PARADE, Brooklyn; Graham Avenue from Broadway to Grand Street; (718) 401–0404; third Sunday in August.

INDIA INDEPENDENCE DAY PARADE, Madison Avenue from 41st to 27th Street; third Sunday of August.

PAKISTAN INDEPENDENCE DAY PARADE, Madison Avenue from 41st to 27th Street; last Sunday of August.

SEPTEMBER

LABOR DAY PARADE, Fifth Avenue from 44th to 72nd Street.

WEST INDIAN AMERICAN DAY CARNIVAL PARADE, Brooklyn; Eastern Parkway between Utica Avenue and Grand Army Plaza; (718) 467–1797; www.wiadca.org; Labor Day weekend.

MEXICAN DAY PARADE, Madison Avenue from 41st to 23rd Street; second weekend of September.

THE STEUBEN DAY PARADE, Fifth Avenue from 61st to 86th Street; (201) 763–7285; www.germanparadenyc.org; third Sunday of September.

AFRICAN-AMERICAN DAY PARADE, Adam Clayton Powell Boulevard from 111th to 142nd Street; (212) 862–8497; third Sunday in September.

MUSLIM DAY PARADE, Madison Avenue from 41st to 26th Street; late September.

OCTOBER

NIGERIAN INDEPENDENCE PARADE, Second Avenue from 54th to 43rd Street; www.oanweb.org; first Saturday in October.

PULASKI DAY PARADE, Fifth Avenue from 26th to 52nd Street; www.pulaskiparade.org; first Sunday in October.

KOREAN PARADE, Broadway from 41st to 23rd Street; (212) 255–6969; first Sunday in October.

COLUMBUS DAY PARADE, Fifth Avenue from 44th to 79th Street; (212) 249–9923; www.columbuscitizensfd.org; second Monday in October.

HISPANIC DAY PARADE, Fifth Avenue from 44th to 86th Street; second Sunday in October.

THE VILLAGE HALLOWEEN PARADE, Sixth Avenue from Houston to 21st Street; www.halloween-nyc.com; October 31.

NOVEMBER

NEW YORK CITY MARATHON, throughout the five boroughs; www.ing nycmarathon.org; first Sunday in November.

VETERANS DAY PARADE; Fifth Avenue from 23rd to 57th Street; (212) 693–1476; November 11.

MACY'S THANKSGIVING DAY PARADE, Central Park West and Broadway from 79th to 34th Street; (212) 494–4495; www.macys.com; Thanksgiving Day.

DECEMBER

TIMES SQUARE NEW YEAR'S EVE, Broadway and Seventh Avenue from 42nd to 57th Street; (212) 768–1560; www.timessquarenyc.org; December 31.

MANHATTAN

MID-MANHATTAN LIBRARY, 455 Fifth Avenue (at 40th Street); (212) 340–0833; Telephone Reference, (212) 340–0849, ext. 3; www.nypl.org

EAST SIDE

58TH STREET, 127 East 58th Street; (212) 759–7358

67TH STREET, 328 East 67th Street; (212) 734–1717

96TH STREET, 112 East 96th Street; (212) 289–0908

125TH STREET, 224 East 125th Street; (212) 534–5050

AGUILAR, 174 East 110th Street; (212) 534–2930

EPIPHANY, 228 East 23rd Street; (212) 679–2645

MACOMB'S BRIDGE, 2650 Adam Clayton Powell Jr. Boulevard; (212) 281–4900

OTTENDORFER, 135 Second Avenue; (212) 674–0947

ROOSEVELT ISLAND, 524 Main Street; (212) 308–6243

TERENCE CARDINAL COOKE-CATHEDRAL, 560 Lexington Avenue; (212) 752–3824

WEBSTER, 1465 York Avenue; (212) 288–5049

YORKVILLE, 222 East 79th Street; (212) 744–5824

WEST SIDE

115TH STREET, 203 West 115th Street; (212) 666–9393

ANDREW HEISKELL BRAILLE & TALK-ING BOOK LIBRARY, 40 West 20th Street; (212) 206–5400; voice mail (212) 206–5425; TDD (212) 206–5458

BLOOMINGDALE, 150 West 100th Street; (212) 222–8030

COLUMBUS, 742 Tenth Avenue; (212) 586–5098

COUNTEE CULLEN, 104 West 136th Street; (212) 491–2070

DONNELL LIBRARY CENTER, 20 West 53rd Street; (212) 621–0619

FORT WASHINGTON, 535 West 179th Street; (212) 927–3533

GEORGE BRUCE, 518 West 125th Street; (212) 662–9727

HAMILTON GRANGE, 503 West 145th Street; (212) 926–2147

HARLEM, 9 West 124th Street; (212) 348–5620

INWOOD, 4790 Broadway; (212) 942–2445

JEFFERSON MARKET, 425 Avenue of the Americas; (212) 243–4334

KIPS BAY, 446 Third Avenue; (212) 683–2520

MORNINGSIDE HEIGHTS, 2900 Broadway; (212) 864–2530

MUHLENBERG, 209 West 23rd Street; (212) 924–1585

RIVERSIDE, 127 Amsterdam Avenue; (212) 870–1810

ST. AGNES, 444 Amsterdam Avenue; (212) 877–4380

SEWARD PARK, 192 East Broadway; (212) 477–6770

WASHINGTON HEIGHTS, 1000 Street, Nicholas Avenue; (212) 923–6054

DOWNTOWN

CHATHAM SQUARE, 33 East Broadway; (212) 964–6598

EARLY CHILDHOOD RESOURCE & INFORMATION CENTER (ECRIC), 66 Leroy Street; (212) 929–0815

HAMILTON FISH PARK, 415 East Houston Street; (212) 673–2290

HUDSON PARK, 66 Leroy Street; (212) 243–6876

NEW AMSTERDAM, 9 Murray Street; (212) 732–8186

TOMPKINS SQUARE, 331 East 10th Street; (212) 228–4747

STATEN ISLAND

DONGAN HILLS, 1617 Richmond Road; (718) 351–1444

GREAT KILLS, 56 Giffords Lane; (718) 984–6670

HUGUENOT PARK, 830 Huguenot Avenue; (718) 984–4636

NEW DORP, 309 New Dorp Lane; (718) 351–2977

PORT RICHMOND, 75 Bennett Street; (718) 442–0158

RICHMONDTOWN, 200 Clarke Avenue; (718) 668–0413

ST. GEORGE LIBRARY CENTER, 5 Central Avenue; (718) 442–8560

SOUTH BEACH, 21–25 Robin Road; (718) 816–5834

STAPLETON, 132 Canal Street; (718) 727–0427

TODT HILL–WESTERLEIGH, 2550 Victory Boulevard; (718) 494–1642

TOTTENVILLE, 7430 Amboy Road; (718) 984–0945

WEST NEW BRIGHTON, 976 Castleton Avenue; (718) 442–1416

THE BRONX

BRONX LIBRARY CENTER, 2556 Bainbridge Avenue (at Fordham Road); (718) 579–4244; Bronx Reference Center, (718) 579–4257

ALLERTON, 2740 Barnes Avenue; (718) 881–4240

BAYCHESTER, 2049 Asch Loop North; (718) 379–6700

BELMONT LIBRARY–ENRICO FERMI CULTURAL CENTER, 610 East 186th Street; (718) 933–6410

CASTLE HILL, 947 Castle Hill Avenue; (718) 824–3838

CITY ISLAND, 320 City Island Avenue; (718) 885–1703

CLASON'S POINT, 1215 Morrison Avenue; (718) 842–1235

EASTCHESTER, 1385 East Gun Hill Road; (718) 653–3292

EDENWALD, 1255 East 233rd Street; (718) 798–3355

FRANCIS MARTIN, 2150 University Avenue; (718) 295–5287

GRAND CONCOURSE, 155 East 173rd Street; (718) 583–6611

HIGH BRIDGE, 78 West 168th Street; (718) 293–7800

HUNT'S POINT, 877 Southern Boulevard; (718) 617–0338

JEROME PARK, 118 Eames Place; (718) 549–5200

KINGSBRIDGE, 280 West 231st Street; (718) 548–5656

MELROSE, 910 Morris Avenue; (718) 588–0110

MORRISANIA, 610 East 169th Street; (718) 589–9268

MORRIS PARK, 985 Morris Park Avenue; (718) 931–0636

MOSHOLU, 285 East 205th Street; (718) 882–8239

MOTT HAVEN, 321 East 140th Street; (718) 665–4878

PARKCHESTER, 1985 Westchester Avenue; (718) 829–7830

PELHAM BAY, 3060 Middletown Road; (718) 792–6744

RIVERDALE, 5540 Mosholu Avenue; (718) 549–1212

SEDGWICK, 1701 Dr. Martin Luther King Jr. Boulevard; (718) 731–2074

SOUNDVIEW, 660 Soundview Avenue; (718) 589–0880

SPUYTEN DUYVIL, 650 West 235th Street; (718) 796–1202

THROG'S NECK, 3025 Cross Bronx Expressway Extension; (718) 792–2612

TREMONT, 1866 Washington Avenue; (718) 299–5177

VAN CORTLANDT, 3874 Sedgwick Avenue; (718) 543–5150

VAN NEST, 2147 Barnes Avenue; (718) 829–5864

WAKEFIELD, 4100 Lowerre Place; (718) 652–4663

WESTCHESTER SQUARE, 2521 Glebe Avenue; (718) 863–0436

WEST FARMS, 2085 Honeywell Avenue; (718) 367–5376

WOODLAWN HEIGHTS, 4355 Katonah Avenue; (718) 519–9627

WOODSTOCK, 761 East 160th Street; (718) 665–6255

BROOKLYN

CENTRAL LIBRARY, Grand Army Plaza (Flatbush Avenue and Eastern Parkway); (718) 230–2100; www.brooklynpubliclibrary.org; Telephone Reference, (718) 230–2100, ext. 5

ARLINGTON, Arlington Avenue at Warwick Street; (718) 277–6105

BAY RIDGE, Ridge Boulevard at 73rd Street; (718) 748–5709

BEDFORD, Franklin Avenue at Hancock Street; (718) 623–0012

BEDFORD LEARNING CENTER; (718) 623–2134

BOROUGH PARK, 43rd Street near Thirteenth Avenue; (718) 437–4085

BRIGHTON BEACH, Brighton First Road (near Brighton Beach Avenue); (718) 946–2917

BROOKLYN HEIGHTS, 280 Cadman Plaza West (at Tillary Street); (718) 623–7100

BROWER PARK, St. Marks Avenue near Nostrand Avenue; (718) 773–7208

BROWNSVILLE, Glenmore Avenue at Watkins Street; (718) 498–9721

BUSHWICK, Bushwick Avenue at Seigel Street; (718) 602–1348

CANARSIE, Rockaway Parkway near Avenue J; (718) 257–6547

CARROLL GARDENS, Clinton Street at Union Street; (718) 596–6972

CLARENDON, Nostrand Avenue near Farragut Road; (718) 421–1159

CLINTON HILL, Washington Avenue near Lafayette Avenue; (718) 398–8713

CONEY ISLAND, Mermaid Avenue near West 19th Street; (718) 265–3220

CONEY ISLAND LEARNING CENTER; (718) 265-3880

CORTELYOU, Cortelyou Road at Argyle Road; (718) 693-7763

CROWN HEIGHTS, New York Avenue at Maple Street; (718) 773-1180

CYPRESS HILLS, Sutter Avenue at Crystal Street; (718) 277-6004

DEKALB, Bushwick Avenue at DeKalb Avenue; (718) 455-3898

DYKER, Thirteenth Avenue at 82nd Street; (718) 748-6261

EASTERN PARKWAY, Eastern Parkway at Schenectady Avenue; (718) 953-4225

EASTERN PARKWAY ADULT LEARNING CENTER; (718) 778-9330

EAST FLATBUSH, 9612 Church Avenue near Rockaway Parkway; (718) 922-0927

FLATBUSH, Linden Boulevard near Flatbush Avenue; (718) 856-0813

FLATBUSH ADULT LEARNING CENTER; (718) 856-2631

FLATLANDS, Flatbush Avenue at Avenue P; (718) 253-4409

FORT HAMILTON, Fourth Avenue at 95th Street; (718) 748-6919

GERRITSEN BEACH, Gerritsen Avenue at Channel Avenue; (718) 368-1435

GRAVESEND, Avenue X near West 2nd Street; (718) 382-5792

GREENPOINT, Norman Avenue at Leonard Street; (718) 349-8504

HIGHLAWN, West 13th Street at Kings Highway; (718) 234-7208

HOMECREST, Coney Island Avenue near Avenue V; (718) 382-5924

JAMAICA BAY, Seaview Avenue at East 98th Street; (718) 241-3571

KENSINGTON, Ditmas Avenue near East 5th Street; (718) 435-9431

KINGS BAY, Nostrand Avenue near Avenue W; (718) 368-1709

KINGS HIGHWAY, Ocean Avenue near Kings Highway; (718) 375-3037

LEONARD, Devoe Street at Leonard Street; (718) 486-3365

MACON, Lewis Avenue at Macon Street; (718) 573-5606

MAPLETON, 60th Street at Seventeenth Avenue; (718) 256-2117

MARCY, DeKalb Avenue near Nostrand Avenue; (718) 935-0032

McKINLEY PARK, Fort Hamilton Parkway at 68th Street; (718) 748-8001

MIDWOOD, East 16th Street near Avenue J; (718) 252-0967

MILL BASIN, Ralph Avenue near Avenue N; (718) 241-3973

NEW LOTS, New Lots Avenue at Barbey Street; (718) 649-0311

NEW UTRECHT, 1783 86th Street (at Bay 17th Street); (718) 236-4086

PACIFIC, Fourth Avenue at Pacific Street; (718) 638-1531

PAERDEGAT, East 59th Street near Flatlands Avenue; (718) 241-3994

PARK SLOPE, Sixth Avenue near 9th Street; (718) 832-1853

RED HOOK, Wolcott Street at Dwight Street; (718) 935-0203

RUGBY, Utica Avenue near Tilden Avenue; (718) 566-0054

RYDER, Twenty-third Avenue at 59th Street; (718) 331-2962

SARATOGA, Thomas S. Boyland Street at Macon Street; (718) 573-5224

SHEEPSHEAD BAY, East 14th Street near Avenue Z; (718) 368-1815

SPRING CREEK, Flatlands Avenue near New Jersey Avenue; (718) 257-6571

STONE AVENUE, 581 Mother Gaston Boulevard at Dumont Avenue; (718) 485-8347

SUNSET PARK, Fourth Avenue at 51st Street; (718) 567-2806

ULMER PARK, Bath Avenue at Twenty-sixth Avenue; (718) 265-3443

WALT WHITMAN, 93 St. Edwards Street (at Auburn Place); (718) 935-0244

WASHINGTON IRVING, Irving Avenue at Woodbine Street; (718) 628-8378

WILLIAMSBURG, 240 Division Avenue (at Marcy Avenue); (718) 302-3485

WILLIAMSBURG ADULT LEARNING CENTER; (718) 302-3489

WINDSOR TERRACE, East 5th Street at Fort Hamilton Parkway; (718) 686-9707

QUEENS

CENTRAL LIBRARY, 89-11 Merrick Boulevard (between Eighty-ninth and Ninetieth Avenues); (718) 990-0700; www.queenslibrary.org; Telephone Reference, (718) 990-0714 or (718) 990-0728

ARVERNE, Beach 54th Street; (718) 634-4784

ASTORIA, 14-01 Astoria Boulevard; (718) 278-2220

AUBURNDALE, 25-55 Francis Lewis Boulevard; (718) 352-2027

BAISLEY PARK, 117-11 Sutphin Boulevard; (718) 529-1590

BAYSIDE, 214-20 Northern Boulevard; (718) 229-1834

BAY TERRACE, 18-36 Bell Boulevard; (718) 423-7004

BELLEROSE, 250-06 Hillside Avenue; (718) 831-8644

BRIARWOOD, 85-12 Main Street; (718) 658-1680

BROAD CHANNEL, 16-26 Cross Bay Boulevard; (718) 318-4943

BROADWAY, 40-20 Broadway; (718) 721-2462

CAMBRIA HEIGHTS, 220-20 Linden Boulevard; (718) 528-3535

CORONA, 38-23 104th Street (between Thirty-eighth and Thirty-ninth Avenues); (718) 426-2844

COURT SQUARE, 25-01 Jackson Avenue; (718) 937-2790

DOUGLASTON/LITTLE NECK, 249-01 Northern Boulevard; (718) 225-8414

EAST ELMHURST, 95-06 Astoria Boulevard; (718) 424-2619

EAST FLUSHING, 196-36 Northern Boulevard; (718) 357-6643

ELMHURST, 86-01 Broadway; (718) 271-1020

FAR ROCKAWAY, 1637 Central Avenue; (718) 327-2549

FLUSHING, 41-17 Main Street; (718) 661-1200

FOREST HILLS, 108-19 Seventy-first Avenue; (718) 268-7934

FRESH MEADOWS, 193-20 Horace Harding Expressway; (718) 454-7272

GLENDALE, 78-60 73rd Place; (718) 821-4980

GLEN OAKS, 256-04 Union Turnpike; (718) 831-8636

HILLCREST, 187-05 Union Turnpike; (718) 454-2786

HOLLIS, 202-05 Hillside Avenue; (718) 465-7355

HOWARD BEACH, 92-06 156th Avenue; (718) 641-7086

JACKSON HEIGHTS, 35-51 81st Street; (718) 899-2500

KEW GARDENS HILLS, 72–33 Vleigh Place; (718) 261–6654

LANGSTON HUGHES, 100–01 Northern Boulevard; (718) 651–1100

LAURELTON, 134–26 225th Street; (718) 528–2822

LEFFERTS, 103–34 Lefferts Boulevard; (718) 843–5950

LEFRAK CITY, 98–25 Horace Harding Expressway; (718) 592–7677

LONG ISLAND CITY, 37–44 21st Street; (718) 752–3700

MASPETH, 69–70 Grand Avenue; (718) 639–5228

McGOLDRICK, 155–06 Roosevelt Avenue; (718) 461–1616

MIDDLE VILLAGE, 72–31 Metropolitan Avenue; (718) 326–1390

MITCHELL–LINDEN, 29–42 Union Street; (718) 539–2330

NORTH FOREST PARK, 98–27 Metropolitan Avenue; (718) 261–5512

NORTH HILLS, 57–04 Marathon Parkway; (718) 225–3550

OZONE PARK, 92–24 Rockaway Boulevard; (718) 845–3127

PENINSULA, 92–25 Rockaway Beach Boulevard; (718) 634–1110

POMONOK, 158–21 Jewel Avenue; (718) 591–4343

POPPENHUSEN, 121–23 Fourteenth Avenue; (718) 359–1102

QUEENSBORO HILL, 60–05 Main Street; (718) 359–8332

QUEENSBRIDGE, 10–43 Forty-first Avenue; (718) 937–6266

QUEENS VILLAGE, 94–11 217th Street; (718) 776–6800

RAVENSWOOD, 35–32 21st Street; (718) 784–2112

REGO PARK, 91–41 63rd Drive; (718) 459–5140

RICHMOND HILL, 118–14 Hillside Avenue; (718) 849–7150

RIDGEWOOD, 20–12 Madison Street; (718) 821–4770

ROCHDALE VILLAGE, 169–09 137th Avenue; (718) 723–4440

ROSEDALE, 144–20 243rd Street; (718) 528–8490

ST. ALBANS, 191–05 Linden Boulevard; (718) 528–8196

SEASIDE, 116–15 Rockaway Beach Boulevard; (718) 634–1876

SOUTH HOLLIS, 204–01 Hollis Avenue; (718) 465–6779

SOUTH JAMAICA, 108–41 Guy R. Brewer Boulevard; (718) 739–4088

SOUTH OZONE PARK, 128–16 Rockaway Boulevard; (718) 529–1660

STEINWAY, 21–45 31st Street; (718) 728–1965

SUNNYSIDE, 43–06 Greenpoint Avenue; (718) 784–3033

WHITESTONE, 151–10 14th Road; (718) 767–8010

WINDSOR PARK, 79–50 Bell Boulevard; (718) 468–8300

WOODHAVEN, 85–41 Forest Parkway; (718) 849–1010

WOODSIDE, 54–22 Skillman Avenue; (718) 429–4700

MANHATTAN

ALFRED EAST SMITH (LOWER EAST SIDE)

80 Catherine Street (off Cherry Street, between Madison and South Streets); (212) 285–0300

Dance classes, open basketball, badminton, gardening club, basic computer courses, kickboxing and karate classes.

ASSER LEVY (MIDTOWN EAST SIDE)

East 23rd Street and Asser Levy Place (at FDR Drive); (212) 447–2020

Indoor and outdoor pool, group fitness classes, martial arts classes, swim classes, guitar lessons, yoga, senior programs.

CHELSEA RECREATION CENTER

430 West 25th Street (between Ninth and Tenth Avenues); (212) 255–3705

Indoor pool, cardio and fitness strength-training equipment, basketball, volley-ball, game room, computer resource center, and a variety of fitness classes.

EAST 54 (UPPER EAST SIDE)

348 East 54th Street (between First and Second Avenues); (212) 754–5411

Extensive schedule of fitness, yoga, and dance classes; indoor pool, track; after-school and senior programs.

HAMILTON FISH (LOWER EAST SIDE)

128 Pitt Street (at East Houston Street); (212) 387–7687

Olympic-size outdoor pool, game room, fitness room, basketball courts, wrestling, computer classes, karate class.

HANSBOROUGH (CENTRAL HARLEM)

35 West 134th Street (between Lenox and Fifth Avenues); (212) 234–9603

Outdoor rooftop sundeck, indoor pool, outdoor and indoor track, aerobic classes, fitness room, seniors programs.

HIGHBRIDGE (WASHINGTON HEIGHTS)

Amsterdam Avenue and West 173rd Street; (212) 927–2012

Basketball courts, game room, computer center, dance and martial arts classes, after-school program.

JACKIE ROBINSON (WEST HARLEM)

85 Bradhurst Avenue (at 146th Street); (212) 324–9607

Olympic-size outdoor pool, fitness room, computer classes, volleyball, teen cooking classes, after-school program.

J. HOOD WRIGHT (WASHINGTON HEIGHTS)

351 Fort Washington Avenue (at 174th Street); (212) 927–1563

Fitness room, computer center, softball and basketball tournaments, game room, two athletic fields, tennis court, handball courts, teen and senior programs.

MORNINGSIDE PARK (WEST HARLEM)

410 West 123rd Street (at Morningside Avenue); (212) 280–0209

Operates primarily as an after-school and senior center.

NORTH MEADOW (UPPER EAST AND WEST SIDE)

Central Park (midpark at 97th Street); (212) 348–4867

Tai chi and yoga classes, youth adventure programs, climbing wall (open-climbing hours are free for eight- to twelve-year-olds; adults $5), basketball clinics, and Field Day Kits. (Borrow a sack of equipment from them for a fun day in the park. The kit includes a basketball, ten cones, three bats, a horse-shoe set, playground ball, Nerf ball, football, Frisbee, two handballs, a soccer ball, jump rope, two Wiffle balls, and hula hoops.)

PELHAM FRITZ (WEST HARLEM)

18 Mount Morris Park West (at 122nd Street); (212) 860–1380

Outdoor pool, computer room, aerobics classes, dance classes, drumming, extensive senior programs, game room, basketball courts.

REC 59 (MIDTOWN WEST)

533 West 59th Street (between Tenth and Eleventh Avenues); (212) 397–3159

Indoor pool, small fitness room.

THOMAS JEFFERSON (EAST HARLEM)

2180 First Avenue (at East 112th Street); (212) 860–1383

Olympic-size outdoor pool, fitness room, basketball courts, athletic fields, martial arts classes, aerobic classes, boxing, handball courts, game room.

TONY DAPOLITO RECREATION CENTER (WEST VILLAGE/SOHO)

1 Clarkson Street (near Seventh Avenue South and Houston Street); (212) 242–5228

Very popular center. Indoor and outdoor pools, handball courts, two fitness rooms, indoor track, boccie court, fitness classes, basketball and flag football leagues.

BROOKLYN

BROOKLYN SENIOR CENTER (FORT HAMILTON)

9941 Fort Hamilton Parkway (at 100th Street); (718) 439–4296

Line dancing, tap dancing, social dancing, arts and crafts, day trips, bingo, computer access.

BROWNSVILLE

1555 Linden Boulevard (between Mother Gaston and Christopher Streets); (718) 345–2706

Indoor pool, computer center, aerobics classes, martial arts classes, game room, basketball clinics, handball courts, track and field, music studio.

METROPOLITAN POOL AND FITNESS CENTER (WILLIAMSBURG)

261 Bedford Avenue (at Metropolitan Avenue); (718) 599–5707

Indoor pool, fitness room, computer center, computer and digital video classes, play schoolroom, and "arguably the best indoor pool in New York City," says the *Village Voice*.

RED HOOK

155 Bay Street (between Henry and Clinton Streets); (718) 722–3211

Outdoor pool, computer center and classes, aerobics, martial arts, yoga.

ST. JOHN'S RECREATION CENTER

1251 Prospect Place (at Schenectady Avenue); (718) 771–2787

Indoor pool, computer center and classes, fitness room, aerobics, tai chi, SAT classes, quilting, senior programs.

SUNSET PARK

Seventh Avenue and 43rd Street (at 42nd Street); (718) 965–6533

Outdoor pool, computer center, fitness room, boxing room, aerobics classes, tae bo classes, game room.

VON KING CULTURAL ARTS CENTER

670 Lafayette Avenue (between Marcy and Tompkins Avenues); (718) 622–2082

Computer center, aerobics classes, game room, dance room, athletic fields, handball courts.

THE BRONX

HAFFEN PARK

Hammersley Avenue at Ely, Gunther, and Burke Avenues; (718) 379–8347

Outdoor pool, tennis courts, senior center, handball courts.

HUNTS POINT

765 Manida Street (between Lafayette Street and Spofford Avenue); (718) 860–5544

Fitness room; dance, aerobics, and karate classes; volleyball and basketball courts; movies on the last Friday of every month.

KINGSBRIDGE

3101 Kingsbridge Terrace (between Perot and Sedwick Streets); (718) 884–0700

After-school teen and senior programs, computer and back-to-work classes.

MULLALY

East 164th Street (at River Avenue); (718) 590–5743

Outdoor skate park.

OWEN DOLAN

1400 Westchester Square; (718) 822–4282

Small facility with some family-oriented classes.

ST. JAMES

2530 Jerome Avenue (at 192nd Street); (718) 367–3658

Computer center, tennis courts, basketball courts, handball courts, teen and senior programs.

ST. MARY'S

450 St. Ann's Avenue (at 145th Street); (718) 402–5160

Indoor pool, computer center, fitness room, basketball courts, aerobics classes, boxing, cooking, karate, tae kwon do, teen programs, scuba classes, tennis courts, athletic field.

WEST BRONX

1527 Jessup Avenue (at 172nd Street); (718) 293–5934

After-school programs, basketball courts, weight room, and tae kwon do classes.

WILLIAMSBRIDGE OVAL

3225 Reservoir Oval East (between 208th Street and Bainbridge Avenue); (718) 654–1851

Fitness room, tennis courts, basketball courts, handball courts, outdoor track, play schoolroom, karate classes, twenty-two-acre playground, senior programs.

QUEENS

DETECTIVE KEITH L. WILLIAMS (JAMAICA)

173rd Place and Liberty Avenue (at 106th Street); (718) 523–6912

Outdoor pool, tennis courts, handball courts, cooking classes, garden, arts and crafts.

LOST BATTALION HALL (REGO PARK)
93–29 Queens Boulevard (at Sixty-second Avenue); (718) 263–1163
Computer center, boxing room, fitness center, karate, kickboxing, rhythmic gymnastics, Gymboree, senior program.

LOUIS ARMSTRONG (CORONA)
108th Street and Northern Boulevard; (718) 651–0096
Fitness room, karate classes, dance classes, boxing, GED program, community groups, basketball, handball.

PASSERELLE
Flushing Meadows Corona Park (between National Tennis Center and Shea Stadium); (718) 760–6937
Fitness room, computer center, REACH program for people with disabilities. "We are more like a visitor center. We invite groups to come to us—school groups, organizations, seniors, et cetera."

ROY WILKINS FAMILY CENTER (ST. ALBANS)
177th Street at Baisley Boulevard; (718) 276–8686
Indoor pool, fitness room, outdoor track, extensive senior program.

SORRENTINO (FAR ROCKAWAY)
18–48 Cornaga Avenue (at Beach 19th Street); (718) 471–4818
Fitness room, computer center, double Dutch program, computer classes, play school, senior programs.

STATEN ISLAND

CROMWELL CENTER
Murray Hulbert Avenue at Pier #6; (718) 816–6172
Fitness room, aerobics classes, computer classes, wood carving and ceramics classes, kid and teen programs.

GREENBELT RECREATION CENTER
Brielle Avenue (between Walcott and Rockland Avenues, across from Sea View Hospital); (718) 667–3545
Tennis courts, basketball courts, soccer field, arts and crafts room, performance space, croquet lawn.

INDEX

About the Author

Born and bred in New York City, **Rob Grader** is a writer, actor, and massage therapist and has lived in four out of the five boroughs (he'll make it to Staten Island one of these days). Rob's other writing credits include *The Cuddle Sutra* (Sourcebooks, 2007), scripts for the National Public Radio series Jazz From Lincoln Center, as well as articles for local newspapers and magazines. He has also created and produced the A&E reality show *House of Dreams*. As an actor, Rob has appeared at many regional theaters across the country; on the television shows *Law & Order, Law & Order: SVU, The Job, All My Children, Who's the Boss;* in the HBO film *American Splendor;* and in a number of national commercials. He's a graduate of the American Repertory Theater's Institute for Advanced Theater Training at Harvard University. As a massage therapist, he has rubbed many sore and aching backs around New York. Rob currently lives, works, and does his darndest not to spend any money in Manhattan. Check out his Web site, www.thecheapbastard.com.